Issues in History Teaching

This book covers a wide range of important issues relating to history education, ranging from justifying the place of history in the curriculum to using information technology in the classroom. The book attempts to incorporate every relevant major issue, including such topics as:

- what should be included in the history curriculum;
- good practice in history teaching;
- Government policies on history matters;
- the links between teaching history and learning about citizenship;
- history and special educational needs.

Written by a range of history professionals, including HMIs, this book offers new and interesting ideas on the teaching, learning and organisation of history in primary and secondary schools.

Professor James Arthur is Professor of Education at Canterbury Christ Church University College. **Dr Robert Phillips** is Lecturer in Education at the University of Wales, Swansea.

Issues in Subject Teaching series
Series edited by Susan Capel, Jon Davison,
James Arthur and John Moss

Other titles in the series:

Issues in History Teaching

Edited by James Arthur
and Robert Phillips

London and New York

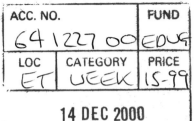
First published 2000
by Routledge
11 New Fetter Lane, London EC4P 4EE

Simultaneously published in the USA and Canada
by Routledge
29 West 35th Street, New York, NY 10001

Routledge is an imprint of the Taylor & Francis Group

Selection and editorial matter © 2000 the editors, James Arthur and
Robert Phillips; © 2000 individual chapters, their contributors.

Typeset in Goudy by Taylor & Francis Books Ltd
Printed and bound in Great Britain by Biddles Ltd,
Guildford and King's Lynn

British Library Cataloguing in Publication Data
A catalogue record for this book is available from the British Library

Library of Congress Cataloging-in-Publication Data
Issues in history teaching / James Arthur and Robert Phillips [editors].
p.   cm.
Includes bibliographical references and index.
(alk. paper)
1. History–Study and teaching (Secondary). 2. History–Study and
teaching (Elementary). I. Arthur, James. II. Phillips, Robert.
D16.2.I88 1999   99-35738
907.1'2–dc21   CIP

ISBN 0 415–20668–5 (hbk)
ISBN 0 415–20669–3 (pbk)

Contents

PART I
Issues in the classroom

4 Teaching historical significance 39

MARTIN HUNT

5 Historical knowledge and historical skills: a distracting dichotomy 54

CHRISTINE COUNSELL

6 Teaching about interpretations 72

TONY McALEAVY

10 **Thinking and feeling: pupils' preconceptions about the past
    and historical understanding**   125
    CHRIS HUSBANDS AND ANNA PENDRY

PART II
Broader educational issues and history

11 **Citizenship and the teaching and learning of history**   137
    IAN DAVIES

12 **'History for the nation': multiculturalism and the
    teaching of history**   148
    IAN GROSVENOR

Illustrations

Contributors

James Arthur is Professor of Education at Canterbury Christ Church University College and is the co-author of *Learning to Teach History in the Secondary School* (Routledge). He also contributed to *History Teachers in the Making* (Open University Press). He was a member of the National Curriculum History Task Group and previously was a member of QCA's National Forum on Values in the Community and Education. He has written a number of books and numerous articles on educational policy in denominational schooling. He has also written *Schools and Community: The Communitarian Agenda in Education* (Falmer Press) and is currently writing *Social Literacy and the School Curriculum* and co-authoring *Citizenship Education through History*, both for Falmer Press.

Hilary Cooper is Principal Lecturer in Education at St Martin's College, Lancaster. Her doctoral thesis on 'Young children's thinking in history' was an empirical study undertaken as a practising primary school teacher. She subsequently worked in the Department of Education at Goldsmith's College, University of London and at Lancaster University before joining the University College of St Martin. She has published widely, particularly in the field of primary history education. Her books include *The Teaching of History in Primary Schools* (David Fulton) and *History in the Early Years* (Routledge). She was an editor of *Teaching History*, 1991–7, and is now consultant editor. Her current research interests include history education in Europe, and children's perceptions of their learning.

Christine Counsell is Lecturer in History Education at the University of Cambridge School of Education. Her in-service training on writing and thinking skills, and her pamphlet, *Analytical and Discursive Writing* (Historical Association), have been influential in expanding teachers' strategies for increasing pupils' capacity and disposition for abstract thought and extended communication. Working with Michael Riley as general editor of the new Key Stage 3 series, *Think Through History* (Longman), she seeks to link these developments with new and systematic attempts at building both historical knowledge and critical thinking in the 'lower-attaining' pupil. She is currently researching the professional knowledge of secondary teachers, examining the way in which history teachers select and conceptualise subject matter components in order to secure progression in pupils' learning.

Wendy Cunnah is a Tutor on the History PGCE programme in the Department of Education, University of Wales, Swansea; she also co-ordinates the special needs programmes within the department. Her research interests focus upon special needs within history teaching.

Ian Davies is a Lecturer in Educational Studies at the University of York. His previous experience includes ten years as a teacher in comprehensive schools in England. He now teaches undergraduates in educational studies (non-QTS), is responsible for the PGCE History course at York, and supervises MA and D.Phil. research. He is the co-editor of *Developing European Citizens* (Sheffield Hallam University Press), the co-author of *Using Documents* (English Heritage) and has published many articles in academic and professional journals.

Ian Grosvenor lectures in History in Education at the School of Education, University of Birmingham. He was formerly Principal Lecturer in Education (Research) at Nene University College, Northampton and Head of History at Newman College of Higher Education, Birmingham. He has taught in primary, secondary and special schools, worked on Local Education Authority anti-racist initiatives, and worked in equal opportunities programmes. He has published articles on the teaching of history, post-1945 Education Policy. Recent books include *Assimilating Identities: Racism and Education Policy in Post–1945 Britain* (Lawrence & Wishart) and *Silences and Images. The Social History of the Classroom*, the latter edited with Martin Lawn and Kate Rousmaniere (Peter Lang).

Penelope Harnett is Senior Lecturer in Primary Education at the University of the West of England, Bristol. Her research interests include the development of primary school children's historical understanding, with particular reference to children's interpretations of visual images. As a Research Fellow at the University of the West of England, Penelope has explored the development of the history curriculum in primary schools during this century and primary school teachers' perceptions of the current history curriculum. She is editor of *Primary History* and has also published teaching materials and children's books.

Terry Haydn is Lecturer in Education and Course Director of the Secondary PGCE Course at the School of Education and Professional Development at the University of East Anglia. He is co-author of *Learning to Teach History in the Secondary School* (Routledge). His research interests are in the field of new technology and the history classroom, pupils' understanding of time, and the working atmosphere in the classroom. He was a Head of Humanities in an inner-city comprehensive school in Manchester before working for several years as a PGCE tutor at the Institute of Education, University of London.

Martin Hunt is currently a part-time Lecturer on the PGCE History course at the Didsbury School of Education, Manchester Metropolitan University, where he was formerly a Principal Lecturer and Course Leader of the one-year PGCE course. He is a co-author of *Learning to Teach History in the Secondary School* (Routledge). He was the Chief Examiner for the GCSE Local History syllabus (1988–97) and is currently a Principal Examiner for the GCSE.

Chris Husbands is Professor of Education at the University of Warwick. He taught in schools in London, Norwich and Hertfordshire, and in teacher education at the University of East Anglia. He is author of *What is History Teaching?* (Open University Press) and co-author of *History Teachers in the Making* (Open University Press). He is co-director of the ESRC Project on *Teacher, Parent and Pupil Attitudes to Affective Education in the EU*.

Tony McAleavy is Principal Inspector for Schools of Gloucestershire County Council LEA and has written widely in the field of history education, including a series of school textbooks. He has a background in secondary history teaching and has acted as a history consultant for QCA.

Anna Pendry is a Lecturer in Educational Studies at the University of Oxford, where she works with PGCE, higher degree and research students. Her research interests are in the field of teacher education, and especially the learning of beginning teachers. She is the co-author of *History Teachers in the Making*, published by Open University Press.

Robert Phillips is Lecturer in Education at the University of Wales, Swansea. He has written extensively on aspects of history education in England and in Wales. His main research interest focuses on the connection between the teaching of history and the cultivation of national identity. He has recently published a book on this theme entitled *History Teaching, Nationhood and the State: A Study in Educational Politics* (Cassell).

William Stow is currently a Senior Lecturer at Canterbury Christ Church University College, where he is responsible for undergraduate and postgraduate primary history training. He has recently completed a Masters in Education, for which the dissertation focused on the development of primary children's understanding of chronology. He is currently studying for a Ph.D., focusing on history teaching and the primary child's sense of chronology in Sweden, Scotland and England.

Ruth Watts is a Senior Lecturer in Education and History Methods Tutor in the School of Education, University of Birmingham. Her research interests are in the history of education, women's history and the teaching of history, and she has published on each of these. She is co-editor of *Crossing the Key Stages of History* (David Fulton) and has recently published *Gender, Power and the Unitarians in England, 1760–1860*.

HMI (England) authors

Carole Baker, Ted Cohn and Mark McLaughlin

Prior to joining the inspectorate, each HMI (England) had significant experience at various levels in education, including in schools, higher education, in-service training and adult education. As an HMI for over fifteen years, each has inspected widely in schools, further education and higher education, including teacher training. Inspection of teacher training involves not only the initial training of teachers, but also the induction of newly qualified teachers and the further professional development of longer serving teachers. In addition, each has written a substantial number of published surveys as well as reports on individual institutions or courses.

Introduction to the Series

This book, *Issues in History Teaching*, is one of a series of books entitled *Issues in Subject Teaching*. The series has been designed to engage with a wide range of issues related to subject teaching. Types of issues vary among subjects, but may include, for example: issues that impact on Initial Teacher Education in the subject; issues addressed in the classroom through the teaching of the subject; issues to do with the content of the subject and its definition; issues to do with subject pedagogy; issues to do with the relationship between the subject and broader educational aims and objectives in society, and the philosophy and sociology of education; and issues to do with the development of the subject and its future in the twenty-first century.

Each book consequently presents key debates that subject teachers will need to understand, reflect on and engage in as part of their professional development. Chapters have been designed to highlight major questions, to consider the evidence from research and practice and to arrive at possible answers. Some subject books or chapters offer at least one solution or a view of the ways forward, whereas others provide alternative views and leave readers to identify their own solution or view of the ways forward. The editors expect readers of the series to want to pursue the issues raised, and so chapters include suggestions for further reading, and questions for further debate. The chapters and questions could be used as stimuli for debate in subject seminars or department meetings, or as topics for assignments or classroom research. The books are targeted at all those with a professional interest in the subject, and in particular: student teachers learning to teach the subject in the primary or secondary school; newly qualified teachers; teachers with a subject co-ordination or leadership role, and those preparing for such responsibility; mentors, tutors, trainers and advisers of the groups mentioned above.

Each book in the series has a cross-phase dimension. This is because the editors believe it is important for teachers in the primary and secondary phases to look at subject teaching holistically, particularly in order to provide for continuity and progression, but also to increase their understanding of how children learn. The balance of chapters that have a cross-phase relevance, chapters that focus on issues which are of particular concern to primary teachers and chapters that focus on issues which secondary teachers are more likely to need to address, varies according to the issues relevant to different subjects. However, no matter where the emphasis is, authors have drawn out the relevance of their topic to the whole of each book's intended audience.

Because of the range of the series, both in terms of the issues covered and its cross-phase concern, each book is an edited collection. Editors have commissioned new writing from experts on particular issues who, collectively, will represent many different perspectives on subject teaching. Readers should not expect a book in this series to cover a full range of issues relevant to the subject, or to offer a completely unified view of subject teaching, or that every issue will be dealt with discretely, or that all aspects of an issue will be covered. Part of what each book in this series offers to readers is the opportunity to explore the inter-relationships between positions in debates and, indeed, among the debates themselves, by identifying the overlapping concerns and competing arguments that are woven through the text.

The editors are aware that many initiatives in subject teaching currently originate from the centre, and that teachers have decreasing control of subject content, pedagogy and assessment strategies. The editors strongly believe that for teaching to remain properly a vocation and a profession, teachers must be invited to be part of a creative and critical dialogue about subject teaching, and encouraged to reflect, criticise, problem-solve and innovate. This series is intended to provide teachers with a stimulus for democratic involvement in the development of subject teaching.

Susan Capel,
Jon Davison,
James Arthur and
John Moss
May 1999

1 What are the issues in the teaching of history?

James Arthur

One of the most critical issues of all in the teaching of history, and one that is raised by a number of contributors in this volume, is the subject's continued presence on the school curriculum. Despite repeated assurances from the Qualification and Curriculum Authority (QCA) that it is committed to securing the place of history in the school curriculum, the Historical Association felt it necessary to launch yet another Campaign for History in February 1998 (the Historical Association ran a previous campaign in 1988). The central objective of this new campaign was to secure the survival of school history through the promotion of the idea that every pupil, between the ages of five and nineteen, has *a right* to a historical education. It is significant that the decision to launch this 'save history campaign' was made in 1997 before the Government decided to loosen the primary school curriculum by allowing schools to spend less time on certain subjects, including history, in order to concentrate a far greater proportion of their teaching time on literacy and numeracy. The consequence of this Government decision, whether intentional or not, has been to reduce the amount of history taught in the primary school and further reduce the need for primary schools to devote their scarce resources to the training of history subject leaders. Whilst it is recognised that the National Curriculum statutory requirements will be reinstated in primary schools in September 2000, it does not remove the fact that history teaching will have suffered in the mean time.

Within the fourteen to sixteen curriculum the number of entries for GCSE history has continued to decline since 1986 by about 1 per cent each year and history's place within the Key Stage 4 curriculum in many schools has consequently been eroded. The choice of courses and qualifications now available to young people at post-fourteen continues to grow and therefore constantly increases the competition that history faces. There are also concerns that some schools structure their Key Stage 4 options in such a way that history is simply not available as a choice for those who wish to take it. In addition, pupils, parents and employers often need convincing that history teaching is both relevant and useful to adult working life. History is also not an easy option either at fourteen or at 'A' Level; the 1996 Dearing *Review of Qualifications for 16–19 year olds* groups history with mathematics and physics as being 'more difficult than

average' and indicates that the subject has one of the highest entry requirements at university. All of this places pressure on the future of school history
and no one should underestimate the real threats and challenges being posed to
the subject, particularly at Key Stages 1, 2 and 4.

It is therefore not surprising that many newly qualified teachers find it difficult to secure history posts in secondary schools to teach the subject for which
they have been trained. History teachers also face the new demands on their
subject teaching presented by the White Paper, *Excellence in Schools* (1997),
with its immediate goals for the school curriculum of encouraging wider access,
higher aspirations and standards, increased literacy levels, inclusive education
and a desire to overcome economic disadvantage. There has also been a vocal
lobby seeking a role for history teachers in the teaching of citizenship education. The Historical Association, for example, has argued strongly for the
expertise of history teachers to be used in order to ensure effective citizenship
education. Whilst a good historical background is necessary if young people are
to understand fully the nature of modern democracy, including their rights and
responsibilities, it is not the Government's intention that citizenship education
should be principally delivered through the history curriculum. Citizenship
education will form a distinct subject area within the curriculum and will not
necessarily be taught by the history teacher as there will not be any prescriptive
model of delivery. The review of the National Curriculum is set to add further
demands on the history teacher, including the integration of Information and
Communication Technology (ICT) and study skills into history teaching. The
purpose of this review has been to pursue a school curriculum that more closely
matches the needs of pupils. As part of this review the QCA established a new
History Task Group in October 1998 to review the history curriculum in
schools.

The History Task Group, 1998–9

The composition of the 1998 History Task Group was essentially the same as it
had been in previous groups that were made up of a clear majority of classroom
teachers. There was one LEA adviser and one representative from higher education. There were of course the usual 'observers' from the DfEE, OFSTED and
the QCA history subject officers. The group met only three times between
October and December 1998 and the agenda was centrally controlled and set by
the QCA for all subject groups. The purpose of the group was made clear at the
first meeting, which was to secure less prescription and more flexibility in the
History Order. In addition, the group was to consider how history made a
distinctive contribution to the school curriculum and in particular to outline a
clearer rationale for the subject by stating what the priorities are at each of the
Key Stages. The teachers on the group were reluctant at first to envisage any
changes to the History Order, particularly at Key Stage 3, but with considerable
'persuasion' and argument from the 'observers' on the group there was a realisation that many history teachers had perceived the programmes of study more as

a syllabus than as a curriculum framework. There was also a realisation that many history teachers had already slimmed the history curriculum down, but not always in a very consistent way across the programmes of study. Nevertheless, it would be mistake to think that the History Task Group generated, far less discussed, a series of issues for history teaching. The group did not have time to deliberate at any length and was more focused on the work of reducing the content specification of the History Order and incorporating statements about the rationale for history teaching, including statements on ICT and access. The group was largely preoccupied with technical points and getting the right phrases for ideas that had been largely formed elsewhere.

There was also extremely limited discussion of citizenship education largely because the Government had not, at that stage, made a decision on the recommendations of the Crick report (QCA 1998c). Another reason was because the QCA had established a group with the title 'Planning for Adult Living' to consider all the non-subject areas, such as spiritual and moral education, but this group was largely dominated by an argument about the place of citizenship education on the school curriculum. I have no doubt that some of the responses to the QCA's consultations, especially those from the Secondary Committee of the Historical Association, figured prominently in the developmental work of the QCA history officers. The final history papers produced by the QCA for the formal consultation on the National Curriculum were edited by a central QCA team to ensure a degree of coherence and consistency across subject areas. The History Task Group was aware that changes to the History Order had to be kept strictly to the essential minimum in order to ensure that it was manageable. Key Stage 3 history therefore remains largely intact. Much has remained untouched and the main changes appear to have been a clarification of requirements through a significant reduction in content specification and a description of the types of learning experiences for history in each of the Key Stages, including the strengthening of ICT and the need for greater differentiation within history teaching.

All of these changes, it is claimed, are intended to allow for greater professional autonomy in selecting content and resources in the teaching of history. The brief work of the History Task Group and the developmental work of QCA has produced a history curriculum with a more explicit rationale, but this must now be combined with the broader aims and purposes of the school curriculum as a whole. History teachers need to demonstrate that their subject is 'relevant' and an integral part of the values, aims and purposes of the school curriculum. These challenges raise a number of potential issues for history teaching, not least of which is whether history teachers should give greater priority to the value of history teaching, as part of the general aims of the school curriculum as a whole, or focus their attention on improving history learning itself. It should be remembered that Government decisions have already removed compulsory Key Stage 4 history and effectively removed the duty of English primary schools, temporarily, to teach history to their pupils. Whilst the existence of the National Curriculum has ensured history's place at Key Stage 3 on the school timetable, it is Government decisions, as we have seen, that could just as easily remove it or reduce it further. It is significant that there has been far less interest in the revision of school history shown by the media, especially concerning the debate about the nature and purpose of history itself. The debate about citizenship education in particular has overshadowed the role of history in the school curriculum.

A collection of issues

This collection of selected essays has been written by a diverse range of scholars in the field of history education and includes important contributions from three experienced history HMIs. Most of the contributors are established scholars who are already well known through their publications. A few are new scholars whose work, as yet less well known, is already beginning to make an impact in the field of history education. The book covers both primary and secondary phases and by no means exhausts the potential issues surrounding the teaching of school history. Each contributor has selected his or her own issue in history teaching. The book is divided into three parts with several chapters in each. The first part addresses issues in the teaching of history in the school classroom. Contributions in the second part examine the relationship between the subject and the broader educational aims in society. The final part is written by three history specialist HMIs who focus on issues in the training of history teachers. Each chapter concludes with some brief questions for discussion and a few suggestions for further reading. The extensive bibliography at the end of this book provides the reader with a valuable resource for further investigation and research of the issues raised. Taken together the seventeen chapters in this volume provide a thorough map of the central issues in the field.

We begin with Robert Phillips, author of the well received and impeccably researched, *History Teaching, Nationhood and the State* (1998) and co-editor of this present volume, who provides us with an understanding of the policy context for all three parts. His detailed research highlights and traces Government policy initiatives in school history over the last thirty years. He describes the debates and issues surrounding the development of the history curriculum and the political involvement of Government in establishing a National Curriculum for history. Robert is also concerned about the future quality of history teaching in our schools, for as he concludes:

> As far as history teaching is concerned, if history teachers are not encouraged to be research orientated, innovative and transformative, then the consequences may be particularly dire, for ultimately the future of a vulnerable subject like ours is dependent upon the quality of teaching.

Robert lays the groundwork in this essay by providing the starting point for the issues raised in each of the three parts.

A second introductory essay by Penelope Harnett, editor of the professional journal, *Primary History*, provides a contextual chapter by way of further background to all three parts. She specifically addresses the history curriculum in the primary school and raises a number of critical issues. She describes evidence of how primary schools are spending less time teaching history than in previous years and suggests that one of the consequences of this is that: 'As different subjects compete with each other for space on the timetable, linking subjects together becomes more attractive, and a return to greater emphasis on topic work more of a possibility.' However, she believes that the experience of the National Curriculum has increased primary school teachers' awareness of the distinctive contribution that each curriculum subject can make to topic work, which will, she believes, prevent a return to the unfocused thematic work that characterised primary school teaching in the past. Penelope's chapter surveys the teaching of history in primary schools and provides an outline of the issues that primary history will face over the coming years.

Part I of the book rightly focuses on the teaching issues arising out of the history classroom. It begins with an excellent essay on teaching historical significance by Martin Hunt. Martin, as well as being co-author of *Learning to Teach History in the Secondary School* (1997) has developed a highly praised PGCE course in Manchester that uses a series of course booklets written by him and which are worthy of publication in themselves. In this chapter Martin examines the case for assessing the significance of events, people and changes in the past and explores the educational outcomes of teaching significance in history. As well as identifying the issues, he also proposes a number of very useful strategies for teaching significance in the history classroom. In addition, Martin effectively relates his essay to an argument for the relevance of history, as he says:

> At a time when there are pressures on history departments to assert the strength of the case for history beyond Year 9, the assessment of the significance of events, changes and people in the past not only deepens pupils' understanding of the world in which they live, but also helps them consider the ageless social, moral and cultural issues that adolescents see as being very relevant.

This essay makes a major contribution to our understanding of historical significance and successfully bridges theory and classroom practice.

Christine Counsell provides us with further bridging: in an important essay she looks at historical knowledge and historical skills as central issues in teaching. Christine is editor of the Historical Association's journal, *Teaching History*, and is an influential scholar on writing and thinking skills in history teaching. She also has a significant voice in defending the place and role of school history through her work for the Historical Association and through the many services she has provided for QCA. In this present essay Christine examines not only the relationship between content and skills but how teachers plan them in their teaching. She also explores the assumptions that teachers have about these two vital issues.

Tony McAleavy, as well as being an LEA inspector for the humanities, is also the author of a number of best-selling historical textbooks for schools. Tony has extensive experience of teaching and advising on history and considers the relationship between interpretations and historical sources in his chapter. In particular he examines how we can use pupil interpretations as a starting point for reflecting on our teaching, and he offers some practical suggestions for the classroom.

This is followed by an important chapter on the developing and under-standing of chronology in history. William Stow, an experienced history educator, together with Terry Haydn, co-author of *Learning to Teach History in the Secondary School* (1997), show here how chronology is an important issue for both primary and secondary teaching of history and suggest some practical strategies for the teaching of chronological understanding. In particular, they give an overview of research into children's understanding of chronology across Key Stages 1–3 and highlight why chronology has a controversial place in debates over methods of history teaching. So important do they consider chronology to be that they make this appeal:

> What is vital is that, at a time when the amount of history taught in primary schools seems set to diminish, this key aspect of historical under-standing is still given prominence. The concept of historical time and its associated skills and links to other concepts is one of the most essential aspects of understanding for the primary child to take forward into secondary education.

This essay analyses afresh the issue of chronology in history teaching.

Terry Haydn makes a second contribution to this volume with his research and writing on ICT, which is of course strengthened in the new History Order. He especially looks at what we can and can not do with ICT applications in history and considers some ways forward for the classroom history teacher. He is conscious that history teachers will normally only use ICT if they are confident that it will improve pupil learning in history. However, he is equally conscious that a failure to consider the use of ICT by the history teacher will result in a loss of opportunities for engaging pupils in history and enhancing their learning. Whilst he believes that history teaching should help young people to handle ICT intelligently, he also warns that: 'Good teachers are always looking for ways to improve their teaching, and are able to adapt and change to meet new chal-lenges and opportunities, but let us not pretend that computers are an unproblematic educational miracle.' Terry adopts a sensible, pragmatic approach to ICT in the history classroom that will be welcomed by many.

Wendy Cunnah is a specialist in special educational needs within history teaching and her contribution considers the issues of both why history is perceived to be a difficult subject and also how history can contribute to the teaching of literacy. She provides a comprehensive survey of the research and ideas concerning access to history, particularly the crucial importance of the pupil's language development and how it aids access to the study of history. The chapter examines the challenges for history teachers of the inclusive classroom and she explores, in that context, why the question should not be 'should we teach history?' but 'how should we teach history?'. Finally, she outlines a number of positive strategies for addressing how children should receive a history curriculum based on need, not learning difficulty.

Chris Husbands, author of *What is History Teaching?* (1996), together with Anna Pendry, his co-author of *History Teachers in the Making* (1998), consider the issue of what existing understanding about history pupils bring to their history lessons. In this context their essay examines some actual historical work of pupils in order to highlight the implications for classroom practice. They conclude by suggesting that:

> If children are to think historically they need to make sense of not just the past but also the adult people in it, and listening to pupils and looking at their everyday work reveals that this is an aspect of their understanding and development with which they need our support. Without such support, they are likely to continue to be overly influenced by their existing ways of thinking.

The authors make the case that teachers should seek to discover the pupils' existing historical knowledge in order that this prior knowledge can be taken into account in planning for teaching and learning.

Part II of this volume addresses national and international concerns, and begins with two essays on the national dimension of teaching history. The first is by Ian Davies, who is a published expert on citizenship education and in the role that history teaching can make to promoting democracy. His essay is timely in relation to the publication of the Crick report (1998) and the Government's intention to ensure that citizenship education is firmly placed on the school curriculum. In particular, Ian looks at the challenges associated with implementing citizenship education through aspects of history. He reveals that, like citizenship education, the status of history in the school curriculum is low and that the potential for overlap between the two is great. Ian believes that history teachers will be given a heavy responsibility for teaching the new requirements for citizenship education, although this remains to be seen. Nevertheless, he draws our attention to the real professional neglect among history teachers that has occurred in making links between history education and citizenship education. As he says: 'a proper sense of citizenship includes knowing about the links between the past and the present'. Citizenship education will remain a much discussed issue for history teaching in the years to come, but the extent to which history should, or may, contribute to the promotion of citizenship education in schools is an unresolved issue that Ian and others will continue to research and study.

The second essay in this section is by Ian Grosvenor, author *of Assimilating Identities: Racism and Education Policy in Post-1945 Britain* (1997). He researches in the field of race and history teaching, and in this chapter he focuses on the issue of 'inclusiveness' and the history curriculum. Ian considers the history curriculum in schools in relation to multicultural education and advocates an inclusive history for the nation. He warns against a 'common cultural heritage approach' to school history and the 'narrow sense of British identity' that may be promoted as a consequence. Ian's 'inclusive' view of the history of the nation presents a radical challenge to history teachers.

This is followed by two chapters on the European dimension, the first written by Hilary Cooper, author of *The Teaching of History in Primary Schools* (1995) and *History in the Early Years* (1995), and former editor of *Teaching History*. She examines history education in Europe, particularly in the age range of five to eleven. Hilary's research in this contribution focuses on how an under-standing of the past by many children in Europe is formed by sources outside of the school – mainly because history is not usually formally taught as a subject until the age of eleven. She links this to how children form their own personal identity and she is generally optimistic by the progress that primary history teaching has made in England compared to Europe.

The second essay on the European experience is provided by Ruth Watts, co-editor of *Crossing the Key Stages of History* (1996) who examines how the European experiences of teaching history can help the teaching of history in England. She provides some interesting information on how English teachers can participate in European activities regarding school history development and teaching. She also makes an appeal to all history teachers to value European co-operation so that they can develop rational, intelligent, critical citizens in thriving democracies, which she believes will ensure that politicians are not allowed to use school history to propagate ideology. She ends with a series of important issues and questions for reflection. The European dimension as an issue in school history teaching is set to be one of growing importance and this essay highlights some of the ways forward.

The final part in this book is written by Carole Baker, Ted Cohn and Mark McLaughlin who are all history HMIs and have written between them a substantial number of published surveys. They have also inspected history teaching in schools, further education colleges and university departments of education. All three HMIs have jointly written the chapters in this section, which address the issues of 'good practice' in the training of secondary history teachers, including that which takes place within the school-based element of the training of history teachers. The third chapter focuses specifically on inspecting the subject knowledge of potential history teachers. These three chapters also describe the work of HMIs in inspecting history teaching and provide some of their findings. The chapters reveal a great deal about the central issues in teaching history and all those involved with the training of future history teachers will acquire a great deal of insight and draw many a prac-tical application from reading them.

Overall, this collection of essays raises a wide range of issues for all those concerned with the quality and standard of history teaching in our schools. The collection by no means exhausts the issues that can be raised as there are many others that require our attention. One major gap, which was under consideration at the time of writing, concerns the history specifications developed by the Awarding Bodies of England, Wales and Northern Ireland for 'AS' and 'A' level history, which are now to be judged against a nationally agreed set of criteria. The accreditation of all 'A' level specifications in all subjects has taken place within the same time-scale, thereby enabling comparisons to be made of specification demand both within and across subjects. Both the development of subject criteria and the accreditation process were considered by the Government to be means of providing universities, employers, teachers and candidates with evidence that the specifications for the revised 'A' level are a basis for a course of study and qualification comparable in rigour to its predecessor.

Despite these gaps it is hoped that this volume will not only supplement *Learning to Teach in the Secondary School* (1997) by Terry Haydn, James Arthur and Martin Hunt, but that it will also be of considerable interest to primary school teachers who have a continued interest in developing their understanding of the issues in history teaching.

2 Government policies, the State and the teaching of history

Robert Phillips

Introduction

This chapter examines the relationship between history teaching and the State, particularly in the late twentieth century. By concentrating upon the 'politics of history teaching', it will explain why history is such an 'issues-based' subject. In order to focus the reader more directly upon these issues, each of the sub-headings below makes reference to some of the most significant texts that have been produced relating to the main policy-related debates over the teaching of history during the period. The chapter derives inspiration from the observation of Aldrich and Dean (1991) that if history teachers do not analyse the history of their own subject, why should they expect their students to think historically?

'Why do governments fear history?'

It is important to consider, initially, *why history matters* and why governments not only in Britain but throughout the world have sought to influence history curricula, prompting Kaye (1996) to ask the question: why do rulers and governments fear history? As this question implies, history is closely related to issues of power, values and cultural transmission. It was Orwell ('he who controls the past controls the future') who made reference to the potential of history to shape minds. Ironically, the year 1984, as we shall see below, turned out to be a significant one in the recent 'history of history'. It prompted Tosh (1984: 8) to claim that school history was a political battleground because the 'sanction of the past' is useful both for 'upholders and subverters of authority'. What history we teach and how we teach it, so the theory goes, has a direct impact upon how young people will view their own identity and, crucially, their country's identity (Phillips 1998a).

Little wonder, then, that at the high point of the controversy over the National Curriculum in the 1990s, Margaret Thatcher should have become directly involved in the debate. In one of the most perceptive of the many articles that appeared in the press at the time, one correspondent argued that Thatcher's involvement was prompted by her own realisation of history's potential to influence, for if she could 'change the way that we are taught history, she will have succeeded in changing the ground rules for a generation to come. It is a big prize' (Martin Kettle in the *Guardian*, 4 January 1990). Political interest in school history was not merely confined to one political party, as politicians from a range of political persuasions expressed a view, including John Major and Tony Blair during the 1996 election campaign (see Brecse 1998).

The reference to the press, politics and politicians highlights the fact that history in the late twentieth century became public property; in the 1980s and 1990s, it appeared that everyone had a say on what history should be taught in schools. This suggests that something was happening in society to initiate this interest. After all, history teaching does not exist in a vacuum; it reflects many of the values and issues perceived to be important in society at large. Some have argued that the British obsession with the past during this period stemmed from a contemporary uncertainty about the present. History had become a subject in demand by a range of competing groups concerned to find identity in a changing (often troubled) world. As Furedi (1992: 8) suggests, there is no longer 'a history with a capital H; there are many competing histories'. This attempt to find certainty through history at times of uncertainty has a long history (Samuel 1998).

The last quarter of the twentieth century was undoubtedly a period of intense economic, political, cultural and social change, sometimes referred to as 'the postmodern condition' (Lyotard 1984). In essence, postmodernism refers to a changing sense and expression of identity. As long-standing ideas, organising principles and traditional values began to be questioned in the late twentieth century (such as Marxism, capitalism, formal religion and a 'canon' of knowledge) tied to traditional forms of identity (for example based on class, the Church, the family), so people sought new forms and expressions of identity, which had profound implications for history. In a controversial and thought-provoking book, Jenkins (1991: 65–6) gives a useful and comprehensive list of these 'other histories' that, in the late twentieth century, were 'all being affected by local, regional and international perspectives'. This was also reflected at this time in the growth of interest in the heritage industry (Lowenthal 1998).

This explosion in the search for 'other histories' posed a challenging question to those charged with responsibility for history in schools: namely, 'what history to teach and why?' This is a question that has challenged philosophers of history throughout the century (Warren 1998). History, by definition, is a vast subject that requires a process of selection and, if we accept that history is a value-laden subject, then the question of selection becomes an acute one, particularly at times of change and uncertainty. It is likely to be even more contentious when the State – through appointed bodies – intervenes to influence the selection process. The 'history of history' in the twentieth century, documented below, will make this clearer.

'An inherited consensus'?

Experienced history teachers and student teachers alike have the rather daunting task of familiarising themselves with a vast amount of documentation relating to the teaching of history. This is because what is taught in history classrooms is heavily regulated by Government. Yet the history of the subject in the twentieth century as a whole suggests that it was not always like this. In fact, for most of the century, a tradition had emerged of non-interference by the State in the details of what was actually taught in history classrooms. As Penelope Harnett demonstrates in the next chapter, governments at various points in the century offered general suggestions and guidance on the direction of history teaching through inspectors or commissioned reports. But they rarely, if ever, sought to prescribe what was taught or how it was taught; as Aldrich and Dean (1991: 99) have shown, for the most of the twentieth century 'history became a matter for historians and history teachers, both as individuals, and as interest groups'.

This traditional non-interference by Government in what was taught in history classrooms can be explained, essentially, by two inter-related factors. First, the type of history taught in school based upon predominantly British constitutional history – what Sylvester (1994) terms the 'Great Tradition' – was essentially non-controversial and 'accepted'. Governments did not interfere in what was taught in history classrooms because there was no perceived reason for them to do so. Second, this 'Great Tradition' or what Slater calls the 'inherited consensus' (see below) both contributed to and reflected back a wider consensus based upon homogeneity, class structure and patriarchal order in society at large. Provided this certainty prevailed, then in turn there was no perceived need to teach anything other than an essentially Anglocentric history. Slater puts this eloquently in an amusing parody of the state of history teaching in English (and, significantly, Welsh) schools in the early twentieth century:

> Content was largely British, or rather Southern English; Celts looked in to starve, emigrate or rebel; the North to invent looms or work in mills; abroad was of interest once it was part of the Empire; foreigners were either, sensibly, allies, or rightly, defeated. Skills – did we even use the word? – were mainly those of recalling accepted facts about famous dead Englishmen, and communicated in a very eccentric literary form, the exam-ination length essay. It was inherited consensus, based on largely hidden assumptions.
>
> (Slater 1989: 1)

A number of developments in the 1960s onwards meant that this 'inherited consensus' began to break down. Post-war immigration and the growth of multi-cultural communities meant that schools had to reconsider history syllabuses that were merely geared towards a predominantly homogenous populace. There was also evidence that history was becoming increasingly unpopular amongst pupils and perceived to be irrelevant; in a famous polemic, Mary Price (1968) warned that if the perceived unpopularity of history continued, it would end up in the curriculum broom-cupboard with subjects such as classics.

It was this concern about the status of the subject that led to the development of 'new history' in the early 1970s. Influenced by educationalists like Bruner, 'new history' placed emphasis not only upon chronology and historical knowledge, but also upon the cultivation of conceptual understanding and skills. In many ways, it was not 'new' at all, as innovative history teachers earlier in the century such as Keatinge (1910) and Happold (1928) had also used these methods. Yet the *Schools' Council 11–16 Project* (SCHP) and its primary counterpart *Place, Time and Society 8–13* were attempts in the early 1970s to shake up history teaching from its lethargy. This 'new history' stressed that in order to understand the subject effectively, pupils had to be shown that history was a distinct body of knowledge and that specific skills had to be cultivated in order to understand it. The SCHP combined local, national and world history topics, and, in order to cultivate conceptual understanding such as change and continuity, selected relatively unusual content matter such as the history of medicine.

'New history' provoked more interest and debate than almost any other 'issue' in history teaching. Its critics (see below) were vociferous in their condemnation of these approaches that, they claimed, did not represent 'history' at all. On the other hand, according to Slater (1989) and Sylvester (1994) 'new history' was beneficial because it invigorated the teaching of history at a time when it was in decline. Although the number of students taking SCHP courses at secondary level was relatively low, its real significance lies in the way that it influenced Her Majesty's Inspectorate (HMI) (DES 1985a) and, perhaps more significantly, the General Certificate of Education (GCSE) that was introduced in 1986 (see below).

Whatever its merits and demerits, it is important to consider that 'new history' emerged during a period of considerable autonomy for teachers over the control of the curriculum. Lawton (1980) called the post-war period down to the late 1970s a 'golden age' of teacher autonomy, and a minister in the 1950s once referred to the curriculum as the 'secret garden' of teachers. Again, as with the apparent 'inherited consensus' during the post-war period, it is possible to exaggerate the existence of a 'golden age' of teacher autonomy. Yet, compared to the 1980s and 1990s, teachers during this period had considerable discretion over the choice of historical content to be taught, which had advantages as well as disadvantages.

'A host of malignant sprites'?

It was not a Conservative but a Labour Prime Minister, James Callaghan, who, in a famous speech at Ruskin College in 1976, raised a number of issues about this state of affairs, arguing that parents, industry and central government should have a say in the control and direction of the school curriculum (Chitty

1989). Yet ten years went by before we saw at least the beginnings of direct governmental interest in the nature and scope of the history curriculum in schools, in the shape of the GCSE in 1986. Two years prior to this, in that symbolic year 1984 which was mentioned earlier, the Secretary of State for Education, Keith Joseph, argued strongly in a speech delivered to the Historical Association (HA) that history was an important subject within the school curriculum. Interestingly, however, perhaps mindful of the sensitivity of the subject under issue, he attempted to steer a middle line between competing philosophies of history teaching. Joseph judged that the time was not yet right for the State to prescribe what should and should not be taught in the history classroom.

Subsequently, the GCSE criteria (DES 1985b) did not stipulate specific content requirements to be included in all GCSE syllabuses. Rather, examination groups should provide 'a wide range of options to give freedom to innovate and to reflect local interests' and that therefore it was 'not desirable to stipulate a minimum core of content' (DES 1985b: par. 4.1). Moreover, in line with SCHP principles, the criteria emphasised that in addition to historical knowledge, pupils should be given opportunities to develop awareness of concepts such as causation, change and continuity, and, in the process, develop a 'wide variety' of skills chiefly associated with the evaluation of historical evidence. Most contentious of all, however, was the requirement that pupils should be encouraged to 'look at events and issues from the perspective of people in the past' (DES 1985b: par. 4.1), i.e. to cultivate a sense of historical empathy.

Empathy had a long history of its own (Knight 1989a). History teachers as long ago as Keatinge and Happold had encouraged pupils to think 'empathetically' through imagination, reconstruction and understanding. Yet the GCSE took this a stage further – pupils were to be examined in their ability to empathise more formally, a combination of skill and conceptual understanding that even historians found difficult to achieve (Lowenthal 1985). The subsequent debate over the teaching of empathy was not confined to professional circles; it provoked a storm of controversy in the press, in the shape of letters, articles and even editorials, concrete evidence that history was now moving away from the academic/professional domain to the public one (Phillips 1998a and 1998b).

The empathy controversy also provided the opportunity for an important ideological grouping to enter the debate, namely the New Right, which comprised an eclectic and varied group of intellectuals, writers and academics who were united in their belief that teacher autonomy over the control of the curriculum had to be broken (Chitty 1989). They were interested in all aspects of the curriculum, but particularly history because of its importance for cultural transmission and the formation of national identity (Phillips 1996). In a series of pamphlets, articles and letters to the press, the New Right critique of history teaching was based upon three major premises: that the teaching of a 'canon' of British history (and particularly English history) had been abandoned in favour of multicultural or world history; that the influence of 'new history' amongst history teachers had led to an obsession with skills and concepts at the expense of historical knowledge; and that, consequently, history had become corrupted by cultural relativism, that is, that nothing of real worth or value was being taught in history classrooms any more. This was evidenced by the teaching of empathy that, in the words of one of the most active New Right campaigners encouraged pupils to be 'sympathetic to everybody else's predicament before making sure that we have a clear idea of our own standpoint' (Deuchar 1987: 15). Consequently, pupils were leaving history classrooms knowing nothing of any real historical worth.

The interesting aspect of this New Right onslaught was that there was a hint of truth about it. In a well argued and thoughtful book, Partington (1980) had justifiably warned of the possible dangers of an over-concentration of skills at the expense of knowledge, as well as the propensity of 'new history' to devalue the importance of chronology and British history. These were genuine and serious issues that many history teachers could sympathise with. And many history teachers had concerns over the teaching of empathy. Yet when the New Right resorted to tactics of blatant derision such as claiming, as did Partington in a later publication, that history teaching had been corrupted by a 'host of malignant sprites' (1986: 69), then history teachers became understandably defensive and sensitive about their subject and their position.

What worried many of them was that the New Right would influence the National Curriculum that had been announced in 1987. The writing seemed to be on the wall when an HMI document produced in 1988 (in marked contrast to that published in 1985 mentioned earlier: see DES 1985a) seemed to endorse many of their views on the teaching of chronology and content (DES 1988). Would the subsequent National Curriculum, in the words of Chitty (1989), be a 'Victory for the New Right?'

'The battle for the big prize'?

The National Curriculum, as Tate has recently pointed out, became 'fiercely contested' because it ran 'counter to the traditions of English autonomy' (1998: 38) over education. Its chief architect, Kenneth Baker, saw in the National Curriculum an opportunity fundamentally to reform the education system and in such circumstances it was bound to arouse strong feelings. History was to prove one of the most controversial of all National Curriculum subjects, not least of all because it attracted direct interference by the Prime Minister and Government ministers. After all, as we said earlier, the National Curriculum represented the 'battle for the big prize', namely the cultural legacy of the Thatcher years (Phillips 1992).

Many challenges, therefore, faced the National Curriculum History Working Group in England established by Baker in 1989 to advise him on the form that the new curriculum should take (NB: there were separate National Curriculum groups for Wales & Northern Ireland, an important point that is discussed later in this chapter). The History Working Group had to abide by the terms of reference laid down by the Government to produce a history National Curriculum that had at its core the history of Britain, the record of its past and in particular, its political, constitutional and cultural heritage; on the other hand, it had to be sensitive to the views of teachers who were proprietorial about their autonomy. The danger was that the History Working Group would end up pleasing no one. In addition, the question of the assessment of historical knowledge was particularly contentious: would the History Working Group advocate a separate attainment target for the assessment of historical knowledge or would they argue for a more sophisticated method of assessing historical understanding?

The story of the History Working Group's trials and tribulations have been recorded elsewhere (Phillips 1998a). In the end, after many meetings spread over eighteen months (during which time the press took a particularly active interest in every dimension of its work) the History Working Group produced a report that was politically very shrewd (DES 1990b). It emphasised that British history was indeed at the core of its proposals, therefore ensuring that it had met the requirements of the terms of reference. However, the report went on to offer a very broad-based definition of British history, to include not only the history of England, but the British isles as a whole, including its multicultural 'inheritances', rather than the singular 'heritage' as had been required by the terms of reference above. It also advocated the teaching of the history of non-European societies and, on the assessment/knowledge issue, the History Working Group recommended a careful balance of knowledge, skills and concepts:

> The study of history must be grounded in a thorough knowledge of the past; must employ rigorous historical method – the way in which historians carry out their task; and must involve a range of interpretations and explanations. Together, these elements make an organic whole; if any one of them is missing the outcome is not history.
>
> (DES 1990a: para. 1.3, emphasis in original)

The reference to 'a range of interpretations' as well as 'inheritances' was significant, suggesting that the History Working Group (like Furedi) recognised that it was no longer possible to merely advocate a singular monolithic 'History'. The initial response from teachers was cautiously positive, despite concerns over workload and autonomy. In a series of conferences held by the HA, teachers throughout the country broadly welcomed the report's proposals (Phillips 1992). It seemed that consensus had returned to the history debate.

Any semblance of agreement or consensus was soon shattered, however, by two well publicised examples of direct political interference by the Government. In contrast to Kenneth Baker who, as a historian himself, was inclined to be sympathetic to the highly complex challenges facing the History Working Group (Phillips 1998c), Margaret Thatcher disliked the History Working Group proposals, particularly the fact that the report had placed too much emphasis upon interpretation and not enough upon British history and the assessment of historical knowledge (Thatcher 1993: 78). She demanded that the report should go out to further consultation, and the subsequent amended 'MacGregor' proposals put greater emphasis on historical knowledge and British history (DES 1990b). Yet, when these were endorsed by the National Curriculum Council following even more consultation, the new Secretary of State for Education, Kenneth Clarke, took action that represented the high point of direct governmental involvement in the whole debate. He announced that he had made 'certain changes' to the final proposals which would ensure that they should focus upon 'the first half of the twentieth century ... to draw some distinction between the study of history and the study of current affairs' (*DES News* 7/91, 14 January 1991).

There was almost unanimous opposition to what was perceived to be blatant political interference in a professional matter. Even the Conservative peer and historian Lord Blake called the decision 'ridiculous' (the *Independent*, 17 March 1991). The HA was understandably incensed by what had happened, describing it as incomprehensible; a senior HA member illustrated the absurdity of the situation by pointing out that 'The building of the Berlin Wall is history; its destruction is not' (*Times Educational Supplement (TES)*: 18 January 1991). Many called upon teachers simply to ignore the new proposals when the National Curriculum history finally became statutory in schools in September 1991 (DES 1991).

Given the controversy and difficulties surrounding its inception, it was not entirely surprising that the history National Curriculum 'Mark I' faced problems from the start. It soon became clear that the curriculum was overloaded, too prescriptive and complicated, particularly in terms of assessment. Consequently, history, along with all the other subjects, was reformed by the review of the National Curriculum under Sir Ron Dearing between 1993 and 1994. Unsurprisingly, during the process of slimming the history curriculum even more, when problems of selection were exacerbated, controversy broke out again. Indeed, the headlines that appeared in the press between 1993 and 1994 were some of the most strident of all. At one point, the *Sun* claimed that the proposals meant that 'Britain's glorious past (was) banished from history lessons'. In fact, an objective analysis of the reformed National Curriculum statutory orders revealed that they kept intact the original History Working Group commitment to a broad-based British history combined with European and world history. National Curriculum history 'Mark II' was implemented in schools in September 1995 (DfE 1995) and, at the time of writing, remain statutory until the second review of the National Curriculum scheduled for 2000.

'Four histories, one nation'?

The debate over history in England had been bedevilled with conflict – a reflection, perhaps, of the wider cultural debate at this time about what constituted Englishness. Yet at the same time the other constituent parts of the UK were developing their own history curricula that, significantly, mirrored the moves towards devolution in Scotland, Wales and in Northern Ireland, and which reflected their 'particular cultural characteristics, political imperatives and historical legacies' (Phillips *et al.* 1999; see also Table 2.1). If we accept that what history we teach may have an impact upon our sense of national identity, then these developments may have significant implications for the future.

The importance of the link between history and national identity becomes clearer when we consider that debates over political devolution were occurring at a time when historiography itself was beginning to reflect a wider 'British' identity. This was reflected in the growth and development of post-colonial history (see Chapter 12) and in historiography that more adequately reflected the histories of the British Isles as a whole. This had its origins in the 1970s and was taken up with vigour by a range of historians in the 1980s and 1990s. Given that this historiography made 'Englishness' only 'one amongst a number of competing ethnicities' (Samuel 1998: 4), one can understand more clearly the History Working Group's call, described above, for a 'broad' approach to the teaching of British history in schools.

In Wales, this 'new' historiography had the effect of promoting exciting, innovative Welsh history that in turn had an impact upon school history. It is extraordinary to think that, prior to the National Curriculum, it could be argued that the 'inherited consensus' or the 'Great Tradition' applied as much to Wales as it did to England. Distinctive Welsh history was, at best, inconsistently taught and insufficiently resourced. Yet the establishment of the National Curriculum History Committee for Wales (HCW) recognised at last the distinctive cultural, linguistic and historical heritage of Wales. Consequently, the HCW recommended (on strong intellectual grounds and, perhaps, to counter the possibility of a 'nationalist' curriculum) the teaching of distinctively Welsh history within a British, European and world context (Welsh Office 1990). As in England, the Welsh history curriculum was subject to the slimming process of the Dearing reforms but the current statutory orders retain the HCW's original model (Welsh Office 1995).

Whereas school history in England, and to a lesser extent in Wales, was characterised in the late twentieth century by central control, the major feature of history in Scottish schools has been autonomy and flexibility. As in Wales, distinctively Scottish history, prior to the 1990s at least, was inconsistently taught, and contributed to widespread ignorance about the past and the consequent distortion of Scottish history through films such as *Braveheart* (see Wood 1998). Thus, a Scottish history review group argued that 'Scottish history should be central to the history education delivered in Scottish schools', which it justified on the basis that a 'shift in consciousness with regard to what it means to be Scottish has taken place' (quoted in Phillips *et al.* 1999). A number of initiatives followed, designed to strengthen the place of history in Scottish schools, including financial support for the publication of Scottish history textbooks.

Table 2.1 Summary of history curricula in the UK

	Key developments	Age 5–11	Age 11–14	Age 14–16	Key organising principles
England	1986: GCSE	Compulsory teaching of British history within European and global contexts	Compulsory teaching of British history within European and global contexts	History optional	Citizenship
	1991: National Curriculum for 5–16-year-olds; history compulsory			Examined mainly through GCSE	Central control
	1995: Dearing review	Dearing review led to greater emphasis on British history	Dearing review reduced content but retained balance between British history and European/world history	Modern World history the most popular option	
	1996: New GCSE criteria			New GSCE criteria stipulate need for balanced British and European /world history	
	1998: Literacy Hour in primary schools	Reduced time for history as a result of Literacy Hour			
	2000: Review of National Curriculum				
Wales	1986: GCSE	Compulsory teaching of welsh history within British, European and world contexts	Compulsory teaching of Welsh history within British, European and world contexts	History optional	Locality
	1991: National Curriculum for 5–16 year olds; history compulsory			Examined mainly through GCSE but also COEA (Certificate of Educational Achievement)	Community
	1995: Dearing review	Cross-curricular 'curriculum Cymreig'	Cross-curricular 'curriculum Cymreig'		Curriculum Cymreig
	1996: New GCSE criteria	No compulsory Literacy Hour		No compulsory Welsh history but new GCSE criteria stipulate need for balance between British and European/world history	
	2000: Review of National Curriculum				

(continued over)

	Key developments	Age 5–11	Age 11–14	Age 14–16	Key organising principles
Northern Ireland	1986: GCSE 1990: Cross-curricular working parties reported 1991: Northern Ireland curriculum introduced 1995: Curriculum review 1996: New GCSE criteria 2001: Review of National Curriculum	Four compulsory modules set within Irish, British and European contexts Cross-curricular Education for Mutual Understanding (EMU)/Cultural Heritage(CH)	Three compulsory modules focused on Ireland, set within British and European contexts Cross-curricular: EMU/CH.	A compulsory twentieth-century Irish history module set in British and European contexts Two European/world-based modules Cross-curricular: EMU/CH	Differing perspectives Mutual understanding Understanding conflict Cultural diversity
Scotland	1983: Standard Grade begins to be phased in 1993: National Guidelines for Environmental Studies include history 1998: Report of Scottish history review group 1999: 'Higher Still' programme begins	Brief and broad guidelines indicate attention should be given to Scottish contexts within a wide curriculum 5–8-year-olds, it is suggested, should focus on local history	Brief and broad guidelines indicate attention should be given to Scottish contexts within a wide curriculum No specific Scottish topics are identified	History optional. History is provided in courses that all include a Scottish emphasis within a British context Exclusively post-1750 (i.e. post-Union).	Autonomy Choice Flexibility

Source: Taken from Phillips, R., McCully, A., Goalen, P. and Wood, S. (1999) 'Four histories, one nation? History teaching, nationhood and a British identity', *Compare: A Journal of Comparative Education* 29(2): 153–69.

Whereas debates over history in England, Wales and Scotland focused upon national identity, priorities in Northern Ireland have been understandably different. Here, policy developments have been concerned with exploring ways in which history can contribute to mutual understanding. This, of course, involves recognising the ways in which history has actually contributed to misunderstanding and conflict in the past (see Walker 1996). Thus, when the National Curriculum was established in Northern Ireland, it included 'Education for Mutual Understanding' and 'Cultural Heritage' as compulsory cross-curricular themes that had very important implications for the history curriculum. The more positive political climate in Northern Ireland created by the Good Friday agreement gave further cause for hope, and led to a number of important curriculum developments aimed at breaking down sectarian conflict. For teachers of history in Northern Ireland there is a particular resonance in the need for resolving what Gallagher (1998: 11) sees as the 'fundamental tension' between those who view history teaching as being pre-occupied solely with the past, a 'kind of prism which views contemporary issues as politics' and those who 'wish to see students' critical skills applied directly to contemporary issues, who wish to see history teaching enter more strongly into the arena of human values'.

'The end of history and the last history teacher'?

Gallagher's comments are highly pertinent, for they point to the different ideologies regarding the aims, nature and justification of history teaching, which it has been the purpose of this chapter to discuss. They also connect usefully to the 'upholders' and 'subverters' camps mentioned by Tosh earlier. Thus, whereas in the late twentieth century some believed that the history curriculum should serve as a means of cultural transmission, with pupils being taught predominantly about the political and constitutional history of Britain, others saw history as a means of teaching pupils to face up to the realities of a changing, diverse and complex Britain. This involved providing pupils not only with the knowledge to understand this complexity but also equipping them with the essential skills for them to survive it.

At the time of writing, working groups are once more preparing guidelines for the review of the National Curriculum scheduled for 2000, reforms which will influence curriculum policy governing the teaching of history well into the twenty-first century. In this final section, like Lomas (1998), I want to discuss some of the challenges facing policy makers and teachers of history as we approach the new millennium.

Three decades after Price's (1968) polemic, history is once more 'in danger' in a number of different respects. At GCSE there is considerable evidence that the numbers of pupils opting for the subject is in decline (see Chapter 4). A number of suggestions have been put forward as explanations for this, including the view that history is conceptually too difficult for pupils, that pupils do not see the 'relevance' of the subject or that senior management in schools give greater priority to other subjects. These are not new sentiments; they were around in Price's time and 'indeed' provided the motivation for her to write her article. At the end of the century, then, it seems that we are once more having to face up, using the phrase of Fukuyama (1992), to 'the end of history'. So what can be done to prevent this becoming a reality?

The first thing to say is that history teachers and policy advisers need to regain confidence in the importance and relevance of the subject for the twenty-first century. The History Working Group put forward a compelling and comprehensive justification for the subject in their report, perhaps the most important being that history allows pupils to better understand the present within the context of the past (DES 1990a). It implies the need to encourage pupils to analyse contemporary events within the context of the past and, at times, vice versa. This is why the Crick report on citizenship and democracy is so important to the subject (QCA 1998c). Its recommendations that pupils should leave school politically literate and being aware of their rights and responsibilities (and how they were derived) gives history teachers an exciting opportunity to re-assert history's relevance to the modern world (see Chapter 11). History teachers should grab the opportunity with both hands.

On the other hand, this does not mean that we should not teach history for history's sake and in turn become hamstrung by divisive and polarised debates that blighted the subject in the 1980s and 1990s. *It is* perfectly possible to use history to teach about heritage as well as diversity, to teach historical knowledge as well as transferable skills, and (following Gallagher) to teach the past for the past's sake, as well as cultivating a sense of informed criticism and objectivity (see Husbands 1996). This seems to me to be more important than ever given the ways in which pupils are being bombarded on a daily basis with historical distortion, caricature and nostalgia through the media (Phillips 1998b).

All this, of course, puts an enormous onus upon the history teacher, and policy makers sometimes forget that the quality of the subject is only as good as those who teach it. For too long in the 1980s and 1990s, it seemed that politicians treated teachers (and history teachers in particular) with contempt. Although there can be no possibility and indeed perhaps not even any merit in turning back the clock to the 'golden age' of teacher autonomy (did it exist anyway?) there is a fundamental need, it seems to me, to 'bring teachers back in' to debates over policy and reform (Hargreaves and Evans 1997).

This involves creating a more positive educational and intellectual climate for history teachers themselves to engage actively with policy-related issues that influence them every day, encouraging history teachers to become what some have called 'transformative intellectuals': teachers who are actively interested in research, new ideas and innovative technology. This puts the ball firmly back in the court of politicians, policy makers and the State: if teachers continue to suffer from sheer exhaustion and lack of time or incentive, then the consequences for education may be grim. As far as history teaching is concerned, if history teachers are not encouraged to be research orientated, innovative and transformative, then the consequences may be particularly dire, for ultimately the future of a vulnerable subject like ours is dependent upon the quality of teaching. It is hoped that the 'history of history' in this chapter and the range of issues described in this book as a whole will go some way towards ensuring that as well as stopping the apparent move towards 'the end of history', we also prevent the scenario of the 'last history teacher' ever becoming a reality.

Acknowledgements

Thanks to Dr Emma Cownie for comments on earlier drafts of this chapter. Table 2.1 also appears in a paper written for *Compare* entitled 'Four histories, one Nation? History teaching, nationhood and a British identity', co-written with Alan McCully, Paul Goalen and Sydney Wood. I am grateful to them and to Taylor & Francis for granting permission to use it.

Questions

1   Why should history be taught in schools?
2   Why did the subject become particularly controversial in the late twentieth century?
3   What are the advantages and disadvantages of a history National Curriculum?
4   What are the challenges and issues facing history teachers in the twenty-first century?

Further reading

Husbands, C. (1996) *What is History Teaching? Language, Ideas and Meaning in Learning about the Past*, Buckingham: Open University Press.
    An intelligent and objective discussion of the aims, purposes and methods of history teaching from somebody who knows what he is talking about.
Jenkins, K. (1991) *Re-Thinking History*, London: Routledge.
    Written from a postmodern perspective: provocative and thought-provoking; a good read even if one does not agree with his views.
Lowenthal, D. (1998) *The Heritage Crusade and the Spoils of History*, Cambridge: Cambridge University Press.
    A masterly and fascinating account of why history has become 'consumed' by the public at large.
Phillips, R. (1998) *History Teaching, Nationhood and the State: A Study in Educational Politics*, London: Cassell.
    Many of the issues raised in the chapter are discussed in this book, which is an analysis of the politics of the 'Great History Debate'; the book uses original source material to describe why history became such a controversial subject within the National Curriculum.

3 Curriculum decision-making in the primary school

The place of history

Penelope Harnett

The key issue to be addressed in this chapter focuses on the place of history within the primary curriculum. During this century the rationale for teaching history has extended, and the contribution that history might make to children's overall development has been more clearly identified. As history's subject identity has become more sharply defined, the subject's position and status alongside the other subjects of the primary curriculum has also undergone significant changes.

For most of the century, Government has not been heavily involved with shaping the curriculum. The Education Reform Act of 1988 marked a sharp break with this tradition and during the last decade the Government has taken a much more prominent role in curriculum decision-making. After ten years of a very prescriptive curriculum, however, there are signs that teachers once again are going to be drawn into the curriculum decision-making process. At issue here is not only who makes the curriculum decisions, but also on what grounds decisions about the history curriculum are being made.

This chapter aims to explore these issues through a historical perspective that will investigate changes in the beliefs and practice of primary school history during this century. It will thus chronicle curriculum developments and also assess their impact on present practice in primary schools. Current developments within the primary history curriculum will be analysed and some suggestions made for future policy and practice.

Discussion will focus on the 'official' history curriculum, that is the State-initiated views of history that have been manifested in a variety of documents. These documents include the Handbooks of Suggestions for teachers engaged in Public Elementary Schools, issued periodically during the first half of the century by the Board of Education and later the Ministry of Education; Government reports, for example the Hadow report (Board of Education 1931) and the Plowden report (DES 1967); documents emanating from Her Majesty's Inspectorate and the Department of Education and Science and different versions of the history National Curriculum. These official sources provide one version of the history curriculum; however, they are of limited value in describing the curriculum as experienced in schools (Goodson 1994). Such sources also cannot take into account the many other ways outside of school, in which teachers and children encounter history and that influence their views of the past (Phillips 1998b).

Why teach history in the primary school?

Throughout the century different educational ideologies have influenced history as a curriculum subject, both in terms of the historical knowledge to be learned and also in terms of pedagogy. At the beginning of the century, the handbook described the purpose of elementary schools as being to provide education in the 'fullest sense of the word'. Such an education involved pupils in learning about their rights and responsibilities, and their obligations to others. Studying history provided opportunities for learning how these responsibilities had occurred and also for learning about the development of the British Empire and explanations for British authority and power in the world (Board of Education 1905).

As the century progressed, views that education should be concerned with developing individual pupil's interests and abilities began to have a stronger influence on the curriculum. The Hadow report's recommendation 'that the curriculum is to be thought of in terms of activity and experience rather than of knowledge to be acquired and facts to be stored' (Board of Education 1931: 75) placed pupils, rather than curriculum subjects, at the centre of the educational process. As a subject within the curriculum, history adapted to this more child-centred approach and was seen as an important vehicle for stimulating pupils' interest and enthusiasm.

Emphasis on the all-round development of the individual remained a feature of primary education in the years following the Second World War. The Plowden report described the important values and attitudes that pupils learned within a school community which was not 'merely a teaching shop' (DES 1967: 187). History provided opportunities for pupils to extend their experience of other values and ways of life through stories, and also through imaginative projects centred on the local environment and family histories.

More recently, history's potential contribution towards pupils' cognitive development has also been acknowledged as history's distinct methodology has become more recognised. In *History in the Primary and Secondary Years*, HMI outlined a range of objectives for progression in historical skills and stressed the importance of children working as historians, asking historical questions and synthesising and communicating information (DES 1985a: 18–19). These objectives reveal official recognition of a distinctive methodology for teaching and learning history in schools.

Prior to the National Curriculum, therefore, there is evidence of several different traditions that were used to justify the place of history within the curriculum. The History Working Group drew on these different traditions in its rationale that described the purposes for school history. Some purposes recognised history's potential contribution to pupils' understanding of their world and place in society; other purposes stressed the value of using history as a stimulus for pupils' imagination and to arouse their enthusiasm for the past. The contribution that historical methodology can make to developing pupils' abilities to acquire and analyse information and to communicate their understanding to others was also recognised (DES 1990b: 1).

The evolving rationale for history education influenced the content of the curriculum and the selection of historical knowledge to be taught in school. Some of the key features of the content of the history curriculum will be considered below.

What history should primary school children learn?

In the early years of the century, history stories of the great and the good provided examples of worthy behaviour that pupils could be encouraged to emulate. The Handbook of Suggestions noted that, 'The lives of great men and women, carefully selected from all stations in life, will furnish the most impressive examples of obedience, loyalty, courage, strenuous effort, serviceableness, indeed of all the qualities of which make for good citizenship' (Board of Education 1905: 6). As the influence of the churches in education was diminishing, history stories provided alternatives to biblical parables in offering pupils models of suitable behaviour. Stories focused on the lives of great British people, and there was also an emphasis on characters who lived in classical times.

A good history story was also seen as a work of literature, and the Board of Education noted in its Handbook, 'whether the story lesson is labelled "Literature" or "History" is immaterial' (Board of Education 1927: 118). This comment also reflects views of historians as 'men of letters' and accomplished storytellers, providing a narrative of the past drawn mainly from documentary sources.

The view of history as the straightforward account of great people in the past, however, began to be questioned. The 1959 Handbook acknowledged,' that history was looked on less as a story and more as a science', and noted that more systematic research in history was undermining the value of history, 'as a basis for moral instruction' (Ministry of Education 1959: 276). Despite such concerns, the Plowden report still recommended stories 'for giving pupils "the habitual vision of greatness"' (DES 1967: 229).

The story tradition has continued to remain popular in primary schools. HMI noted that stories with a historical setting were used to initiate work in about half the 9-year-old classes and two-thirds of the 11-year-old classes that they observed (DES 1978a). This practice continued to be endorsed by HMI who commented that, 'Story and narrative are central to history teaching' (DES 1988: 19).

Unsurprisingly, in the early years of the century there was a strong emphasis on British history. The Board of Education suggested an Alphabet of Dates for pupils to learn containing the key events in British history that would provide pupils with a chronological framework (Board of Education 1923). Concern for chronology was a recurrent theme in the handbooks (Board of Education 1927; Board of Education 1937). Syllabuses for older pupils were often constructed to provide a chronological account of British history and this structure was also adopted for primary aged pupils in many schools where history was taught as a discrete subject.

Evidence from HMI, however, suggests that many pupils failed to acquire an understanding of chronology, and that ways in which history was taught, particularly topic and thematic approaches, often led pupils to have a very fragmented understanding of the past (DES 1978a; DES 1982). In more recent documents from HMI, chronology has continued to feature strongly (DES 1985a; DES 1988), and a description of possible progression in pupils' understanding of chronology has been outlined (DES 1985a).

As the century progressed, developments in the study of history opened up fresh fields of historical enquiry that began to be reflected within the history curriculum. Political history was studied alongside social, economic, cultural and other aspects of history. Investigating different ways of life in the past appealed directly to pupils and also enabled them to contrast the past with their own contemporary experiences.

Curriculum initiatives such as the Schools' Council History 13–16 Project (at secondary level) widened the content of history in schools, providing opportunities for pupils to study the history of other countries and cultures, together with contemporary history (Schools' Council 1976). Developments in exam syllabuses for secondary education also opened up the content of the history curriculum. The direct impact of such initiatives on the primary history curriculum may have been limited, but these initiatives did create an increasing range of opportunities for studying history that were reflected within the outcomes of a course of history for all pupils aged between five and sixteen suggested by the HMI. These outcomes, with their inclusion of a broad sweep of historical knowledge, drawn from different periods of time and from different cultures, present a sharp contrast with the Alphabet of Dates published earlier in the century, which focused on British history (DES 1988).

However, despite this diversity of histories, primary school pupils generally concentrated on British history with some attention paid to ancient civilisations such as the Romans, Greeks and Egyptians. Family and local histories were significant features of the history curriculum for younger pupils and were emphasised in the Hadow report (Board of Education 1931) and later Plowden report (DES 1967). Such approaches were consistent with the importance attached by the Hadow and Plowden committees to histories that would have a direct appeal to pupils' imagination and interest.

Prior to the National Curriculum, therefore, primary school pupils' experiences of history had largely concentrated on British history, with an emphasis on local studies and family history. Historical stories were considered important and there was a long-standing concern about pupils' fragmented experience of history and lack of chronological awareness. These were all elements that were addressed by the History Working Group in its report on the history National Curriculum (DES 1990b).

Linked with the debate concerning the content of the history curriculum, there has also been discussion on effective ways to develop pupils' understanding in history. This chapter will now consider the different ways in which history has been taught and organised in the primary school.

How should history be taught in the primary school?

In the early years of the century, a common format for the history lesson was the teacher telling or reading a story, followed by a question and answer session with the pupils. There were traces of earlier practices of catechistic learning in this question and response format. Written questions at the end of stories also demonstrate the importance attached to the acquisition of facts, rather than the expression of opinion.

Stories were recommended as a stimulus for pupils' imaginations, providing opportunities for pupils to extend their experiences and appreciation of other values and ways of life. The handbooks advised that pupils were to accept stories as straightforward accounts and not to sit in judgement (Board of Education 1905: 89). This approach contrasts with current views on the role of story in history education. Rather than a passive acceptance of the past, HMI have described how stories can be used to introduce pupils to different interpretations of history, involving pupils in speculation and raising questions about the course of events (DES 1985a: 6).

History has often been taught through a topic approach which links together a variety of subjects such as drama, model-making, handwork and geography. This approach has its roots in the child-centred philosophy embedded within the Hadow report (Board of Education 1931). Stimulating pupils' enthusiasm and interest were key features of such an approach, which prioritised pupils' active involvement in initiating areas of learning above learning in different curriculum subjects.

Such views remained prominent in educational circles after the war. The Plowden report recognised that 'children's learning does not fit into subject categories' (DES 1967: 203), and commented that this 'spilling over of history into other aspects of the curriculum is probably the most general advance of recent years' (DES 1967: 226). Organising history within a topic approach continued to remain popular. In its working paper, *Primary Practice*, the Schools' Council suggested pupils' experiences of history and geography should be grouped together within the study of people, past and present (Schools' Council 1983). The value of grouping subjects together as in the humanities was emphasised by HMI, who also stressed that the integrity of the subject needed to be maintained and its unique qualities protected (DES 1988).

The distinguishing features of history as a discipline, however, were often neglected within such topic approaches. HMI commented that much history in primary schools was badly planned with too great a concentration on copying out from textbooks. Importantly, they also emphasised that history's curriculum content should be selected, 'not only to suit the interests and abilities of the children and to provide for the progressive development of the basic skills, but also because it is important in its own right' (DES 1978a: 8.25). HMI recommended that more attention should be given to identifying historical skills and concepts, and outlining a possible model for progression of pupils' learning in history.

Developments were already occurring in these areas; for example, Coltham and Fines (1971) related history teaching to the definition of historical objectives. The belief that pupils could work as historians, asking similar questions and using similar sources of evidence underpinned the work of the Schools' Council History Project (Schools' Council 1976). For younger children, the project 'Time, Place and Society' identified key concepts such as communication, power, values and beliefs, conflict and consensus, similarity and difference, continuity and change, and causes and consequences as organising principles for teachers to plan their work with pupils (Blyth *et al.* 1976).

The use of historical sources such as pictures, museum collections and places of interest was advocated in the Hadow report (Board of Education 1931). The possibility of using these sources did permit the opening up of the subject to wider interpretations, but it is difficult to assess the extent to which they were used in many over-crowded and under-resourced classrooms.

The 1959 handbook included a section on documentary sources and descriptions of local and family sources, but also seemed to suggest that the use of source material might be beyond the capabilities of many primary aged pupils: 'But too much must not be asked of the imagination of children who may be disheartened after hearing of the beauties of Athens, to see a photograph of what may seem to them to be "old ruins"' (Ministry of Education 1959: 282). In this instance, source material is regarded as a stimulus to pupils' imagination, not as an essential tool for learning history and helping pupils to analyse evidence from the past.

Recognition of primary school pupils' abilities to analyse source materials began to emerge more fully in the 1970s, influenced by J.S. Bruner's belief that pupils could learn the structure of any subject, provided it was introduced to them in a meaningful way that was appropriate to their stage of development (Bruner 1960). In terms of primary history, pioneering work was undertaken by individuals such as West who encouraged pupils to make deductions and inferences from pictorial sources and devised activities to develop their awareness of chronology (West 1981a). Using historic pictures, Blyth researched young pupils' understanding of key concepts of change, power, evidence and sequence (Blyth 1988). Such research contributed towards a growing recognition of a distinctive pedagogy for history, where key skills and concepts were identified and particular ways of teaching and learning encouraged.

This emerging historical pedagogy is discernible in HMI's description of possible progression in pupils' learning of historical skills and concepts (DES 1985a). The description provided a framework for learning in history for the History Working Group to consider as they constructed the history National Curriculum.

This brief survey has sought to describe some of the ideologies that have influenced the history curriculum in primary schools during the century. Before the history National Curriculum a strong rationale for teaching history was emerging, together with distinctive views on the content of the history curriculum and ways in which it should be delivered. The history National Curriculum embraced many of these traditions, making them statutory requirements for all schools.

1988: the Education Reform Act and the history National Curriculum

The curriculum structure introduced by the Education Reform Act in 1988 considerably enhanced history's status within the primary curriculum. The statutory requirement to teach history alongside the other foundation subjects provided all primary aged pupils with the opportunity to study history, whereas in the past this had been rather a piecemeal experience. History was clearly defined as a subject within the National Curriculum, with distinct subject boundaries that separated history from other curriculum subjects (Phillips 1998a).

The introduction of separate subjects created many challenges for primary schools, particularly in their curriculum organisation and resourcing. The Key Stage 1 history curriculum could be adapted to existing themes within the Key Stage 1 curriculum, but the introduction of specific history study units at Key Stage 2 influenced history's relationship with other subject areas in competing for space within an over-crowded timetable. At Key Stage 2 there was a tremendous amount of history to be squeezed in through the nine study units to be taught across four years. Ensuring progression was also a key consideration, and this was particularly important in primary schools where there were many mixed-age classes.

All pupils were to have the opportunity to study history and this included provision for the very young in Key Stage 1 (five to seven years). The entitlement of 5-year-olds to learn history was important and reveals a deep commitment to the notion of Bruner's spiral curriculum. This was a radical departure from much existing practice. History had not featured on the timetable of many infant schools and HMI observed that history in two out of three infant classes received little or no attention (DES 1989). Earlier reports had also commented on the difficulties of teaching history to very young pupils and emphasised a story-telling approach (Board of Education 1931; DES 1967).

History's status within the Key Stage 1 curriculum was further strengthened by the publication of standard assessment tests (SATS) designed to test pupils' progress in key historical skills and concepts. The SATS offered teachers a range of interesting material to assess Key Stage 1 pupils' historical understanding, yet have been largely unused since by the time of their publication it was becoming increasingly evident that pupils at Key Stage 1 were being over-burdened with standard assessments. However, the existence of the SATS materials does reveal the acceptance within official circles that history was an appropriate subject to study with young pupils (SEAC 1993a).

The history National Curriculum included opportunities for studying local and family history, as well as the history of more distant places. Pupils were also to be introduced to studying history from a variety of perspectives including political, economic, technological and scientific, social, religious, cultural and aesthetic (DES 1991; DfE 1995). In this respect, the history curriculum was building on much existing good practice. Likewise, the inclusion of predominantly British history was a continuation of earlier traditions.

However, the initial versions of the history National Curriculum did provide more opportunities to study aspects of the histories of other countries at Key Stage 2, which have since disappeared following Dearing's review of the curriculum. An increasing focus on British history has also occurred at Key Stage 1, with an emphasis on pupils learning about personalities and events drawn from British history (DfE 1995).

Justification for the emphasis on British history within the National Curriculum has been discussed in an earlier chapter. Analogies could be drawn between the current history National Curriculum's concentration on British history and the history curriculum taught in schools in the early years of the century. Yet the context for the curriculum has changed: at the turn of the century as Britain moves closer into union with Europe, and as more decisions are taken on a global basis, it could be argued that the curriculum needs to open pupils' knowledge and understanding of other areas of the world.

In terms of organising the curriculum, the topic tradition has remained strong. At Key Stage 1, whilst acknowledging the importance of developing historical knowledge and understanding, more thematic approaches for organising the history curriculum, in line with existing early years practice, have been consistently advocated in all the recommendations and subsequent revisions of the curriculum (DES 1990a; DES 1991; DfE 1995).

At Key Stage 2 the topic tradition was represented within the supplementary study units, which included options to study such themes as ships and seafarers, food and farming and land transport as well as local studies (DES 1991). Further revisions of the curriculum, however, have removed the thematic approaches and, although the local history study unit remains, the remaining history study units are all focused on a historical period. (DfE 1995).

A distinctive pedagogy for history was outlined within the Attainment Targets (DES 1991) and, later, the Key Elements (DfE 1995). Key skills and concepts were identified and an attempt made to describe progression in pupils' historical understanding through the Statements of Attainment (DES 1990b; DES 1991) and Level Descriptors (DfE 1995).

The active involvement of pupils in constructing their own knowledge of the past through asking questions, selecting and organising information, and communicating their understanding in different ways featured strongly within the different versions of the National Curriculum. A range of historical sources for pupils to work with at different Key Stages was also included. (DES 1991; DfE 1995). The history National Curriculum focused on the interpretative nature of history, according it a separate Attainment Target in 1991, 'Interpretations of

History', which later developed into Key Element 3 in the revised version (DfE 1995). The emphasis on interpretation contrasted strongly with earlier approaches to history as straightforward accounts of the past. It stressed the importance for pupils to develop their awareness of historians' tentative conclusions about the past, and also encouraged pupils to become involved themselves in constructing their own versions and understandings of past events and ways of life.

The concern for chronology that had been present in the advice and reports relating to history teaching throughout the century was reflected within the Attainment Targets (DES 1991) and Key Element 1, which indicated ways in which pupils could be encouraged to develop a chronological framework at the different Key Stages (DfE 1995).

These requirements outlined in the Attainment Targets and Key Elements were a landmark in the development of history teaching within the primary school. They marked a radical overhaul of much existing practice in history and opened up opportunities for primary pupils to develop their own historical enquiries from a range of sources and to question their understanding and knowledge of the past.

The content of the history National Curriculum was challenging for many teachers. Teachers' own personal knowledge of history varied. Many teachers had learned little history and had a very sketchy knowledge of many of the history study units. The history National Curriculum also required teachers to become familiar with fresh approaches to teaching the subject and towards assessing pupils' historical knowledge and understanding. Many teachers needed to develop their own awareness of historical concepts and ways of working before they could fully implement the history curriculum.

The National Curriculum therefore created a demand for further professional development from many primary school teachers, and in-service courses and conferences were very popular. Resourcing the history curriculum was also a major concern. There was a dearth of material, particularly for Key Stage 1 history, and publishers were very much to the fore in producing not only resources, but also advice on methods for teaching history in school (Blyth *et al.* 1991; Mason and Purkis 1991).

Despite the many challenges, the introduction of the history National Curriculum was generally well received within primary schools. HMI have noted a consistent improvement in the standard of pupils' work in history during the 1990s. However difficulties remain: in the 1995–6 phase of inspection subject HMI noted that planning, organisation and management were poor in nearly a quarter of the schools visited and a third of schools had ineffective assessment and recording systems. Resources were also a cause for concern; one in five schools had serious deficiencies in the quality of resources available (Hamer 1997).

Back to basics? History within the contemporary primary curriculum

The 1990s witnessed tremendous changes in the organisation of the primary school curriculum. History was not unique as a subject that placed fresh demands on primary school teachers. Revisions of the curriculum in 1995 reduced the content of many curriculum subjects and also simplified the assessment requirements. A slim volume containing the curriculum for Key Stages 1 and 2 replaced the subject ring binders of the original National Curriculum. Following the revisions there was a recognition within official circles that the curriculum needed to be consolidated and further changes are not envisaged until the curriculum review in the year 2000.

The Dearing Review maintained the existing structure of the primary curriculum with its core and foundation subjects. More recent developments, however, now appear to be affecting the structure and organisation of the curriculum in primary schools further. Against a background of concern for standards in literacy and numeracy, the Secretary of State for Education, David Blunkett, announced his decision to lift the statutory requirement for schools to follow the Programmes of Study for foundation subjects (Blunkett 1998). This initiative was supported by Her Majesty's Chief Inspector for Schools, HMCI Chris Woodhead, who announced that from September 1998 inspections would concentrate on the core subjects of mathematics, English and science, together with information technology, and no criticism would be passed on schools failing to cover the existing requirements for the foundation subjects (Woodhead 1998).

The status of all the foundation subjects was thus considerably reduced and different subject groups organised campaigns in the press and media to raise public awareness of these developments. The Historical Association launched its Campaign for History in January 1988; *The Times Education Supplement* has published a strong lobby for music within the curriculum. At the time of writing, different foundation subjects are jostling with each other to maintain their presence and status within the primary curriculum.

However, there is still a statutory requirement to provide a broad and balanced curriculum and Blunkett commented that, whatever curriculum arrangements schools choose to adopt, they will still be 'expected to find a place for these subjects in their curriculum' (Blunkett 1998). Guidance on how this might be achieved has been described in *Maintaining Breadth and Balance*, which identifies the key features involved in the study of history and suggests ways in which the history National Curriculum might be reduced, prioritised or combined with other subjects within the curriculum. However, the strategies suggested by the Qualifications and Curriculum Authority (QCA) could all be interpreted as reducing the overall content and amount of time spent on history within the primary school (QCA 1998b). Such a reduction in content would be welcomed by many primary school teachers who, whilst enjoying teaching history have continued to find coverage of all aspects of the history curriculum difficult (Watson 1998).

The introduction into primary schools of the literacy strategy from September 1998, and the numeracy strategy from September 1999, will potentially reduce the amount of time available for teaching the foundation subjects further. At the time of writing there is evidence to suggest that this is already occurring in some schools. Responses to a Historical Association questionnaire sent out to primary schools indicate that some schools are spending less time teaching history than in previous years (Lomas 1999).

As history's position within the primary curriculum is squeezed, it might be tempting to review common threads linking history with other curriculum subjects. For example, the School Curriculum and Assessment Authority (SCAA) has identified the links between history and language (SCAA 1997b), and throughout the century the links between history and literacy have been described within official documents. Stories have formed the backbone for pupils' learning in history, and the contribution that historical fiction can make to pupils' understanding of the past has been recognised (Little and John 1986; Cox and Hughes 1998). The last decade has witnessed increasing publication of children's historical fiction (Martin 1999) and reading schemes are also including more stories set in the past.

The Literacy Hour offers pupils the opportunity to explore a range of different historical texts: diaries, biographies, eye witness accounts, information books, myths, fables, legends, poems and fiction (DfEE 1998b). Whilst the focus of teaching and learning will be essentially on the development of literacy skills, pupils' knowledge and understanding of the past may also be enriched.

History also provides opportunities for pupils to extend their research and information retrieval skills and their abilities to write in a variety of contexts. Various studies have investigated strategies to encourage pupils to take notes, organise historical information and to communicate their understanding within a variety of writing frames (Wray and Lewis 1998; Nichol 1998).

It is important to forge some of these links between history and English, but Blyth also reminds us, 'there is a danger that, in this unequal association, mighty English could become the lord and humble history the serf, with such matters peculiar to history as evidence, truth and timescale submerged' (Blyth 1998b: 2).

Similarly, history's distinctive subject identity may be diminished if too close links are created with a further current educational priority: citizenship education. The Advisory Group on Citizenship cites many instances where history could relate to learning outcomes in citizenship. Unlike previous models of citizenship where pupils were encouraged to learn and to accept without question their rights and responsibilities, the Advisory Group emphasises pupils' active participation as citizens. This would involve pupils in developing enquiries, discussion, and making informed decisions that incorporate many of the principles embedded within the key elements of the history National Curriculum (QCA 1998c). The history curriculum, however, could not be fully delivered through citizenship education: learning history also requires the acquisition of some historical knowledge, which would not necessarily occur if the focus was on citizenship.

As different subjects compete with each other for space on the timetable, linking subjects together becomes more attractive, and a return to greater emphasis on topic work more of a possibility. Recommendations by the QCA to the Secretary of State suggest that a future curriculum will be less prescriptive and more flexible, providing greater opportunities for teachers to plan their own curriculum appropriate for their school and pupils (QCA 1998a).

It is unlikely, however, that the re-emergence of topic work will signal a return to the unfocused thematic work of the past. The National Curriculum has increased primary school teachers' awareness of the distinctive features of different curriculum subjects and a whole generation of primary school teachers are familiar only with ways of organising subjects within the current curriculum framework. Consequently, thematic work will probably be much more sharply subject focused rather than child-centred as it was in years prior to the National Curriculum.

If teachers take on more responsibility for curriculum decision making in primary schools, central government may still play a prominent role in providing advice and support. The schemes of work for history are the most recent from a long list of publications offering guidance in planning, implementing and assessing the history National Curriculum (NCC 1991; NCC 1993a; NCC 1993b; SEAC 1993b; SCAA 1997a; SCAA 1997b; QCA 1998b).

Into the millennium

The chapter has described some of the developments and tensions within the official history curriculum. However, the history curriculum forms only a part of children's experience and knowledge of the past (Kimber *et al.* 1995; Phillips 1998b). We are all surrounded by our past and interest in the past is all pervading. The environment has been shaped by earlier generations; contemporary beliefs and ways of life have all been influenced by past events and those who have lived before. Images of the past from films, documentaries, books and TV programmes are constantly being thrust before our eyes. An expanding heritage industry provides opportunities to experience the past through visits to historic sites, museums, theme parks and involvement in historic re-enactments.

Studying history through the 'official curriculum' can enable children to make sense of all these experiences. The official history curriculum offers opportunities to critically interpret the past; to question, reflect and make judgements on what has happened before.

These opportunities that history offers for critical reflection need to be emphasised as teachers take on more responsibility for their curriculum. Experience of a highly prescriptive and centralised curriculum in the 1990s has extended teachers' awareness of the specific features of different subject areas. The challenge for teachers in the twenty-first century will be to see how they can develop from a prescribed curriculum, a curriculum that takes into account the needs and interests of children, provides a broad and balanced range of experiences and yet also will introduce pupils to the key features of different subject areas.

Questions

1   Should history be included as a subject within the primary curriculum?
2   What are the strengths of teaching history through either a subject-focused or a topic-centred curriculum?
3   What links can be made between history and other curriculum subjects within the primary curriculum?
4   List different opportunities that occur for pupils to learn about the past in their everyday lives. How can the 'official' history curriculum extend and enrich these experiences?

Further reading

Ashley, M. (ed.) (1999) *Improving Teaching and Learning in the Humanities*, London: Falmer Press.
   The book encourages readers to reflect on the humanities curriculum in primary schools and investigates the impact of different values on curriculum decision-making in this area.
Cooper, H. (1995) *History in the Early Years*, London: Routledge.
   The development of pupils' historical learning is clearly outlined in this important book, which draws on case studies and research to provide a justification for history's place in the primary curriculum. Curriculum planning and organisation are also addressed.
Hoodless, P. (ed.) (1998) *History and English in the Primary School. Exploiting the Links*, London: Routledge.
   The many ways in which learning in history and English can complement each other are described in this book. Different chapters focus on the development of reading, writing, speaking and listening skills through historical activities.

Part I

Issues in the classroom

4 Teaching historical significance

Martin Hunt

Introduction

The use of Key Element 2d in the revised National Curriculum can offer a useful vehicle for emphasising the significance of the content studied and the extent of its contribution to the pupils' education. At a time when there are pressures on history departments to assert the strength of the case for history beyond Year 9, the assessment of the significance of events, changes and people in the past not only deepens pupils' understanding of the world, in which they live, but also helps them consider the ageless social, moral and cultural issues, which adolescents see as being very relevant. In spite of the potential problems of generalisations and abstractions, which the study of significance encourages, it can be argued that, given an appropriate methodology, pupils will respond positively towards this concept.

The case for emphasising significance in the teaching of history

The revised National Curriculum for history, introduced in 1995, made many changes from the 1991 documentation. Fundamental was the primacy given to the Key Elements in the underpinning of the delivery of the subject. While much of the emphasis of the original National Curriculum was retained, there were some important developments. These included a greater emphasis on chronology, more attention to historical enquiry through the use of sources, and the acknowledgement of the skills of organisation and communication. All of these were most welcome. And then, less heralded, almost as an extra in Key Element 2, was something new but equally welcome for the possibilities it presents to the history teacher. This is, that pupils should be taught to assess the significance of the main events, people and changes studied.

Although the documentation contains very little explanation for this addition, its inclusion can encourage a greater emphasis on the value and relevance of learning history in the secondary school. The understanding and use of the other key concepts in Key Element 2 (e.g. change, causation, differing attitudes) has for some time been seen as helping to underline the significance of historical events and processes. When a pupil's recall of specific detail diminishes, it is the understanding that comes from conclusions about the significance of events, people and changes that creates the eventual educational value. In that sense Key Element 2d is making explicit one of the reasons for studying these key concepts. Tim Lomas, in his Historical Association pamphlet, *Teaching and Assessing Historical Understanding*, includes a separate section on significance alongside cause and consequence, time concepts, evidence, and similarity and difference (Lomas 1990: 41–6). Those five pages are very enlightening and are almost unique in the literature that has appeared on this concept.

The need to re-establish the value and relevance of the subject is pressing. 'Significance' is a difficult concept for many pupils to understand and for most will be interchangeable with the word 'importance', although this is not a precise synonym. Even so, the importance of the content, which the pupils study in history, needs to be emphasised as history fights for its place in the post-14 curriculum. To long-serving history teachers it will seem that history has been under threat for most of the last thirty years. Now, again, after the false hopes of a guaranteed status at Key Stage 4, the subject has been successively downgraded to the extent that it is but one of many subjects competing in the options choices for the GCSE and other post-14 courses. Furthermore, the popularity of vocational courses available at 14 is a factor in the decline of history candidates. In 1995 there were 239,524 GCSE history candidates yet by 1999 the entry had dropped to 210,113 (*The Times*, 1996 and the *Guardian*, 1999). At a time when schools are seeking to maximise results to enhance their place in 'league tables', it has become crucial that the importance of the content and processes involved in the study of history is made very clear to both pupils and parents alike. In the post-Dearing situation that now prevails, history departments are increasingly conscious that the challenges presented by the options system are far more competitive than in the days before the National Curriculum. John D. Clare probably echoed the experiences of many when he wrote of departmental crisis talks, when 'option choices' for history dropped by a third. It was realised that all the pupils found history enjoyable but 'few reckoned it IMPORTANT' (Clare 1997).

A fundamental strategy is to try to ensure that the pupils are very clear about the importance or significance of what they study in history and how this contributes to their general education, in the same way that a core curriculum subject does. There is a strong case for history teachers to be more pro-active in selling not just the content of history but the varied and extensive educational outcomes that can arise from the study of people in the past and the significance of what they did. Indeed, Howells argues effectively that there is a case for statements about the significance of the content being incorporated into the planning both of schemes and of individual lessons (Howells 1998: 17). Ben Walsh, feeling a responsibility on the history teacher to ensure pupils are aware of the wider outcomes, admits, 'I certainly have been guilty on many occasions of knowing what my core purpose was in a given activity, but forgetting to tell my students' (Walsh 1998: 7). Similarly, Chris Husbands makes the point that pupils must see the relevance and importance of the subject to their own lives when he writes, 'if they [the pupils] cannot explain why some historical periods and events have a significance and resonance *for them* ... then knowing about the past is reduced to a sort of quiz game' (Husbands 1996: 133).

In stressing its importance the subject has to combat various contemporary influences – modern images of history – that tend to trivialise its educational value. The use of history as a source of comedy, entertainment, theme parks and leisure activity can easily detract from the seriousness of the subject. Humour is an important part of selling the subject and, given the central focus of history is people, people's foibles and idiosyncrasies are a legitimate resource for the teacher. And long may this be the case. However, the use, or perhaps the over-use, of a humorous presentation of historical content carries with it the danger of trivialising the subject at a time when it is necessary to impress upon pupils and their parents the importance of the subject and the real educational bene-fits that can arise from its study. The challenge for the history teacher is to use humour, but to seek to emphasise at all times *the serious and significant value of the study*. The function of professional history, wrote Richard Evans, 'has always been towards puncturing the clichés of popular myth than towards maintaining them' (R. J. Evans 1997: 207). And so at secondary school level the professional history teacher will seek to emphasise, for example, the enduring significance of the break with Rome in Henry VIII's reign rather than his table manners and other less attractive features of his 'commercial' persona.

Carmel Gallagher, addressing the April 1998 SHP Conference, said, 'the biggest challenge I think that history faces is proving its relevance'. She went on to suggest that the teachers themselves feel they have lost the relevance debate and asks, 'What is the relevance to young people's lives of three-quarters of what we teach? Are pupils clear about why they are learning certain aspects of history? Do we have clearer criteria for the selection of content?' (Gallagher 1998).

If teachers are to stress the significance of events, people and changes, then the choice of the content to be covered will influence what is stressed. As the prescriptive nature of the National Curriculum is relaxed, the need for criteria for the selection of content is strengthened. Partington suggested the following interrelated criteria (Partington 1980: 112–16):

1   Importance – to the people in the past;
2   Profundity – how deeply people's lives have been affected;
3   Quantity – how many lives have been affected;
4   Durability – for how long have people's lives been affected;
5   Relevance – contribution to an increased understanding of present life.

While such criteria have been criticised for being too intellectual (Wilson 1985: 44–5), they are not likely to exclude the content to which adolescents are drawn, namely the major events that made a great impact and ones that raise moral, social and cultural issues. So it may be argued that it is incumbent upon teachers, as prescription is relaxed, to be sensitive to the implications of the chosen content and to the various ways the significance of events, people and changes can be interpreted. Indeed, perceptions of which events should feature in a syllabus will change over time. Changing perceptions may result from new evidence, or current developments may change the significance of events. Alternatively, new circumstances could give a changing emphasis to established content. For example, at the time of writing a range of constitutional issues are being debated, relating to the powers and the composition of the House of Lords, decentralisation and regional government, devolution for Scotland and Wales, and a complex new deal for the governance of Northern Ireland. All of these current issues could alter views about the significance of events in the past, including the presentation of content under the title of the National Curriculum study, 'The Making of the United Kingdom'.

Another extensive debate being currently pursued concerns the balance between the role of the State in the provision of welfare and the role of the individual. Again, while the reforms of the Liberal governments of 1905–14 and the impact of the Beveridge report will remain significant events, there may well be revised perceptions about what was significant about them. Pupils need to be encouraged to understand how and why perceptions change, and why with time a topic could be seen to be more or less significant.

What educational outcomes arise from the study of significance in history?

The creation of a case emphasising 'significance' in the learning of history requires a distinction between the educational outcomes, which can be achieved by the teaching of the concept and those more generally ascribed to the learning of history. Unsurprisingly, there is overlap, but the contention is that, even where this occurs, an emphasis on the significance of events, changes and people will enhance the quality of learning and generally clarify in the minds of the pupils the value of studying history.

Attention to the significance of events, changes and people in the past can provide a useful balance against the compartmentalised episodic approach, which has to result from breaking down a prescribed area of study into individual, manageable lessons. By helping pupils *understand the wider perspective and the long-term themes to which the individual topic contributes*, a balance is restored. There will be times when pupils can only understand the real significance of what they have covered in earlier years after they have studied some of the more recent history usually taught in Year 9. Such understanding can be helped by reference back to earlier topics, making pupils aware of the wider themes and those events that stand out as being significantly different from the typical. Whether it be changes in the way Britain is governed, changing relations with Scotland and Ireland, changes in trade and industry, or scientific and technical developments, what pupils have been studying throughout Key Stage 3 will seem more coherent when such developments are pulled together. It will give added point to what has been covered at a time when Year 9 pupils are becoming mature enough to appreciate the connections with their own lives. It is encouraging to note that some recent textbooks are beginning to present such overviews in imaginative and attractive ways.

Assessing the contribution of people in the past encourages pupils to develop their understanding of human actions and motives as well as the attitudes and the ideas that gave rise to such actions. Topics that invite such judgements include the feudal system, the use of child labour, the slave trade, law and order, public welfare, revolts and reforms. With these topics, and many others, the history teacher can *draw out the significance of specific events to the wider consideration of human conduct and motivation.* This is one of the aspects that pupils themselves see as being particularly relevant. Discussions with Year 9 pupils would suggest that often the topics which most interest them are those requiring judgements about the actions of people in the past. When given a choice of a range of topics, the ones a group of Year 9 pupils were keenest to talk about were topics such as the slave trade, the rise of Hitler, the Holocaust, Martin Luther King and civil rights. Adolescents' interest in human actions was also brought into sharp focus by Jenny Parsons, Head of History at Rednock School. In explaining the high take-up of history in her school, she noted:

> It is the moral and spiritual aspect of history, which is one of the most pressing reasons for its appeal. Emphasis on debate, discussion, controversy and moral issues interests many students and makes them accept the relevance of history today.
>
> (Parsons, 1998)

Assessing the significance of the role of the individual in the past has for many years been a feature of the learning of history. Brief biographies of great men and women were a feature of history over a century ago, where the significance lay in the emphasis on the moral value implicit in their greatness. More recent approaches seek to set the contribution of the individual in the context of the time in which they lived. Evans concluded that it is precisely the interaction between the individual and his or her circumstances that makes the study of people in the past so fascinating (R. J. Evans 1997). *Benefits accrue to pupils from the consideration of a range of questions when assessing the significance of an individual, which can prompt some perceptive answers.* Questions such as, to what extent was the individual the product of the times? How unique was the contribution? How might the course of history have been different had it not been for the influence of that individual?

Considering the big picture, and the wider themes that can span the centuries, will necessitate the use of generalisations and with them *the need to understand and use a range of abstract concepts, such as freedom, equality, inflation, slavery, taxation, class, depression and many more.* Using such concepts to assess the significance of real people in real situations will help pupils to understand such terms. Furthermore, as citizenship is back on the educational agenda, assessing the significance of certain events and changes in the past can make an important contribution to this aspect of a pupil's education. *They raise fundamental questions, which it is important for an adolescent to consider.* It is accepted that some such questions could also arise in some other areas of the curriculum such as Personal and Social Education, but history lessons are more likely to deal with the wider political and social philosophical questions. The contention is that, even with the time constraints within which the subject is taught, the relevance and value of studying history will be enhanced when such questions as those set out in Table 4.1 are raised.

The strategies included in the final section of this chapter are designed to indicate ways of achieving such outcomes in a way that renews emphasis on the value and relevance of studying history.

What are the potential problems in the learning of significance?

There can be little doubt that assessing significance has the potential for difficulties, yet there are real rewards and it requires the skill of the history teacher to overcome the potential problems pupils will have in assessing historical significance. By so doing, it should be possible to demonstrate the relevance and educational value of studying significance in history. So what are the potential problems? They may be classified into four groups: the negative, the sceptical, the psychological and the practical.

The negative

A fairly basic problem, with which most history teachers have to deal, is the notion that exists in some pupils that the past is irrelevant to their lives. This argument seems to gain ground when the topics being studied are more remote in time. It has an apparently undeniable truth, that 'you cannot change what has happened', which could attract those who are not inclined to work at the tasks the study of history demands. It is an argument that most history teachers will have heard and most need to counter. 'What's the point of studying this, sir?' Pupils need to be convinced that they cannot escape the past. The evidence and the influence of the past surround them. Without making some sense of the past, there will be many aspects of their own lives that are incomprehensible. What they are allowed to do by law and what is not allowed – what are their rights and responsibilities – are directly connected with past events. Factors that directly influence the quality of their lives are again only understandable in terms of what has gone before. Where they live, what they eat, how they travel and many other aspects of their daily lives, are all determined by past events, not just social and economic but political and cultural as well. There will be some pupils who imply in their responses that little is of significance in the past because peoples of past ages were, in the opinion of these pupils, far less intelligent than people today. These are the pupils, who, in

Table 4.1 Making links with issues related to citizenship, social and moral development

Concept	Key questions/issues	Significant historical events/changes
Citizenship		
Rights and responsibilities	What should be the rights of an individual? What are reasonable responsibilities to be expected of an individual or nation?	Feudal system; Magna Carta; Bill of Rights
Taxation	Why pay taxes? Should we evade taxes? What is an unjust tax?	Poll tax; Ship Money; hearth tax; window tax; income tax; VAT
Equality	What do we mean by equality? Are there limits to the creation of equality?	Levellers; slavery abolition; toleration acts; acts against race and sex discrimination; French, American and Russian revolutions
Liberty, freedom	What are the limits of liberty? What is the difference between freedom to and freedom from?	Elizabethan religious settlement; feudalism; slavery and slave trade; settlement certificates; mill apprenticeships; opposition to tyranny
Society, community	Why do people form societies or groups?	Medieval guilds; religious communities; trade unions; co-operative movement
Laws	Why do we obey the law? When would it be right to break the law?	Peasants' Revolt; Pilgrimage of Grace; Jacobites; Luddites; strikes; Prohibition
Sovereignty	Who should have the last word on what should be the law?	Model, Elizabethan and Stuart parliaments; triennial acts; successive parliament acts
Democracy	How democratic can a country be?	Reform acts; electoral change; Chartists; suffragettes; local government changes
Social/moral development		
Right/wrong; good/evil	What is the basis of what is right or wrong, good or evil?	Slave trade; exploitation of workers, children and women; press-gang; witch-hunts; anti-Semitism; imperialism; humanitarianism
Needs	How do we ensure the varied needs of people are met?	Monasteries; poor laws; charities; growth of the Welfare State
Choice	How much should you be able to choose what you do?	Compulsory education; tax and census returns; registration of births etc.; licences; Puritan legislation in Cromwell's time; conscription
Welfare and well-being	Should the State have a role in people's welfare, or should it be left to charity? Should an individual be left to look after him/herself?	*Laissez-faire*; education, health reform; welfare; housing

Shemilt's analysis, mistakenly confuse 'cultural and technological supremacy with biological supremacy' (Shemilt 1984: 50–1). For them satisfaction is achieved in their presence in the age of computers, organ transplants and satellite communication. Such a dismissive view of the past would inhibit any serious consideration of the complexity and relevance of the recurring issues of past and present.

To some the recurrent issues of the past are all too familiar. To those pupils, who have direct and indirect experience of poverty, unemployment, racism, crime and disorder, together with various manifestations of inequality, the influence of the past is very evident. In some cases it may be too pressing and some might prefer a history that is seen as escapist, remote from their own lives, where they can identify in some vicarious manner with past successes and triumphs in the same way as some will support successful football teams, which are based many miles from where they live.

The sceptical

A further set of problems, which could affect any emphasis on the significance and relevance of the past, comes with a sense of disillusionment. Such a view is fired by the frustrations, which stem from any recall of past events, to justify continued conflict. On several occasions, Tony Blair has criticised what he sees as the excessive influence of the past in the Irish Question. He has a point. The study of history is diminished if its significance is seen in the perpetuation of past conflicts. 'Tradition' and 'culture' have a clear downside.

Disillusionment is also evident when there is clear evidence that any lessons from the past have not been learned. The adolescent, watching the television news, will see a continuing tale of war, famine, murder, fraud and abuse, to which may be added the problems of drugs, pollution and global warming.

A different kind of scepticism is also familiar to the history teacher. As the 'new' history has introduced younger pupils more and more to the uncertainties of history, the limitations of evidence and the variety of interpretations, we can now add the subjective nature of what is significant in the past. Pupils are to learn that it is possible for there to be different selections of significant facts about some events or situations and that all of them can be equally valid. There is no one unquestionable set of significant and true facts about a situation or event (Lomas 1990: 41). Some pupils find this very frustrating, when they see learning as the acquisition of a body of knowledge they can own and recall. Such pupils need to be reminded that many events are not a matter of dispute and that the significance of many of them is generally agreed.

The psychological

Perhaps more fundamental problems to be encountered in the teaching and learning of significance lie in the conceptual demands, which this aspect of the Key Elements makes of pupils. An important feature of assessing significance is the ability to go beyond the specific to the general, to be able to abstract from the detail the wider, more enduring issues, and to be able to make links and connections across time and between past and present. All of these are frequently listed as the characteristics of the able pupil. As such, are they deemed too difficult for the average pupil? Research over the past thirty years has shown that much depends on the methodology used (Husbands 1996: 15, 27 and footnotes). Recipients of the more traditional transmission mode of teacher talk found great difficulty when asked to make conceptual leaps to deal with abstract concepts and formulate and substantiate their own opinions. However, when pupils have been encouraged to become involved in applying knowledge, making and supporting judgements, extending their vocabulary through pupil talk and decision-making, and making connections with charts and diagrams, then very different results are achieved. Recent research by Tim Lomas, quoted by Walsh, suggests that pupils are put off history less by its conceptual difficulty and more by the amount of work they have to do, and the impression that much of it is simply 'grinding through' material (Walsh 1998: 6). Hopefully some of the strategies described later indicate ways round this potential problem.

The practical

Finally, there are the most fundamental potential problems: the very practical ones related to the pupils' breadth of knowledge and the command of language being sufficient to be able to assess the significance of past events, people and changes. Often the significance of an event can only be seen in the light of subsequent events. Teachers will therefore need strategies to try to overcome this, helping pupils to make the links and connections, relating the familiar to the unfamiliar.

Language is the last and arguably the most fundamental potential barrier to being able to understand and articulate an assessment of significance. The language demands of history are several and diverse, yet the study of significance has its own language problems that need to be anticipated. The very word, 'significance', will present difficulties for some pupils, who may well be happier with 'important' or perhaps 'influence'. Many will find 'turning-point' easier, where it is appropriate. As has been emphasised in the previous section, the significance of events can often lie in their contribution to developments in subject areas not usually taught in Key Stages 3 and 4 – politics, economics, philosophy, sociology and theology. Yet many of the concepts associated with these subjects will be needed by the pupil assessing significance, e.g. equality, poverty, non-conformity, inflation, class, etc., and of course part of the value of the subject is learning to use these words in their historical context. A further area of problematic language is encountered when pupils attempt to describe, comment upon and compare past and present attitudes and values – ideas of fealty and divine right, or unfamiliar notions of evidence of guilt or apprenticeship. And yet, as M.D. Wilson persuasively argues, there is clear evidence that pupils of limited ability can surprise their teachers with demonstrations of their understanding provided they find the subject content of value and interest. Colin Harrison, quoted by Wilson, writes:

> If children can gain an insight into such concepts as justice and truth, for example, by consulting and discussing extracts from difficult books, including primary sources to which the less able do not normally have access, then the materials will have served their purpose.
>
> (Wilson 1985: 57)

Successful teaching of Key Element 2d is more likely if the potential problems are anticipated. With a methodology and a content that strikes a chord with young people, most then can be encouraged to see the value and significance of what they are studying.

What strategies can be used in the teaching of significance in history?

There is plenty of scope for emphasising significance within the usual pedagogic routines such as question and answer, the final thinking question of a sequence or within lesson conclusions, which emphasise what has been learned and consider what is significant about the topic that has been studied. Yet the timing will differ. There will be occasions when consideration of significance can precede a topic, while on others it will be beneficial to encourage the pupils to make links with previously covered topics and units to underline the wider issues such as attitudes and responses to poverty, crime, technological change, oppression and disease. At the completion of a unit, pupils could be asked to justify their selection of the six most important events covered.

Emphasising significance can frequently mean increasing pupils' awareness of the range and comprehensive nature of that significance, as shown in some of the examples below. Teaching the concept gives great scope for decision-making. This can take the form of 'exclusion exercises', such as the creation of time-charts or diagrams with only so many items permitted so that pupils have to select the most significant. Alternatively, another form would be the writing of a brief, hundred-word précis of an event or person for an encyclopaedia (Lomas 1990: 43). Decision-making can encourage group-work, presentations of a case, e.g. for an award for the most significant invention. There are role play possibilities as characters from the past assert the significance of their contribution. GCSE candidates are increasingly invited to make decisions, which encourage their assessment of the significance of events, changes and people. The following ideas may well be adapted to other content.

Explanation cards

Encouraging explanations of why an event, cause or consequence is significant.

This could be done by presenting the pupils with a list or a set of cards for group-work (which could include some 'dummies', or less likely explanations) and asking the pupils to select the more likely ones and be able to explain their choice.

Example: Why was the 'Great Fire of London', 1666, a significant event in history? From Table 4.2, choose the *three* best explanations of the importance of the Great Fire in history.

Table 4.2 Explanations of why the Great Fire of London is a significant event in history

More hygienic housing conditions meant that London never suffered a plague again. Lessons learned for other towns and cities.	Catholics were accused of starting it. Showed how rumour and false information can be used by propagandists for a particular cause.	People learnt how to make better use of their natural resources. The Fleet river was less polluted and water was used more effectively for fire-fighting.	Fifty-one new churches were built, many by the architect, Sir Christopher Wren. They included a new St Paul's, built between 1675 and 1710.	More permanent buildings were erected, showing the value of red brick and stone in replacing the old timber buildings. More fire-proof but still elegant.
Showed the need for a proper fire brigade and also for house insurance schemes.	The newly built London was now better placed for its role as a commercial centre, with the growth of banking and trade.	Wren had plans to create a planned city with wide streets and more elegant buildings, but these were not to be as the need for rapid re-housing meant the old street system was retained.	Through the primary evidence of the time, such as Pepys's diary, we can learn about how people organised themselves at a time of crisis.	London missed a great opportunity to build a modern new city. Had they followed Wren's plans there might have been less traffic problems today. Note lack of vision and the effect of individual self-interest, which hampered progress.

Deciding on the most important of a set

The significance of events of the Second World War. The following is a list of nine of the events of the Second World War. There is an element of gimmickry in the following example, but nevertheless it can be a thought-provoking exercise.

A   Take each in turn and discuss why it was a significant event.
B   Which of them do you consider to have been the *most significant* event?

Give reasons for your choice.

1   The replacement of Neville Chamberlain by Winston Churchill as British Prime Minister.
2   The evacuation of the British troops at Dunkirk, 1940.
3   The Battle of Britain, 1940.
4   Operation Barbarossa: the German invasion of Russia, 1941.
5   The USA's declaration of war on Germany, 1941.

6   The Battle of El Alamein, 1942.
7   The Battle of Stalingrad, 1942–3.
8   The D-Day landings in Normandy, 1944.
9   Hitler's suicide, 1945.

In the follow-up discussion it would be interesting to explore why certain choices have been made. Pupils could also discuss, as an aspect of historical interpretations, which choices might be made by pupils living in the USA, France, Germany and Russia.

Concept cards

The pupils are presented, in pairs or groups, with a set of cards (see column A of Table 4.3), on each of which is a single word concept, e.g. taxation. The first task of the pupil is to match the cards to a duplicated list of topics, which they have covered in their history lessons at that point (Column B). Raleigh is included as an example. Second, taking each concept in turn, they have to explain why they have made a particular match. Additional discussion could consider how this activity helps the pupils understand the significance of the historical events they have studied. A further development could be to ask them to match the concept cards (Column A) to a list of topics from current national and world events to see if they can transfer their understanding.

Table 4.3 Concept cards and possible matches

Column A	Column B	Your matches
Equality	Walter Raleigh	Empire, colonialism, trade
Poverty	Peasants' Revolt	
Non-conformity	Ship Money	
Puritanism	The Jacobites	
Slavery	Ku Klux Klan	
Taxation	Martin Luther	
Empire	The slave trade	
Inflation	The Levellers	
Democracy	Whitney's cotton gin	
Monarchy	Guy Fawkes	
Racism	Martin Luther King	
Class	Oliver Cromwell	
Unification	Magna Carta	
Reform	Francis Drake	
Civil Rights	Execution of Charles I	
Liberty	Abraham Lincoln	
Colonialism	Defeat of the Armada	
Profit	Malcolm X	
Rebellion	Norman Conquest	
Trade	John Brown	
Feudalism	Cardinal Wolsey	

Categorising the nature of significance

Following the contention that an important part of 'selling the subject' is to keep reminding pupils of the relevance and wider significance of history, there may be times when the message can be presented as an exercise. Not all topics will generate the quantity and range of the points listed in the example, but most will be capable of a similar list.

Which of the twelve explanations in Table 4.4 do you think is *the most important?* Explain your choice.

Ending with a current contemporary issue

There is considerable merit in being able to show how many of the issues of the past are still present today. Reference to such may have its greatest effect if the pupils come to realise that what to them may seem the experiences of a past, unenlightened age are still a relevant cause for study and concern today.

Example: Year 9 pupils have been studying the use of child labour in early nineteenth-century Britain. Using sources, they had to identify and understand the arguments that were advanced by both employers and some parents in defence of such a system. As a conclusion to the lesson, the pupils were then shown, on an OHP, almost identical arguments being offered for the use of child labour in the sub-continent of India, which they had heard about in a recent new item

Table 4.4 Reasons why the study of the slave trade and its abolition is important

1. It explains how Black people came to live on the American continent.	2. It helps us to understand why there was a civil war in the USA.	3. It explains how cotton was produced cheaply for the new machines and factories.	4. It makes us think about how Black people were treated and how the traders and slave owners tried to justify what they did.
5. It allows us to make up our own minds about what we think of slavery.	6. It shows how money from the trade created most of Liverpool's banks, which provided loans for the development of railways, mines and factories.	7. It helps us to try to understand why people like the abolitionists worked to bring an end to the slave trade and then slavery itself, and what motivated them.	8. It helps us to understand how people could make a lot of money (big profits) by using a cheap labour force bound by law not to run away (slaves and mill apprentices).
9. It helps us to understand how public opinion can be used to bring about change – use of pamphlets, poems, pottery, petitions, public meetings and speeches.	10. It helps us to understand further words such as freedom, liberty, profit, cheap labour and humanitarianism.	11. It helps us to explain the background to the Civil Rights movement in the USA and the underprivileged position of Black people in America and Europe.	12. It helps us to understand the role of the evangelical movement, the Quakers and the humanitarian movement in the late eighteenth and early nineteenth century.

about the manufacture of footballs. The nineteenth-century study helped them to understand the context and complexity of the issue.

Conclusion

History teachers in the secondary school are very aware of the need to emphasise the value of studying the subject. While it has been a long established practice to make links between the past and present, the requirement placed on pupils to assess the significance of events, changes and people in the past encourages the exploration of the range of ways in which the past has significance for adolescents and their education. The emphasis on significance will help them understand the physical world they see around them: the location of certain trades and industries, the different types of churches, the various types of transport and consequences of scientific and technological change. They will learn why certain parts of the world speak English, and about those factors that have contributed to today's multicultural society. They will be encouraged to consider the enduring questions of how a country looks after its poor, sick and aged. They will try to make some sense of why there is conflict between nations and within them. More than that they will be encouraged to develop a vocabulary necessary for such understanding. History teaching is enlivened when pupils feel they can engage with issues that they see as still relevant to their lives today. It is also enlivened when pupils, either individually or in groups, are asked to make decisions. The consideration of significance promotes not only the ability to explain and support a case, but also encourages teenagers to consider where they stand on some of the significant and enduring issues that arise from the study of people in the past.

Questions

1   What makes an event significant? Do you agree with Partington's criteria? What would be the basis upon which you decide which topics should have fuller treatment?
2   Does an emphasis on events that are generally accepted as being significant mean that school history will necessarily concentrate on the 'big events' – the wars, revolutions and invasions – at the expense of local history?
3   Do you think that allowing teachers to have a greater choice in the content of the history they teach could diminish the relevance and significance of learning history?
4   Can the concept of 'significance' be incorporated into schemes of work and lesson plans? Using the criteria mentioned in this chapter, or your own, identify and describe what you consider to be the significance of some of the topics you are planning to teach.

Further reading

Lomas, T. (1990) *Teaching and Assessing Historical Understanding*, London: Historical Association.

One of the few publications about the teaching of history that specifically addresses in some detail the concept of significance alongside the more familiar concepts of cause, time and evidence, and as such anticipated the revised National Curriculum.

Partington, G. (1980) *The Idea of an Historical Education*, Slough: NFER.

Contains an extended discussion of 'what makes an event significant?', which is only very briefly touched upon in this chapter. His criteria have been criticised but are possibly now more fashionable with the establishment of the National Curriculum. See especially Chapter 5.

5 Historical knowledge and historical skills

A distracting dichotomy

Christine Counsell

Introduction

By the late 1990s all of history teaching discourse in England and Wales has become infused with an assumed duality – that of 'knowledge' and 'skill'. Dominant professional languages matter because they end up informing new mechanisms for accountability, be they National Curriculum levels, OFSTED inspection criteria or GCSE assessment objectives. It is so easy to become a prisoner of such languages, to assume that if we espouse given models of progression and assessment they will automatically offer us the stages, strategies and goals for moving pupils forward.

This chapter argues that history teachers and researchers need to analyse much more closely the relationship between those things that we have traditionally called 'content' and 'skill'. Such labels conceal great reaches of hidden mental activity that might be better characterised in different ways.

Skill and knowledge: an uneasy alliance

During the 1970s and 1980s, history teachers, curriculum developers and researchers completely reconceptualised school history. Through the work of thinkers such as Coltham and Fines (1971) and a variety of Schools Council Projects – most notably the Schools Council 13–16 Project – many history teachers began to think differently about what constitutes progression (Shemilt 1976, 1987). Instead of emphasising the cumulative memorising of a body of facts, curriculum developers produced and researchers analysed new cognitive domains that were deemed to be more closely derivative of the practice of the academic discipline itself (e.g. Booth 1987; Ashby and Lee 1987).

The 'new history' brought a new professional language, one which experimented with new taxonomies of 'skills', 'concepts' and 'attitudes'. These influenced everything from GCSE assessment to resources and textbooks, and ultimately the National Curriculum itself. Yet throughout this revolution, substantive knowledge has remained high on the agenda in examination boards and assessment schemes at both GCSE and Advanced Level. It sits rather uneasily alongside other objectives but it never goes away. Much of teachers' agonising over how to interpret assessment schemes, be they GCSE or National Curriculum, is about how to handle the relationship between, and appropriate weightings for, so-called 'content' and so-called 'skill'. Substantive knowledge still moves awkwardly in the professional language of many history teachers.

A new kind of 'teaching as exposure'?

In his 1991 study of junior school pupils and their teachers, Peter Knight argued that pupils were merely being 'exposed' to slabs of content. Learning activities did not seem to fit any discernible pattern or purpose linked to the nature of the discipline. There appeared to be no model, conscious or tacit, of skills or concepts that might provide thresholds for planning and assessment (Knight 1991). Knight's concept of 'teaching by exposure' can be transferred to skills and concepts, too. The assumption that by 'doing' the various skills of history pupils will necessarily get better at them is just as likely to be flawed. There are plenty of pupils in secondary history departments in England and Wales in the 1990s who have a constant diet of activities relating to causation and evidence, and who are regularly assessed against those aspects of the National Curriculum Level Descriptions that relate to them. Yet the majority of pupils still find history prohibitively difficult at GCSE. These are the very pupils for whom the skills and concepts revolution was designed to serve. I do not dispute the idea that mastery of such skills and concepts ought to inform our goals; I want to suggest, rather, that we have built up a package of uncritical and questionable assumptions about how pupils might reach them.

Some divergent thinking about progress in skills

In 1994 I was in charge of a humanities faculty in an urban secondary school. During October, one of my colleagues taught a history lesson to a mixed-ability Year 8 class. This was a Newly Qualified Teacher with whom I would regularly 'team-teach', as part of his professional development programme. One pupil, 'Marie', a lower attainer, was carrying out an activity on the German Reformation.

In Marie's group (Marie and two boys) an argument was taking place over the position of a picture-card showing Tetzel selling indulgences. The boys wanted to place the card underneath a heading they had just made called 'things to do with money'. Their case seemed strong. Who could argue that Tetzel's selling of indulgences was not to do with money? Marie, however, was having none of it. She wanted to put the card under a new heading called 'triggers'. The class were familiar with the term 'triggers', having encountered it in many other topics. It was not Marie's invention, but she had chosen to use it in this setting. The pupils were familiar with this problem of overlap (it had often been a teaching point) but in this particular lesson the pupils had been explicitly instructed to press their arguments on to a conclusion. They had to settle for the category label with the strongest rational claim.

Marie was challenged now. How could she argue that her choice of category was superior to that of the boys? It was at this point that she tried a new line. Perhaps it was not possible to have *both* of these categories in one explanation. One could *either* have the heading 'things to do with money' (along with other things) *or* one could have the heading 'triggers' (along with quite different things). To bolster her case she found herself using other picture-cards on the table to jog her memory about the kinds of events and situations that go under 'triggers', pointing to peasant discontent and wider political pressures within the Holy Roman Empire. Previous lessons had given her some 'fingertip knowledge' of these narratives. The pictures and their captions helped her to define the mini-narratives in her memory and to call them up.

Marie's achievement was impressive. Her argument, backed up with detail, amounted to a defence of one classification system over another. This moment came as a result of a very long-term programme of systematic planning for progression to take place. All along, her exposure to new substantive knowledge and opportunity to process or 'play' with it had dovetailed closely with systematic work in helping her to define or 'see' abstract issues. Some observers, using the language of 'historical 'skills', would say that the lesson described above was an example of the pupils practising multi-causal explanations or seeing the relationship between causes or applying common categories of cause. Indeed they were, but this was not the language of the incremental stages that brought the pupils to this point. By the time I was managing this faculty, having lived through the first National Curriculum (and having experimented with all the latest ways in measuring paths of conceptual progression before that) I had completely abandoned much of the language of progression within discrete skill domains. Overwhelming frustration with inadequacies in all given models (such as movement from mono-causal explanation to multi-causal explanations; or from stereotypical empathy to differentiated empathy of the early GCSE) led to a different way of thinking about progression. Like many teachers I was theorising in a messy, but cumulatively helpful, way from my own experience. It was useful to start with the big ideas in history, but in terms of how to reach them (that is, how to plan for progression) my colleagues and I came to use very different terms. We spoke of 'active linking' or 'finding shapes', always alerting pupils through the kinds of pattern that history's natural discourse repeats. Becoming secure in the language and structure of a 'rebellion story' or a 'social change story' required both acquaintance with the detail as singularities and with the generalising concepts that helped us to talk about them.

The problem with 'skill'

The term 'skill' is problematic in the first instance because it tends to be used by teachers as a catch-all for all manner of understandings and processes, some specifically historical, others general. Once teachers use it to describe everything from 'listening skills' to skills in evaluating historical evidence, its value as a professional term is diminished.

A more specific difficulty within history education is the absence of a common distinction between those aspects of the subject that relate to evidential method or enquiry and those that relate to understanding of the big ideas that history generates, such as causation, consequence, change, continuity and so forth. Although the latter is sometimes thought of as 'conceptual understanding', it is just as often characterised as a set of 'skills' (suggesting a process), such as the ability to construct multi-causal explanations or the ability to explain the connection between causes and effects. This means that it is never quite clear what is meant. Is the teacher trying to improve and assess the pupil's ability to discuss evidence as an abstract issue or his ability to apply it in particular situations? Researchers in this field are usually rather more careful with their terminology, eschewing the term 'skills' and thinking, instead, of concepts or ideas which pupils hold. Many speak of 'second-order' historical concepts, meaning the big ideas that shape historical questions such as causation, change, continuity and so forth. Interestingly, Dickinson, Lee and Ashby include 'evidence' along with these concepts rather than referring to this as skill or mechanism. Their research focus is on the ideas that pupils seem to be working with (often tacitly) rather than procedures they can carry out (Dickinson, Lee and Ashby 1997).

The past two decades have seen strong interest in attempts to use second-order historical concepts as a means to provide a structure for progression in history. The principle behind such models, if not the detail, has been influential in National Curriculum and GCSE assessment objectives alike. Conceptual gradations within GCSE examination mark-schemes are common. The 1991 National Curriculum was built around five areas of second-order understanding – cause and consequence, change and continuity, similarity and difference, evidence and interpretations.

Teacher reaction to the 1991 model was explosive. Phillips (1993) conducted surveys and interviews of teacher opinion that created a damning picture. Comments ranged from 'complex', 'impractical', 'verbose' to 'awful', 'daft', 'mad'. Few, however, suggested that the very idea of managing progression and assessment around these ideas might be flawed. Indeed, the reaction of some teachers to the Level Descriptions of the 1995 National Curriculum has been to disaggregate the Levels and so recreate the very structure against which they protested in 1991! Difficulty in interpreting either Statements of Attainment or Level Descriptions is still frequently attributed to the lack of an elusive 'precision' (QCA 1997). If only the statements were right (the argument seems to run), or more closely tied to real progression in each skill area, somehow assessment would make sense.

Part of the problem is that 'progression' is a problematic word. It is used, loosely, to indicate both goals and journeys. Research into children's ideas may well tell us much more about goals than journeys. The broad ideas that pupils hold at any one stage may belie the detailed gaps and confusions that need to be worked on if pupils are to be moved on. After two decades of working with these ideas it is time to ask more fundamental questions. I have three main concerns about the professional impact of addressing progression through discrete, content-free 'concepts' or skills. None of these suggest that these concepts are unhelpful or unfitting goals, but only that over-reliance on specific second-order concepts as a progression framework may limit the effectiveness of planning, teaching and assessment.

Dangers of over-reliance on models of progression within discrete cognitive domains

1 It can mask hidden reaches of mental activity that may be the proper focus of teacher attention

The extract from a 15-year-old's work (see Figure 5.1) was produced after extensive work on reliability, utility and typicality of sources, as was common in the late 1980s. This was the teaching focus. This pupil's difficulties, however, proved to be much more basic and mundane. The writing shows that Michael was unable to distinguish between a proposition *as an example* and as *a generalisation or main point*. The piece of writing is full of examples. It is crawling in the particular and lacking in the general. He does not know how to *show* us that they were examples. He does not know how to make a main point and then indicate where the support lies. Work on 'Big Points and Little Points' later transformed this pupil's approach, equipping with him with the ability to select and arrange material and to make his reasoning for such selection transparent. This proved to be his real difficulty and therefore the place where the solution lay (Counsell 1997).

   This is the kind of pupil who seems refractory in his ability to understand anything. Only by abandoning attempts to extend his thinking within one particular domain and by adopting a completely different way of looking at the problem did the breakthrough come. The result was an improved ability to

---

Problems with generalising prevent him from finding or showing the significance of his ideas.

What can we learn from the sources about why vagabonds were treated so harshly?

Robert Shakysberie pretended to have the palsy and that mad the aldermen cross and that why they wiped him. There were thieves too and four hundred people were idel.

Figure 5.1 A 15-year-old, 'Michael', attempts to answer a question on sources, but problems with generalising prevent him from finding or showing the significance of his ideas. Written in 1987 at Rednock School, Dursley

construct evaluations of source material using extended and connected thinking. The journey could be characterised by a strong teaching emphasis on naming and playing with the structural relationships between components in an account (for example, through text-marking and experimentation with classifying and labelling). It was part of a successful journey *towards* evidence-handling and source-evaluation, but the teaching and learning activities *en route*, and the interim assessment undertaken, were not best described by these concepts. Pupils do not necessarily get better at something just by doing a lot of it.

2 The relationship with substantive content is left unexplored

When teachers are using concept- or skill-based models for assessment purposes, such as in a GCSE mark-scheme or using aspects of the National Curriculum Level Description, a frequent question concerns the quantity and specificity of information that it is appropriate for the pupil to deploy at a particular stage. Perhaps the question should be asked in a slightly different way, however. What is at issue is the amount of propositional knowledge or content awareness that *made it possible* for a pupil to operate at this stage.

To some extent, the content–skill dichotomy and its associated problems are mirrored in school science. Amongst science educators, the distinction is sometimes described as that between 'propositional knowledge' and 'procedural knowledge'. In a study of pupils' understanding of magnetism, Gaalen Ericksen attempted to analyse the relationship between content, process and progression. Groups of pupils aged four, seven and ten were conducting experiments with magnets:

> What sort of knowledge were these pupils displaying in this assessment task? ... Typically this type of knowledge of pupils' actions in an inquiry setting has referred to as procedural (or process-oriented) as opposed to propositional (or content-oriented). But this distinction between method and content has become increasingly blurry.
>
> (Ericksen 1994: 89)

In the same vein, Millar and colleagues have argued that it is misleading to portray the methods of science as discrete processes. In particular, within what they call 'inquiry tactics', content knowledge has an interactive effect since selection and control of variables depends on the pupils' knowledge of the phenomena being examined (Millar 1991; Millar and Driver 1987). What kind of interactive effect takes place in history between their general second-order ideas and their substantive knowledge? Too mechanistic an analysis is not likely to be helpful, but it raises questions, if not about the goal of progression itself, then about how it might be secured.

In their study of pupils' rational understanding in history the CHATA researchers identified a broad pattern of progression with such categories as 'bafflement', 'explanation in terms of personal wants or reasons', and 'explanation in terms of the wider context of ideas and material life' (Dickinson, Lee and Ashby 1997: 118–19). This gives teachers a valuable language for defining a focus, but it is possible that the pupils' ideas were shaped, to some extent, by their period knowledge. Those performing at the higher levels, for example, took account of the temporal context in which people in the past were operating. In trying to explain the actions of the people in the past they saw the Anglo-Saxon 'ordeal by fire' as fitting into beliefs about hierarchy and so were beginning to take into account the wider framework of social and material life. Indeed, Lee concludes with the suggestion that a useful further research might 'explore the relation between substantive knowledge and second-order progression' (ibid.: 123).

3 It derogates the role of the teacher's own theorising

Many existing progression frameworks derive from external, unsituated testing. They do not necessarily reflect professional knowledge. This does not mean that there is not a place for this type of research, but over-reliance on models constructed and tested by others outside the classroom may detract from the critical, analytical evaluation all teachers need to carry out if they are to diagnose individual weaknesses and to remedy them. Teachers sometimes need to reconceptualise in order to name a problem. Flexibility and inventiveness in professional language is essential. 'Michael', in the example above, would not have had his breakthrough if I, as his teacher, had not stood back from the particular cognitive domain (evaluating evidence) and re-thought, completely, the basis of his confusion.

The problem with knowledge

Despite unceasing tabloid vilification saying the opposite, by the 1990s most history teachers would agree that knowledge is important, that both knowledge and skill matter, that one needs to be taught 'through' the other and so on. Yet whenever 'content' is compared with 'skills' as a teaching objective it continues to get a bad press. The onslaught of pressures created by time, accountability mechanisms, a prescribed curriculum and troublesome pupils all make teaching history very challenging. The blame is frequently laid at content's door. Thus, for example, as late as 1995, in Peter Knight's findings from interviews with twenty-nine history teachers concerning their views about National Curriculum history, there was general agreement about damaging effects of excessive or prescriptive content. One teacher stated:

> It is not the body of content that's important, it's the skills that the children develop. Is it relevant for 14-year-olds to know about the Act of Union ? The detail is too complex for children of that age.
>
> (Knight 1996: 49)

Content is often held up as a separate concern from skills, even as a possible distraction. As such, it must be the bogeyman. It is worth examining very closely some of the reasons for these perceptions.

First, prescribing any body of historical knowledge is seen to be dangerous. The reasons for this are obvious. Choice of topics and periods is hugely sensitive and will always be contested particularly where a national curriculum is imposed on a multicultural society. These are important and complex concerns. They reflect history's power. Pupils can feel excluded and alienated by a diet of history that excludes or derogates what they see as 'their' past. Equally, for other pupils, a lack of opportunity to study the stories, traditions, communities and nations *other* than their own could give them a damagingly limited cultural outlook. To decide what history is to be taught, at school, regional or national level, is to exercise phenomenal power. Better, then, say the nervous, not to prescribe it at all.

The second common objection is often linked to the first. This is the view that the choice of content for history teaching is somehow unimportant. On the face of it, this seems easy to defend. After all, many a mature historian has survived into a successful academic career without knowing very much about whole periods or themes. It therefore seems easy to state that the content is somehow unimportant, and that it is just the 'domain' in which we practise things.

So, historical content is damned for being both dangerous and unimportant. As if that were not enough, content is also damned for being a chief culprit in making history too difficult or unnecessarily boring. This is the most interesting charge of all. Anyone who has wrestled with teaching 9Z on Thursday afternoon will comprehend it. Pupils switch off when they hit overload or when they fail to connect with abstract, alienating detail. Therefore this kind of detail, or this particular detail, or any detail I have not chosen myself, must somehow be at fault. To reach the conclusion that such detail is not 'relevant', and that this offending thing called 'content' is the root of the problem is understandable. Such reasoning then merges with the 'not important' argument, and 'content' is doubly damned.

It is not that these judgements deserve censure but rather that professionals need to analyse both the rationale for and the consequences of such judgements. The first warning of 'dangerous' is one to which curriculum policy-makers and teachers must forever be alert. To feed children a view of the past, uncritically (and even a choice of content for the purposes of a prescribed curriculum amounts to a 'view'), is to close down other possibilities, other stories and other ways of telling them. Yet to try to solve this by opting for a criterion-based history curriculum seeking the ultimate balance in all cultural, ethnic, gender and social aspects is not to protect the pupil from indoctrination. It is just creating another kind of story reflecting an assumed consensus in contemporary concerns. It is arguably just as dangerous for any teacher to seek the holy grail of an ethnically, culturally, socially neutral history curriculum, however redemptive of past imbalances.

If the answer cannot lie in a perfectly balanced or politically-acceptable-to all-parties-curriculum, then where does it lie? One answer to this particular difficulty was created by the first National Curriculum of 1991. Attainment Target 2, as it was then called, or 'Interpretations of History', was an astonishing innovation whose significance has been hugely underestimated. What this new curriculum device did was to make the danger of history the object of study itself. Here was the perfect solution: the way in which history reaches us, through textbook, teacher, film, family folklore or heritage tea-towel becomes the focus for our critical attention. The aim was not to judge its reliability, but simply to examine how it came to be. The Working Group's final report asserted that 'historical theories and interpretations are there to be constantly re-examined ... there are no monopolies of the truth' (DES 1990: 11). To teach interpretations well is to show pupils that history *is* dangerous.

What, then, of the charge that choice of historical content is unimportant? When the content of the curriculum is viewed in the context of learning process rather than outcome, when its function in children's learning is explored, it becomes impossible to see content choice as unimportant. Much of our ability to make meaning from historical sources and accounts comes from the ability to spot analogy. As study continues, analogies multiply. This supplies a frame of reference without which most passages of history are unintelligible. The acquisition of historical knowledge is cumulative in its impact:

> We see the world in terms of our picture of it, and that picture is not a mere agglomeration of random sensory chaos but the outcome of a classificatory process which has grouped and separated experiences according to a sense of like/unlike.
>
> (Rogers 1987: 16)

One way of analysing a teacher's work is to examine what the teacher does to highlight resonance, to 'warm it up', and to prepare for future resonance. The lesson on the Reformation outlined at the start of this chapter was part of a unit of work on the German Reformation. It was deliberately positioned before the teaching of the National Curriculum Study Unit on 1500 to 1750. This was an example of deliberate manufacture of resonance. Rather than despair that the bottom 40 per cent of the ability range cannot handle the religious concepts of the Reformation, it makes sense to build understanding of key religious mentalities very systematically so that during the subsequent study of the Reformation in England, Wales and Scotland all pupils will be comfortable with the political significance of innovations in theology. The more pupils know the more they are in a position to learn. To say that the learning of content is unimportant is to ignore its subtle role in future learning.

This brings us to the third and final charge – that an emphasis on knowledge acquisition will tend to boredom and difficulty. I deal with these two problems together because they are exactly the same thing. Pupils get bored when they get stuck. They persevere with the most impossible of quests when they are fired up and excited. To suggest that a particular detail or fact is or is not 'relevant' to a pupil is to indulge in slightly careless curricular thinking. All history is potentially relevant to adolescent and adult living: it is about the behaviour of men and women in society. What we really mean when we say something is irrelevant is that either the information overload, or the unfamiliarity of the material, or the sheer banality of its presentation, make the pupil switch off. It is either too strange or too familiar! If we are to overcome the kinds of difficulties that the majority of pupils still present, we need both to construct and to analyse short and long-term journeys into the difficulties themselves. Somehow, the strange must be made familiar, and the familiar strange. The critical question is how do (or might) teachers ensure that the virtuous circle of cumulative knowledge acquisition replaces the vicious circle of boredom and difficulty?

Making the abstract interesting: the role of status and structure

In any classroom activity, from listening to a story, to planning a role play or evaluating a source, pupils are dealing with a great deal of contextual knowledge. Some of the problems that pupils encounter can be seen in terms of difficulties they are having in utilising existing understandings or in appropriating new ones. They may lack an existing knowledge framework that will make the new knowledge make sense. Background chronology may be too fuzzy for the pupils to frame a meaningful question, the word 'Parliament' may lack sufficient resonance for a pupil to 'hear' it in a crucial video clip, awareness of eighteenth-century mentalities might be too undeveloped to see the significance of a source detail, and so on.

How far do teachers address these difficulties directly? Much of the time they are addressed only indirectly. Teachers' lesson objectives sometimes refer to knowledge but the process by which the knowledge might be appropriated is unclear. It is left to the processing activity – the writing, speaking or listening activity – to make the knowledge 'go in'. It is still a kind of faith in 'exposure'. In one sense, this is not a foolish hope. When we process items (that is, when we 'do' something with them), information is converted into more enduring knowledge shapes. But typical lesson objectives remain vague about how or to what extent this is expected to happen.

Most history lesson objectives relate to one of two issues. The emphasis is either upon the *status* of accounts (whose side is it on? is it reliable? in what setting was this written/painted? what kind of account is this? how would this person have told the story differently? let's try to see this from her point of view …) or their *structure* (which factors were the most important? what *were* the key factors? how shall we summarise the main issues? does this example fit into this account? are these issues political or social? is this label any good or is it more confusing?). I deliberately ignore the issue of whether or not the pupils are constructing such accounts or whether they are reading/hearing/using those of others. These are irrelevant distinctions here, especially as reading and writing, listening and speaking, watching and making are usually closely woven in even the shortest of activity sequence. The distinction here is between two types of history teaching *emphasis*:

1   Who is saying/writing this and what difference does that make? (status)
2   How do (or might, or should, or don't) these things fit together and what
    shall we call them? (structure)

Of course, from many perspectives this distinction is flawed (status deter-mines structure and structure may determine status). Even in terms of teaching, these types merge into each other (writing an imaginative account will involve thinking about selection and arrangement; deciding how to define the issues a source raises will involve consideration of its provenance). Yet this is why the notion of teaching *emphasis* is helpful. It is an important way of analysing types of teaching focus, the things the teacher chooses to stress, and its potential for solving pupils' difficulties.

The defining characteristic of school history teaching ever since 'new history' principles were enshrined in the first GCSE criteria in 1986 is an emphasis on status. The use of the documentary source, and, more recently, the use of interpretation, as a teaching focus, has made questions about reliability and utility of accounts, their provenance and purpose, the staple of the history classroom. Whilst there is little doubt that the active, critical, rigorous tech-niques that came with this revolution have made it possible to enthuse a wider range of pupils about the interest and value of history, it has brought new diffi-culties with it too. There is a danger that by emphasising *only* the status of an account, pupils' fundamental difficulties with the knowledge references it presents can be obscured. I am not talking about the problem of conflicting preconceptions, but rather the problems some pupils have in finding *any reso-nance at all* in key words – their inability to recognise allusions to familiar story shapes or structures. The example given earlier of the pupil 'Michael' illustrates this problem. Here, the teaching emphasis had been entirely, and very thor-oughly, upon the status of the accounts being used. Yet Michael had much more fundamental difficulties in collecting up and processing that information. Other ways of seeing and shaping things were necessary if he was to construct any meaningful commentary, even about the nature of evidence.

To think about the structure of an account is to think about the organising role of words, sentences and whole texts. Pupils can be taught to see the role of one piece of information *vis-à-vis* another. There are many teaching strategies that help pupils to see (*literally* to 'see') the delineation of issues. Stark, physical devices such as small text cards or stacked and linked images on a computer screen allow for manipulation of identifiable ideas. Sorting and arranging activi-ties help pupils to group, organise and name or label issues. When learning how to use conventional classifiers such as 'political' or 'economic', to see the scope and limits of a term like 'rebellion' or to explore the conflicting and overlapping ways in which contemporaries and/or historians used the terms 'gentleman' and 'nobleman', many pupils need much extra help in defining the object of study. When the scope and power of such a word becomes the focus of pupil reflection and class discussion the pupil's difficulty is turned into a teaching solution (Counsell 1997).

Such strategies are often associated with helping pupils to construct coherent prose but they are just as much reading strategies, being a development of the valuable Directed Activities Relating to Texts ('DARTs') strategies already widely used by history teachers (Lunzer *et al.* 1984). By defining and labelling ideas – either their own or others – and making this the primary focus of pupil discussion or teacher explanation, the abstract comes to the foreground of the lesson. Time to dwell directly on the appropriateness of the noun 'rebellion' or the adjective 'political', in relation to a few limited, defined and commonly 'visible' issues helps some pupils, sometimes for the first time, to know what everyone is talking about.

There are many other ways of achieving this, but these examples illustrate a core principle. Knowledge is not free-floating information that gets in the way, but a mental resource for future learning. Substantive knowledge becomes an organising device, an analytical tool for creating and discerning structures, and especially when those pupils who fail to learn through exposure are systematically taught to see its organising functions. Nor is there any need for this to detract from work on the status; in fact, to teach pupils to analyse by playing with terms and labels is to give them increasingly flexible tools for naming things and for realising, straight away, that such labels are contingent, slippery, shifting and problematic.

This is simply another way of describing the area of understanding identified by Key Element 5 of the 1995 National Curriculum for history, or 'Organisation and communication' (DfE 1995). 'Key Element 5', like all the Key Elements, is not a 'skill' to be taught and ticked off; it is simply another angle on the approaches and dispositions pupils must adopt to make sense of history. Some pupils may need more direct emphasis on its issues than others. Sometimes differentiation (if it is really to secure access as opposed to making things easier) is about lifting out the Key Element 5 dimension in any task – selecting, arranging and experimenting with labels – and giving it more direct a focus. To make the abstract interesting and so to build knowledge at the same time is to foster that virtuous circle in which pupils start to gain the power of a store of knowledge as a set of building blocks for understanding or analysing new material.

Layers of knowledge: fingertips and residue

One result of the uneasy status of historical knowledge in history-teaching discourse has been the lack of thorough, shared professional debate about the function of knowledge in progression. Most general guides on progression refer to such things as 'expanding knowledge and understanding of the past' and 'increasing understanding of historical terminology' (Grosvenor and Watts

1995: 25), but how one bit of knowledge might contribute to another is not an area about which teachers and authors have theorised in depth. Even having acknowledged that knowledge might be important in some way, most commentators fall back on hierarchies of skill with which to define progression.

The National Curriculum Mark 3 of 2000 will leave teachers with even more freedom to select and combine content elements for programmes of work. If teachers can shake off assumptions that historical knowledge consists of neutral, value-free, atomised pieces of information to be learned, and, instead, see knowledge as a cumulative process of active critical construction, it will be timely to theorise about the function of knowledge in securing learning across longer time-scales.

Deep within the professional knowledge of effective teachers, there are no doubt all kinds of tacit criteria for positioning content elements within wider planning. In the early part of the term, I might choose to teach particular political concepts and institutions, precisely so that the pupils can manage these with ease and confidence during a depth study that I plan to undertake some weeks later. This, in turn, helps me to judge the kind of content detail or the range of particular examples that it is necessary for pupils to understand during the earlier study. This type of professional reasoning gives a clearer rationale for choice and order of content components, micro and macro and short- and long-term time-scales. It may be helpful to conceptualise knowledge-building as a layering process and to judge its effectiveness by its power in securing new understandings, especially for those pupils who struggle.

All kinds of professional language may be helpful here and it would be useful to explore the type of reasoning, or the tacit, teacher theories that exist already, in order to build a stronger professional body of knowledge about the analytical facility that greater knowledge can bring. For example, one very helpful distinction is that between the temporary or 'working' knowledge that pupils build up during a detailed study, and the broader and lasting understandings such as broad chronological awareness, awareness of institutional structures or cultural values of a period. The first might be called 'fingertip' knowledge. It is the kind of detail that one needs in ready memory and that is acquired through familiarity after extensive enquiry. It does not matter if much of the detail then falls away. The second type can be likened to the residue in a sieve. It is not just the ability to remember that the Tudors came before the Stuarts and that they used Parliament a lot. It is also that loose, amorphous objective of 'a sense of period' – the retention of all manner of mental furniture, gleaned from a rich visual and active experience of period stories and scenes. Such a residue is bound to enrich current and future study by preventing anachronism and sharpening judgement, even after the particular stories and scenes have long receded.

'Fingertip' and 'residue' do not create an absolute distinction. The distinction becomes helpful in relating the function of each type of knowledge to other kinds of learning. One kind of knowledge can be used by the teacher to create another. One of the purposes of 'fingertip' knowledge is that it *leaves* a residue. I once had a close knowledge of the details of late eighteenth-century

British politics. Dates and events were not a problem. Now I can no longer do any of this. I have forgotten huge amounts of detail. The knowledge has never been 'warmed up'. In one sense it is as though I never knew it. But to leap to the conclusion that my learning was somehow a waste of time would be absurd. What I *have* retained is a broad understanding of the institutions of the period and some of its central themes.

This is why it is essential to think of knowledge in the context of medium- and long-term planning. What professionals need is a language for describing such knowledge for the purposes of planning. It is rather meaningless to state, in a lesson objective (although we do it all the time), that the objective is 'By the end of this lesson pupils will have gained knowledge of Henry VIII's wives' or ' ... of the Act of Supremacy'. What matters is the teacher's awareness of the *role of that knowledge in future learning* – the types and layers of knowledge that will endure and the types that will function as temporary working knowledge the details of which will, quite naturally and properly, fall through the sieve. This defines and delineates the amount or type of knowledge the teaching is trying to deal with. Lesson objectives are more helpful when they indicate the proposed function of a knowledge area within wider planning. Words like 'anticipate', 'revisit', 'prepare for' tell us much more about the layer of knowledge being worked on – the teacher's rationale for its specificity or generality.

It is somewhere here that we begin to get close to the complicated task of the effective history teacher. Coming to know is a valuable experience in its own right but it may be a different thing from the concomitant awareness that results and endures. A study in depth in Year 8 or Year 10 is valuable in its own right for the opportunities that in-depth knowledge gives, allowing the pupil, for example, to examine sources closely and critically. Yet 'overview' understandings probably lurk in every 'depth' study. The paradox that needs to inform the planning of school history is that *pupils do not necessarily acquire 'overview' knowledge by doing 'overviews'*. This is why it is essential to distinguish between curriculum outcomes and teaching processes. Although it may seem logical to 'teach the pupil an overview' if one wants an 'overview', it is not that simple. 'Depth' knowledge, memorable and thrilling in its period detail, creates certain kinds of overview knowledge. In turn, overview understandings might support pupils' work in a depth study. It likely to be the *interplay* of 'depth' and 'overview' components within a work-scheme that is critical to quality, not their mere incidence (Riley 1997; Counsell 1998).

The similarity spotters: teaching for resonance

I have argued above that existing models of progression are probably not flawed in the broadest sense, that is, in the set of goals or directions towards which teachers are aiming. The problem lies in characterising the journeys pupils might make in order to get there. What tacit professional knowledge exists about how to move pupils forward? What do teachers actually do from lesson to lesson? What types of moves do they make that come from their knowledge of the subject and their experience of pupils, and which might tell us more about the actual engines of progression? It is important for the profession to look more closely at how effective teachers secure transfer of understanding in a time sequence if we are to find better conceptual frameworks for describing what happens.

In a small-scale, qualitative study, three experienced teachers were interviewed in 1996 about their planning and practice (Counsell 1996). They were video-taped teaching a sequence of two lessons and then interviewed again about the moves they had made in that sequence, using the entire video as a means to stimulate recall of their detailed moves in the lesson (Calderhead 1984). Video evidence, interview transcripts and planning documentation were then analysed together in an attempt to construct a model of these teachers' choice and ordering of subject matter components.

The teachers differed widely in their preferred styles, using very different balances and blends of story-telling and explanation, group discussion and activity, but it was nevertheless possible to theorise about strong common themes. The lessons of all three teachers were littered with implicit and explicit references to organisation of historical content. These formed the teacher's main way of reminding pupils of the existence of a content area. One teacher referred repeatedly to 'this story', and 'the German's view of the story'; another to 'show me the link', 'this type of link', and 'the way the Irish would now see this link'. These teachers were weaving content into memorable shapes ready for future use. What the teacher wanted to stress about organisation or about status was affected by the role of this content element in the wider lesson or the wider planning sequence.

In fact, a key criterion that made these lessons make sense was that of the use of similarity as an explanatory tool. These teachers were similarity spotters. The function of the lessons was to turn the pupils, bit by bit, into similarity spotters, too. Similarity with previously studied structures, patterns and labels is the only thing which makes the maelstrom of historical information make sense, which turns the past into history. A teacher, like any other communicator, is utterly dependent upon resonance. *Unlike* any other communicators, the teacher, who has responsibility for long-term progression in pupils' learning, is chief resonance-manager. He can only have a meaningful dialogue with a class or can only explain ostensibly new material if he knows that something will resonate with what has gone before. Multiple resonances in language need to exist if the pupil is to understand anything at all. This is how terms like 'Parliament' or 'settlement' make sense. The teacher has the task of making this kind of complex resonance possible, through activity, through talk or through any strategy available. Every lesson is concentrated, densely packed allusion. The planning and teaching make the difference between such allusion being fascinating and completely impenetrable.

This notion of similarity should not be misunderstood as an attempt to homogenise history. It is only by being aware of potential similarity that we are capable of noticing difference. Difference has no meaning without similarity. A focus on the nature of difference (in region, across period, in structure) is critical to history's concern with the particular. To discern difference is to be aware of potential links, connections or patterns across time and space (Rogers 1987). Without these there would be no differences to spot and nothing to remark upon. To understand anything is to see it as a case of something more general.

And this is precisely the point of history *teaching*. Teaching is about showing pupils (or putting them in situations where they will discern) similarities that they might not otherwise perceive. An awareness of similarity enables pupils to make judgements that are significant to the discipline's concerns. The pupil is able to say 'I judge this to be a significant cause' or 'I judge this a critical piece of evidence' because they have a pattern that they are either copying or consciously forming. To teach any discipline is to help pupils to see more clearly the common interpretive devices that allow it make sense: to identify the conceptual devices that unify. To do history is to 'see' its information in a certain way. We have to become familiar with its validation claims, the organisational shapes and patterns of its discourse structures. Whether these are left as implicit or explicit, as routine procedures or meta-cognitive reflection, depends on the emphasis a teacher is trying to achieve at any given point (e.g. LeCocq 1999).

The three teachers described above, despite their apparent variations in practice and widely different justificatory rhetoric, were all active managers of memory. All used story, with its compelling mixture of the familiar and strange, as a knowledge-carrier, working with both practised routines and new reflections about status and structure, until these pupils had a great deal of 'fingertip' knowledge that would, in turn, play a critical part in immediate and future reflective activities.

Long-term planning and intensity of resonance

The notion of resonance goes deeper than the common idea of 'transfer' of learning. 'Transfer' implies the ability to practise an old skill in a new content domain. Resonance, at its simplest, simply suggests unconscious recognition – the hidden familiar tag that keeps motivation up for a few seconds longer before the pupil rebels or falls asleep. Models of planning that are likely to be most effective are those that create an intensity of resonance. This is one way of characterising the influential, but as yet unexamined, work of Michael Riley. Like so many, in recent decades, whose professional knowledge has been constructed and disseminated through creative in-service training and through the creation of new curriculum materials rather than through formal research, it is difficult to identify a body of work that attests to it. Yet anyone who has worked extensively with history teachers in the late 1990s will have witnessed the impact of his thinking. All of Riley's thinking is, in effect, about resonance. His popular idea of 'fruitcake history', which attracted thousands of history teachers to workshops during 1997 and 1998, was built around the trio of 'interest, accessibility and challenge'. Both the accessibility and the challenge were made possible by careful management of the planning context on a variety of scales. Riley has also been influential in reshaping the history teacher's use of the word 'enquiry' to mean a structured lesson sequence that deliberately plants and then picks up resonances so that substantial 'fingertip knowledge' is developed throughout the journey, leading to less anachronistic and more historically grounded outcomes (Byrom 1998b; Gorman 1998). Detaching, the word 'enquiry' from common professional assumptions about frighteningly open-ended investigations, Riley tamed the idea of 'enquiry' and linked it directly to a pedagogic rationale for layers of knowledge. His practical examples make the acquisition of knowledge both the servant and the result of enquiry skills.

Conclusion: beyond knowledge and 'skill'

A conceptual distinction between substantive content and historical process is always going to be necessary and helpful for many purposes, but it is important to remember that this is *all* it is – a conceptual distinction. It may be necessary to be more precise about different types of teaching emphasis and how these interact to secure learning. What *kinds* of similarity do teachers help pupils to spot? If these resonances integrate what we habitually call 'content' and 'skill', is there a more effective way of characterising them for the purposes of defining teaching or of assessing whether learning is taking place?

Classic, typical models of progression in causation, such as that provided by the influential Teaching History Research Group (Scott 1990), do not describe the staging posts that led to Marie's success in analysing the causes of the Reformation. She can apply a variety of categories of cause, and she can even begin to debate the way in which different types of classifications cut across each other, but she has not arrived there by going through the equivalent stages in the lower levels of Scott's model, still less through the suggested hierarchy of work with 'reasons and results' identified in either of the 1991 or the 1995 National Curriculum. What she has done is a great deal of early, meta-cognitive work on the structuring of different types of accounts. This has helped her to cope with multiple possibilities of classification. Through a balance between activities that require active conceptualisation (making up headings) and borrowed conceptualisations (learning the 'big' words), her teachers aimed to help her to articulate different types of substantive and second-order classification. Meanwhile, increasing experience of more and more layers of substantive content (through much story-listening, story-telling and making of new stories or themes) was critical to giving Marie the language and the *interest in that language* that fostered abstract reflection.

This account is not as neat as stages in a model of 'progression in causation', but it is a more rounded picture of the mechanisms that were used to accelerate progression. Marie was the kind of pupil who was particularly vulnerable to the 'non-progression' that can result from mere 'teaching by exposure'. There is much more to learning about causal analysis than merely doing causal analysis.

The danger of drifting into 'teaching by exposure' will always be with us.

Once new professional ideas ossify into paths and patterns, it is so easy for the focus of professional reflection to be removed from the things pupils find difficult. Knowledge is an enabler. Yet we have scarcely begun to examine how, exactly, it can be harnessed to enable those pupils who find history hard. Avoidance is no solution. Rather than avoiding the abstract, the abstract must somehow become interesting. A useful first step is to view the shapes and patterns of historical knowledge as a quarry for structural and linguistic activities that drive at the heart of a pupil's observed difficulties in handling new material. Pupils' interest and curiosity can be made to thrive in the most surprising of places.

Questions

1   What do 'lower-attaining' pupils in Year 9 seem to find most difficult in history? What kinds of learning activities and teaching emphases in Years 7 and 8 might equip such pupils to *overcome* some of their difficulties by Year 9?

2   Analyse the amount and type of knowledge that pupils need to hold in their heads in order to tackle a typical GCSE source-based question. With what hidden, overview understandings and references do pupils need to be familiar, even in those 'source-based' exercises that emphasise testing of evidential skills? How and where do we expect them to have acquired this knowledge?

3   What kinds of structured enquiries or lesson sequences seem to deepen pupils' 'fingertip knowledge'? What are the characteristics of medium-term planning that give pupils a 'secure sense of period'?

4   Why do some pupils seem to be able to evaluate source material for reliability or typicality whereas others find it difficult? What, exactly, is the difficulty?

Further reading

History teachers need to be aware of the origins of different types of progression models. A stimulating starting point in the area of organising concepts such as causation is the work of the Teaching History Research Group. See J. Scott (ed.) (1990) *Understanding Cause and Effect: Learning and Teaching about Causation and Consequence in History*. Compare your own thinking about the way in which pupils make progress in causation with the Research Group's model. In the area of evidential understanding, see D. Shemilt (1987) 'Adolescent ideas about evidence and methodology in history' for a post-Piagetian model of progression in evidential skill.

For a different way of viewing progression see P. Rogers (1987) 'The past as a frame of reference'. Rogers argues that useful historical knowledge accumulates through awareness of similarity. For a wide range of examples or real planning for progression from different history departments integrating different aspects of knowledge and skill over a long-term planning, see C. Counsell, and the Historical Association Secondary Committee (1997) *Planning the Twentieth Century World*.

6   Teaching about interpretations

Tony McAleavy

Introduction

A requirement to teach about interpretations of history is part of the National Curriculum in England and Wales and the GCSE criteria. This article traces the evolution of policy on interpretations since 1991. It also explores the classroom implications of this aspect of the history curriculum and considers why work on interpretations has been perceived as problematic.

Interpretations of history and the English and Welsh history curriculum

As Philips and Harnett have shown in Chapters 2 and 3, the history National Curriculum was introduced in schools in September 1991 after a prolonged period of debate about the nature and purpose of school history. One of the most innovative aspects of the new history curriculum was a requirement to teach pupils about interpretations of history. The History Working Group was established by the Government to draft the new history curriculum. In April 1990, this working party reported to the Government and recommended that work on interpretations should be a required part of school history. The History Working Group's *Final Report* hinted at two reasons why interpretations were given so much attention. The reason given the greater prominence was related to the dangers of ideologically slanted school history. The report explained that the emphasis on interpretations was intended as a bulwark against the political abuse of school history. By insisting that teachers presented different interpretations of controversial topics the Working Group hoped to encourage pluralism and democratic values:

> Many people have expressed deep concern that school history will be used as propaganda; that governments of one political hue or another will try to subvert it for the purpose of indoctrination or social engineering. In some other societies the integrity of the teaching of history has been distorted by such objectives and there will always be those who seek to impose a particular view of society through an interpretation of history.
>
> (DES 1990b: 11)

A second justification for the study of interpretations can also be found in the report. The History Working Group talked about the use of historical sources in the classroom and made the then commonplace distinction between 'primary' and 'secondary' sources: sources 'dating from the time and place being studied' and later reflections on the events of the past. The call for compulsory work on interpretations was motivated by a belief that school history made insufficient use of secondary sources, and particularly the work of academic historians:

> Pupils' use of primary sources in learning history should also be complemented by the study and evaluation of the writings of historians. The use of these and other secondary sources appears to have been unduly neglected in schools and ought to be given greater prominence than has traditionally been the case.
>
> (DES 1990b: 177)

The publication of statutory orders in March 1991 provided teachers with the official view of how they should approach work on interpretations. There was no obligation for pupils to study particular interpretations or controversies. Instead, the detailed requirements were to be found in the assessment arrangements. The 1991 curriculum established three assessment objectives, known as Attainment Targets (ATs). Performance in work on interpretations was described in AT2, 'Interpretations of history', within a ten-level framework.

These level statements provided teachers with a picture of the intended learning outcomes from work on interpretations. AT2, therefore, defined the parameters for classroom activities in this area. The statutory orders contained illustrative descriptions of the kind of activities that pupils could undertake. At Level 4, for example, pupils were asked to explain how differences between accounts of life in Ancient Egypt could be caused by a lack of evidence. At Level 7, characteristic of an able 14-year-old, pupils were investigating how far a film gave an accurate account of events in the history of Germany.

A variety of interpretations

As we have seen, the History Working Group was keen to increase the use of the work of academic historians in school history. While giving primacy to the work of historians, the History Working Group also recognised that interpretations should not be exclusively restricted to historiography.

> The study of history necessarily includes *interpretations* of history and its nature. This has three distinct but related aspects:
> i   an acquaintance with the writings of historians and a knowledge of typical historical controversies, relating to the content of the course;
> ii an understanding that history has been written, sung about, painted, filmed, and dramatised by all kinds of people for all kinds of reasons; and

iii   an understanding that some histories have a high profile, others are hardly known.

(DES 1990b: 11)

In 1991 the National Curriculum Council (NCC) published *History Non-Statutory Guidance* to accompany the history National Curriculum in England. This document was less enthusiastic about historiography in school history. It stressed the need for pupils to encounter a variety of interpretations and made it clear that too limited a diet of historiographical interpretations would be both dull and difficult: 'A narrow view of AT2 which confined it to the writings of historians would remove opportunities to study a wide range of interpretations and make this AT more difficult for many pupils' (NCC 1991, Section B: 6).

History Non-Statutory Guidance encouraged teachers to consider a great variety of interpretations: historical novels, museum displays, film and television, and oral history. This theme was taken further in 1993 when the NCC set out the types of interpretation that pupils could be expected to consider during the Key Stage (see Table 6.1).

In practice, teachers were reluctant to introduce historiography, as they saw it, prematurely to mixed-ability pupils. They were much keener to take the broader view of interpretations that had been endorsed by the NCC. In particular, at

Table 6.1 Types of interpretation

Types of interpretation	Examples
Academic	Books and journals by professional historians
	Excavation reports
	Lectures
Educational	Textbooks
	Museums
	TV documentaries
	Artists' interpretations
Fictional	Novels
	Feature films
	TV dramas
	Plays
Popular	Folk wisdom about the past
	Theme parks
	Nostalgic depictions in advertising
Personal	Personal reflection

Source: NCC 1993a, 1993b; see also McAleavy 1993.

Key Stage 3, films were often used as an interpretation that could be evaluated by pupils. Many teachers took Hollywood depictions of Robin Hood or Cromwell and invited pupils to use their historical knowledge in order to assess the accuracy of the film. This was an opportunity for discussion about how purpose and intended audience could make a big difference to the nature of an interpretation.

Is there scope for introducing real historical debate at Key Stage 3? There is sometimes too great a gulf between professional historians, archaeologists, historians and museum curators. While artists, writers and dancers routinely work in schools, there is much less of a tradition of academic historians working with schoolchildren as part of their work in history. This is a missed opportunity.

Perhaps the answer is to focus on aspects of the work of academic historians that are neither too difficult nor too technical. It can also be helpful if we try to explain to students how disagreements can come about rather than expecting them to arbitrate on the disagreement. There are many debates that are perfectly accessible to 11–14-year-olds. Here are a few examples:

- Historians are not sure how the Anglo-Saxons took control of Britain in the decades after the departure of the Roman army.
- Nineteenth-century historians thought that King John was cruel and wicked, but today historians say that he was an effective King.
- There is a debate about whether there was a blitz spirit in wartime Britain.

Opportunities for work on interpretations

Auditing a scheme of work is one way of ensuring that pupils are introduced to a good range of interpretations. Pupils can also be enabled to make comparisons across types, comparing, for example, a film about life in Roman times with an information book on the same topic.

Different units of study will provide different possibilities for work on interpretations. Roman or medieval work lends itself to a consideration of the way archaeologists interpret the past. Some periods, such as Tudor times, have a great wealth of historical fiction and film drama. There is an abundance of folk wisdom about life in Britain in the 1930s and 1940s and in Victorian times. Popular views of the past are more restricted in the context of topics that are distant in time or space.

Discussion points

Look at the scheme of work in a school you know for Key Stage 3. Assess provision for coverage of a range of modern interpretations. Does the scheme of work provide the following opportunities:

- Pupils identify and comment upon differences between the way different textbooks or information books address the same issue. They can be invited to explore the issue further to see which view they find more convincing.
- Pupils learn how archaeologists interpret the past from its physical remains. They can also learn how museum curators and keepers of historical monuments conserve and interpret archaeological evidence.
- Pupils are introduced to debates among historians about aspects of the past. They can learn how historians use documentary sources to answer questions about the past.
- Pupils reflect upon the way dramatic reconstructions of the past are put together – dramatic reconstructions can include both 'living history' events and historical drama on TV and in film.
- Pupils can discuss a specific 'controversial' historic personality and consider the evidence for different opinions about that person.
- Pupils consider commonly held popular views about the past and try to find out how accurate these views are.

What can we ask students to do?

The 1993 NCC guidance made some practical suggestions about how teachers should plan interpretations work. Three points were made that have a continuing relevance for classroom approaches to interpretations:

1   The analysis of interpretations was more likely to be effective if it was part of a wider study. Having built up a level of contextual knowledge about a topic, students were better placed to make comments about the plausibility of an interpretation. There was, therefore, a strong connection between the level of background knowledge about a historical issue and students' capacity to reflect purposefully on an interpretation.
2   Students' own interpretations can be a useful way of introducing more general ideas about interpretations. A great number of standard classroom activities in history require pupils to create their own interpretations. Teachers can encourage pupils to stand back and reflect on their own interpretations. They could consider, for example, how they have used evidence to create their own pictures of a past situation or event.
3   Rather than rushing to judgement about the quality of interpretations, pupils can be asked to think about the process of forming an interpretation. The work of historians, museum curators, archaeologists, film-makers and others can be de-mystified and explained.

   The NCC put a gloss on the level statements of AT2 and identified three 'threads' or key conceptual areas relating to interpretations that could be used by teachers when planning classroom activities:

- Interpretations combine fact and fiction, imagination and points of view.

- Interpretations are dependent, if they are of historical worth, on evidence.
- Differences between interpretations can be explained by reference, among other things, to purpose and intended audience, and to the background of the author of any interpretation. (NCC 1993a and b; see also McAleavy 1993).

Discussion points

Is it possible to develop classroom activities to increase understanding of the following ideas relating to interpretations?

- Interpretations differ because people use evidence in different ways and will select and place emphasis on different aspects of the evidence.
- The amount of evidence available to different interpreters will vary. Access to evidence will also change through time and this will lead to differences in interpretation.
- There are often gaps in the evidence and people must use creativity and imagination to provide an interpretation.
- Differences of purpose and intended audience will lead to differences in interpretation.
- The personal background and beliefs of people making interpretations will influence their work and lead to differences.

Interpretations and the 1995 review of the National Curriculum

The ideas about interpretations in the 1991 National Curriculum represented an interesting but highly ambitious set of ideas. There was no research basis for the level statements. They represented a leap into the pedagogical dark, particularly in this innovative area of interpretations. It was hardly surprising that the structure established in 1991 contained some flaws. One of the weaknesses of the AT2 statements was in the degree of emphasis on the provisional nature of historical knowledge. Some experienced teachers were not convinced about the merits of introducing ideas about knowledge as a construct to very young or less able students. The Level 2 statement, for example, described how students would recognise conflicting 'versions' of the past. This was supposed to encapsulate the performance of average 7-year-olds or significantly below average 11-year-olds. Teaching these ideas at this level was seen by many teachers as unrealistic and unhelpful.

The National Curriculum was revised in 1995. The main purpose of the overall review was to reduce the content of the curriculum in order to make teaching and assessment more manageable. The revision of the history curriculum went beyond this brief and involved changes based on lessons learnt since 1991. Work on interpretations remained a central part of the curriculum but the emphasis on the provisional nature of historical knowledge was substantially reduced. It is interesting to compare the equivalent level statements relating to work on interpretations.

Discussion points

Look at Table 6.2, which contrasts expectations relating to interpretations in 1991 and 1995. How have the expectations changed? What kind of classroom activities are likely to elicit performance along the lines described in the 1995 statements?

Table 6.2 Comparison of 1991 and 1995 expectations of classroom performance

1991 Level Statements	*1995 Level Statements*
Level 1: They understand that stories may be about real people or fictional characters.	Level 1: They know and recount episodes from stories about the past.
Level 2: They show an awareness that different stories about the past can give different versions of what happened.	Level 2: They are beginning to identify some of the ways in which the past is represented.
Level 3: They distinguish between a fact and a point of view.	Level 3: They identify some of the different ways in which the past is represented.
Level 4: They show an understanding that deficiencies in evidence may lead to different interpretations of the past.	Level 4: They show how some aspects of the past have been represented and interpreted in different ways.
Level 5: They recognise that interpretations of the past, including popular accounts, may differ from what is known to have happened.	Level 5: They know that some events, people and changes have been interpreted in different ways and suggest possible reasons for this.
Level 6: They demonstrate how historical interpretations depend on the selection of sources.	Level 6: They describe, and are beginning to explain, different historical interpretations of events, people and changes.
Level 7: They describe the strengths and weaknesses of different interpretations of an historical event or development.	Level 7: They explain how and why different historical interpretations have been produced.
Level 8: They show how attitudes and circumstances can influence an individual's interpretation of historical events or developments.	Level 8: They analyse and explain different historical interpretations, and are beginning to evaluate them.

Interpretations at GCSE

The 1995 National Curriculum made certain assumptions about how pupils might progress in their understanding of interpretations:

- pupils can identify different ways in which the past is represented and interpreted;
- they can give reasons for these differences;
- they can analyse and evaluate interpretations.

The development of the 1995 National Curriculum coincided with a major revision of the national GCSE criteria, and these assumptions about progression became part of the GCSE requirements.

GCSE in history was introduced in 1986, with the first examinations in 1988. The governing principles for GCSE history were revised in 1995 by the Schools Curriculum and Assessment Authority (SCAA). In this revision SCAA sought to build upon National Curriculum developments and introduced, for the first time, an explicit requirement for work on interpretations at GCSE. SCAA stated that the aims of GCSE history should include the development of candidates' capacity to 'draw conclusions and appreciate that these and other historical conclusions are liable to reassessment in the light of new or reinterpreted evidence'. SCAA also produced new assessment objectives that would be used for the award of marks in all GCSE syllabuses. The objective that related to source analysis was defined in such a way that made compulsory work on interpretations.

In addition to the explicit requirement for candidates to work on interpretations, the new criteria put a new emphasis on the use of contextual knowledge. SCAA wanted candidates to bring together their background knowledge of any topic and their capacity to analyse sources or interpretations relating to that topic. The first full GCSE examinations set under these new regulations were taken by candidates in summer 1998. An analysis of these examination papers reveals some significant patterns.

Candidates were often given clearly two conflicting interpretations about a particular topic and asked to comment on how such differences could come about. Sometimes these conflicting interpretations were both modern, on other occasions one was contemporaneous with the event and the other was a modern view. Very little background detail was provided about the provenance of particular interpretations and it is difficult to see how candidates could give anything other than a fairly stereotypical explanation for the apparent differences. The following ascriptions are taken from a modern world history question on Roosevelt and the New Deal:

'From a school textbook about Roosevelt and the USA, 1991.'
'From a history of the New Deal by a British historian writing in the 1980s.'

This is typical of the level of background detail that examiners provided, regardless of the syllabus or the examination board. It was important that students recognised the significance of these brief descriptions as part of the process of explaining differences between interpretations.

Examiners often provided students with a quoted view of a topic – usually one invented by the senior examiners – and inviting candidates to endorse or reject the view based on their own knowledge of the topic and evidence provided as part of the examination. These questions often came at the end of a series of questions about sources and interpretations, and they were heavily 'weighted' in terms of available marks, indicating that examiners anticipated an extended answer. Here are examples from different syllabuses and different examination boards:

> ' "It was the introduction of anaesthetics which made complex operations safe and successful." Is this interpretation a fair one? Explain your answer using the sources and your own knowledge (12 marks).'
> ' "The lives of ordinary Soviet people improved greatly in the 1930s." Use the sources, and your own knowledge, to explain whether you think this statement is accurate (10).'

These are intellectually quite demanding questions. They ask candidates to marshal simultaneously their prior knowledge, their reading of the stimulus material and their view of the validity of the interpretation. Under examination conditions, candidates must then synthesise this into a single coherent piece of writing.

What are we to make of these questions and the demands placed upon GCSE students by interpretations work? The activities are difficult – try one for yourself – and the simultaneous juggling of prior knowledge and constructing of an interpretation is no mean feat. If we are not careful, interpretations questions will reinforce the perception of difficulty that so bedevils secondary school history.

The activities are difficult; they are also fairly dismal. Interpretations are defined in narrow terms as either brief quotations or possibly pictures and cartoons. There is no sense of the rich range of possibilities mentioned earlier in the context of work at Key Stage 3.

Perhaps most disappointing is the lack of contextual detail that might help the student to make sense of interpretations. Course-work could, in part, be used to redress this. In course-work teachers can take control and can give students some of the background they need to see how an interpretation works.

As has been mentioned, GCSE questions on interpretations often involved extended writing. The recent work of Christine Counsell, although not written with interpretations in mind, provides some interesting ways forward.

Both the National Curriculum at Key Stage 3 and the GCSE required pupils to undertake extended writing. In 1997 Christine Counsell produced a highly imaginative and thought-provoking guide to techniques supportive of extended writing in history (see Counsell 1997). Although she said very little explicitly about interpretations, much of her work was directly relevant to teaching about interpretations. There was a 'meta-cognitive' quality to her guidance; she wanted pupils to become more aware and reflective about structure and organisation when producing historical writing. In other words, when pupils produced their own interpretations they would benefit from 'explicit attention to the mechanics of the communication process' and this, in turn, will 'help pupils to think about what they are doing' (Counsell 1997: 12). Counsell identified a number of facets of the interpretative process that pupils were likely to find difficult and suggested practical strategies in these area. These interpretative difficulties included:

- identifying relevance when selecting from a large amount of historical information;
- sorting and categorising information into a coherent structure;
- understanding the difference in status between generalisations and supporting particular examples.

Counsell explained how sorting exercises of different kinds could be used to aid greater clarity in historical thinking. She outlined, for example, how students could be asked to categorise statements as either 'big points' (= generalisations) or 'little points' (= supporting particular examples). These techniques are directly relevant to work on interpretations. They can be used not only to help pupils think about their own interpretations but also to assist them in critically evaluating the interpretations of others.

Interpretations and citizenship

As we look forward to the challenges of history education for the future it seems that education for citizenship will play an increasingly significant role. At the time of writing there is much discussion about how the curriculum in England and Wales should be modified to provide more systematic opportunities for the development of citizenship. At the same time secondary history teachers continue to feel that their subject is often marginalised by the overall curriculum arrangements. The advent of citizenship may offer a way forward. It is clear from the Government's report on citizenship (QCA 1998c) that history has much to contribute to this curriculum area, and that work on interpretations is an area of particular significance in this respect. Crick placed history at the top of his list of National Curriculum subjects that could enhance citizenship:

> The emphasis in History on the use of evidence and processes of enquiry can help pupils to discuss and reach informed judgements about topical and contemporary issues which are the lifeblood of citizenship and to develop the confidence to take informed action.
>
> (QCA 1998c: 53)

The Crick report explored approaches to controversial issues. His comments on desirable outcomes in this area relate directly to work on interpretations in history. He called for pupils to develop:

> a willingness and empathy to perceive and understand the interests, beliefs and viewpoints of others; a willingness and ability to apply reasoning skills to problems and to value a respect for truth and evidence in forming or holding opinions.
>
> (QCA 1998c: 57)

This new emphasis on citizenship takes us back to where we started. The History Working Group report of 1990 justified time spent on understanding interpretations of history in terms of its contribution to democratic values and active citizenship. As the debate continues on the place of history in the secondary curriculum the words of the History Working Group remain relevant. The Group described how work on interpretations could counter ideologically driven attempts to restrict pluralism and democracy:

> The best possible safeguard is an education which instils respect for evidence. Pupils should come to understand that ... there are no monopolies of the truth. If our history course can lead to such a level of awareness it will be a valuable training for future citizens of a democracy.
>
> (DES 1990b: 11)

Discussion points

1   How well are students prepared for those GCSE questions that test understanding of interpretations?
2   How far do you encourage pupils to think about their own historical work, including their extended writing in history – as examples of interpretation?
3   Do you and your colleagues try to link together work on interpretations with citizenship education?

Further reading

Evans, R. (1997) *In Defence of History*, London: Granta Books.
Hobsbawn, E. and Ranger, T. (1992) *The Invention of Tradition*.
Lowenthal, D. (1998) *The Heritage Crusade and the Spoils of History*, Cambridge: Cambridge University Press.
—— (1985) *The Past is a Foreign Country*, Cambridge: Cambridge University Press.

7   Issues in the teaching of chronology

William Stow and Terry Haydn

Introduction

This chapter aims to put the debates on the role of chronology in school history in the context of recent events and practice, to explore exactly what it is that we want children to understand about time, and to give an overview of research into children's understanding of chronology. It will examine how this might inform the effective teaching and learning of history in primary and secondary schools. What do teachers and student teachers need to consider when approaching this aspect of teaching history?

Why chronology is an issue in history teaching

Chronology has a controversial place in debates over methods of history teaching. The controversy predates the introduction of the National Curriculum for history. A much lambasted feature of history teaching in the past was the extent to which the memorisation of dates was regarded as a prerequisite to historical understanding. Yet it was also argued that without knowledge of a framework of dates, history would become a meaningless discipline, and that the balance of emphasis in history teaching was beginning to swing too far away from chronology. Harnett notes that the 1937 Board of Education *Handbook of Suggestions* for history advocated the provision of a chronological framework for the study of the subject, and expressed the concern that history should not be learned as a series of unconnected events (Harnett 1998: 87). More recently, the curriculum wars over school history (Little 1990; McKiernan 1993; Phillips 1998a) thrust the issue of chronology on to the front pages of the tabloid press, and the editorial columns of broadsheet newspapers. The *Daily Express* highlighted an ICM survey which found that only 4 per cent of 14-year-olds knew the date of the Battle of Trafalgar, and only 2 per cent the date of the first Roman invasion of Britain. An editorial in *The Times Educational Supplement* argued that pupils needed 'the old points of reference to be restored':

Their acquaintance with the order in which kings and queens reigned provided a matrix against which to understand the time scale of the past. That matrix is increasingly being lost. Today it is possible to meet children who think history is about dinosaurs.

(*The Times Educational Supplement*, 23 January 1989)

There were divisions of opinion on the role of chronology within the profession. Some schools were moving away from the 'trundle through the ages' school history syllabus, in order to do some topics in more depth, or incorporate the 'What is History?' element of the Schools Council History Project (SCHP) (Patrick 1987, 1988). Although the project, with its move away from doing a solid 'period' of history, was influential, it did not sweep all before it, and many history teachers stayed with traditional, more chronologically based syllabuses. There was a further erosion of chronology as an organising principle for the subject, with the GCSE emphasis on selected 'themes' rather than straight 'periods' of history. Moreover, with the move towards the critical examination of sources at the expense of the essay in GCSE examinations, narrative was further weakened in history. It would be possible to gain maximum marks in a source-work question on the Second World War, without necessarily knowing how the events of the war unfolded, who was on whose side, or who won.

This was to cause a backlash or counter-revolution from history teachers and historians concerned that the balance between history as sources, and history as stories, was being distorted, including some chronology 'fundamentalists' who seemed reluctant to sacrifice as much as a single English monarch from the school history curriculum. Popular press coverage of the national debate on school history (Phillips 1998a: 122–4) suggested a yearning to go back to the (apocryphal) days when all pupils studied British history from Julius Caesar to Elizabeth II, and could recite the names of all monarchs in chronological order. Margaret Thatcher and Kenneth Baker were respectively 'appalled' and 'disappointed' at the lack of emphasis on history as chronological study in the Interim Report of the History Working Group charged with drafting a National Curriculum for history (Thatcher 1993: 596; Baker 1993: 206). Chronology had become 'a problem' because, as Slater noted, the greater emphasis on skills, conceptual understanding, and the nature of history as a discipline, made it difficult to cover the same breadth of content. Although a defender of SCHP, he noted that 'not all teachers were happy with its fragmented content, lacking in continuity and apparent focus' (Slater 1989: 2). The need to allocate further curriculum time to course-work and the 'A' level personal study project, and the growth of modularisation in university history courses meant that there was some concern about 'black holes' in students' chronological frameworks of the past at both 'A' level and undergraduate level.

How was the History Working Group to handle these divisions? Perhaps mindful of HMI' s warning of the 'serious risks' inherent in ignoring chronology as an organising principle (DES 1988), and of the need to maximise consensus for the proposed National Curriculum for history, the Working Group advocated a school history course that would 'respect chronology and be broadly chronological in structure' (DES 1990a).

Thus, the advent of the National Curriculum in 1991 marked a return to a more secure position for chronology. Although the history curriculum through ages five to sixteen was not to be rigidly chronological, in practice, pupils between the ages of eleven to fourteen studied British history from 1066 to the twentieth century. The public controversy over the importance of dates, and which dates pupils should be expected to know, tended to obscure the fact that there is more to chronology than the memorisation of dates, and more to children's understanding of time than chronology.

The inclusion of attainment targets in the National Curriculum for history, in addition to programmes of study, made it much more explicit to teachers what children should be expected to achieve in the subject. The ability to sequence events was a key feature of Attainment Target 1 (DES 1991), but knowledge of dating systems and time-related vocabulary was not stipulated in the attainment targets. Hence, it would be possible for pupils to get to Level 10 in all strands of the attainment targets, without necessarily knowing which century they were living in, what 'reign' and 'anachronism' mean, or understanding what 'AD' means or stands for.

If some elements of children's understanding of time had been forgotten by the National Curriculum for history, Mark 1, this was rectified by the 1995 revision of the history curriculum (DfEE 1995). In addition to chronology's status as one of the five Key Elements, all of the level descriptions in the revised attainment targets for history include some reference to children's understanding of time, from 'showing their emerging sense of chronology by sequencing a few events and objects, and by using everyday terms about the passing of time', at Level 1, to being able to 'analyse the relationships between events, people and changes, and between the features of past societies … making appropriate use of dates and terms' (DfEE 1995) at Level 8. With the curriculum currently under review and a new version due in schools from September 1999, is the position of chronology secure? Or will it become marginalised again, especially in primary schools, as recent guidance from QCA (1998c) might indicate?

The importance of chronology in the teaching of history

The concept of chronology has a central place in the development of a child's historical understanding. It is the distinctive marker of history, setting it apart from other disciplines based on the interpretation of evidence. For historical evidence itself derives its meaning from the time-frame in which it is set. As Lomas states: 'Without a grasp of the concept of time, there can be no real understanding of change, development, continuity, progression and regression' (1993: 20). Wood argues that the ability to sequence is a fundamental feature of historical understanding, and that 'the past is chaos' to pupils, until sequenced (Wood 1995: 11).

Bruner argues that a key task in the process of education is 'to learn structure, which in short, is to learn how things are related' (Bruner 1960: 7). In terms of how children make sense of the past, their ability to sequence events, and gauge their distance from the present, is one of the ways in which they can develop a working structure or mental framework of the past, and establish at least one dimension of how events are related to each other. Thus the history teacher needs to ask, 'When did this happen? What is its relation to the present day, where does it fit in with the other things which we have done in history, and [the sometimes forgotten element] what is its significance – how does it relate to us, to the present and the future?' (see Chapter 4).

In addition to being an indispensable component of historical under-standing, time is also a highly complex one, comprising a variety of areas of understanding, including mathematical, linguistic and logical. Adults refine their sense of chronology continuously: as they learn more about themselves, their sense of personal time changes; as they learn more about the past, their sense of historical duration alters; and as the breadth of their understanding of the past develops, so their ability to make links between the various chronolo-gies within their own minds increases. It could be expected, therefore, that it would be a challenging area of historical understanding for children to acquire. Partington (1980: 225) notes that children do not acquire concepts of time quickly or easily. Wood (1995: 11) points out that the development of the concept of time is inextricably bound up with proficiency in language, and that we make it difficult for pupils because we have a wide range of different systems for describing time. In addition to dates, we have vague phrases ('long ago', 'in olden times'), words that describe time spans ('generations', 'decade', 'reign'), location by event ('when Granny was alive', 'before the revolution'), terms for sizeable but inexact amounts of time ('aeon', 'mesolithic') and for smaller, more precise units of time ('Victorian', 'Tudor').

In addition to helping pupils to place people and events in the past in a temporal framework, the history teacher also has to recognise the limits of chronology, in terms of pupils' historical understanding. We do not want chil-dren merely to develop the ability to construct chronicles of the past, we want them to be able to fashion coherent explanations, and to begin to understand other relationships between events other than temporal ones. In the words of Tawney, 'Time, and the order of occurrences in time is a clue, but no more; part of the historian's business is to substitute more significant connections for those of chronology' (Tawney 1978: 54). This is also the business of the history teacher.

It is also important for history teachers to be absolutely clear about what is meant by chronology, and for them to make this explicit to their pupils, in order to draw a distinction between chronology as the sequencing of events, and chronology as it is sometimes used (as in the National Curriculum Key Elements), as a term to describe pupils' general understanding of 'historical time', including dating systems, and time-related vocabulary. In its strictest sense, it is variously defined as 'the arrangement of dates or events in order of occurrence; the determining of the proper sequence of past events' (Collins

1995), *or* 'the science of computing time or periods of time and assigning events to their time dates' (Oxford 1993).

It derives in the first instance from two Greek words: *chronos*, meaning time, and *logia*, meaning a branch of knowledge. It can therefore be legitimately placed in a wider sense of an understanding of time. Thornton and Vukelich considered there to be three main aspects to this: clock time, calendar time and historical time. The first two are self-explanatory, while they described the third as something that 'requires one to depict a person, place, artefact or event in the past using some form of time language' (Thornton and Vukelich 1988: 70).

Friedman (1982) contests the notion of parcelling these different aspects, regarding them as heterogeneous concepts with much common ground between them. Certainly the adult 'total' understanding of time combines all these elements with a deepening sense of personal time. Friedman (1982) and others have argued that understanding clock and calendar time are prerequisites to developing a sense of historical time, but in the context of teaching history, it is the latter that must be the focus of attention.

Oakden and Sturt saw three strands to historical time:

i   The child's understanding of time – words and symbols such as are in use in everyday life;

ii   his [*sic*] power to form the conception of a universal time scheme … and his ability to use the dates by which such a scheme is symbolised;

iii   his knowledge of the characteristics of definite epochs in the time scheme, and his ability to place these epochs roughly in the correct order.

(Oakden and Sturt 1922: 310)

How do these ideas relate to current curriculum arrangements for history? Chronology is one of the five Key Elements of history in the National Curriculum (DfEE 1995). At Key Stage 1 this consists of two parts: the ability to sequence events and objects, and to use the appropriate everyday vocabulary to describe passing time. At Key Stage 2 children's senses of chronology can be expressed and developed by their placing 'events, people and changes in the periods studied within a chronological framework' and by their using 'dates and terms related to the passing of time … and terms that define different periods' (DfEE 1995). At Key Stage 3, the words 'conventions that describe historical periods and the passing of time' are added. There is a third strand of historical time in the National Curriculum that requires pupils to know about (and analyse at Key Stage 3) 'characteristic features of particular periods and societies, including the range of ideas, beliefs and attitudes of people' (Key Element 2a).

Clearly the development of an ability to 'arrange dates or events', 'determine a proper sequence of events' or 'compute time or periods of time' touches on the development of an understanding of those events or of what those 'periods' refer to and what their characteristic features are. Thus chronology in the classroom can legitimately be widened to mean the development of an understanding of historical time.

What does research indicate about children's understanding of historical time?

Research has shown that young children struggle to understand these abstract markers of time. In reviewing the research undertaken into children's thinking in this area, the model used by Oakden and Sturt (1922) is used, as it mirrors in many ways the frame of development of chronology evident in the National Curriculum (DfEE 1995). The three areas investigated by Oakden and Sturt were: everyday terminology of time; the conception of a universal time scheme and the use of dates; and knowledge of the characteristics and the sequence of different epochs.

The language of time, as the overt symbol of the child's understanding of time, has probably received the most attention in research. Among the developmental studies, Harner (1982), researching the use of language of time in the early years, noted that the complexity of expressing the future tense in the English language could be a barrier to the development of understanding. Friedman (1982) suggested that, by the age of six, children are aware of regularities in time, and use the names of the more everyday elements of time. Pedagogical and classroom-based studies have been focused more on the development of children's understanding after the age of six. Oakden and Sturt (1922) suggested that children find it difficult to move beyond ordinary vocabulary to an understanding of periods and their sequence. According to Levstik and Pappas (1987), whose research was undertaken in the USA, it was only at the age of ten or so that children used specific descriptors, such as 'the Incas' to mark time. However, Thornton and Vukelich (1988), who also focused on the USA, suggested that from the ages of nine to eleven children started to use period labels. More recently, Lynn (1993) and Harnett (1993) both identified nascent, if confused, understanding of the labels of historical periods. Researching the understanding of children who had experienced six years of National Curriculum history, Stow (1998) indicated that very able 6-year-olds were able to use period labels, while the majority of eight- to nine-year-olds were capable of using these with some confidence and understanding. All of these studies and those by other authors (Jahoda 1963; Bernot and Blancard 1953; Thornton and Vukelich 1988; West 1981a) have suggested that the cultural and educational context will influence the pace at which a child develops an understanding of the language of time.

The conception of a universal time scheme is seen by many as a late development. Piaget (1927) considered it to be it to be a feature of adolescence, linked to the passing of time within the life of the child. Friedman (1982) also tied it to adolescence, and the classroom-based studies confirm that this 'total understanding' of time is something that occurs after the age of eleven. There are, however, differences of opinion over the use of dates. Earlier researchers

(Oakden and Sturt 1922; Bradley 1947; Jahoda 1963) suggested that knowledge and understanding of dates was only a characteristic of understanding at or beyond the age of ten to eleven. More recently, Harnett (1993) reported that children in her study, although finding the activity of dating pictures to be threatening at any age, were aware at the upper end of Key Stage 2 of dating conventions including centuries and (in some cases) BC. Furthermore, Stow (1998) suggested that children's confidence in and understanding of dating may be increasing. In his study, many 9-year-olds were able to place periods in the correct century, and most 11-year-olds could recall and accurately use dates associated with a period. It is worth noting again that the children featured in this study are the first generation of school children to have experienced the National Curriculum for history throughout their school lives.

Research into children's knowledge of the characteristics and sequence of periods also suggests a change in recent years. In their original study, Oakden and Sturt found that children younger than eleven showed 'an apparent lack of interest' in period names (Oakden and Sturt 1922: 335). It was only after this age that knowledge of periods and the subdivisions of time that they represent was developed. Bradley (1947) queried this, and suggested that there was a gradual increase in awareness of this aspect towards the age of eleven. Thornton and Vukelich (1988) indicated the development of the ability to label periods of time as occurring between nine and eleven. Harnett (1993) and Lynn (1993) both noted an increasing confidence in identifying characteristics of illustrations by period in children up to the age of eleven, and a particular ability at that age to recognise pictures from the Victorian era. Most recently, Stow (1998) indicated that children as young as six and seven were able to identify and categorise pictures according to some periods, particularly Roman, and that many 9-year-olds had confidence in their knowledge of the shared characteristics of Tudor, Roman and wartime illustrations. This suggests a downward shift in the age at which children are demonstrating this aspect of understanding.

West's (1981a) work has been instrumental in raising awareness of the value of sequencing as an indicator of time knowledge. He regarded it as 'an essential aspect of any recognisable ability to understand historical time' (West 1981a: 122). He found a gradual increase in the ability to sequence, although he was sure of the positive influence of teaching and practice on the development of this ability. Lynn (1993) and Harnett (1993) both reported children's successes in identifying and sequencing pictures that were characteristic of period, although Harnett again indicated that children found the activity threatening. By contrast, Stow (1998) found that the 6- to 7-year-olds in his study confidently tackled the activity (with mixed success), and that by the age of eight to nine many of the children could confidently group and sequence pictures from five different historical periods (Roman, Tudor, Victorian, 1940s and 1990s). The understanding of period seemed to develop more readily than a confidence in dates.

In general, more recent research on children's understanding of time has tended to move away from the idea of age-related models such as those of Piaget.

The research of Shemilt (1980), Booth (1983) and Lee, Ashby and Dickinson (1996a) suggested that sometimes young pupils were able to cope with quite difficult concepts, and had more sophisticated understanding than much older pupils. Maturation was only one factor, together with familiarity with material or content, teaching context, and interaction with other pupils. It was no longer a question of waiting for pupils to be old enough to be able to cope with ideas about time; there was a growing belief that the way in which the teacher approached the teaching of time could influence children's levels of under-standing. In the words of Thornton and Vukelich (1988: 74) these abilities 'are crucially dependent upon instruction ... it seems likely that such specialised time language (as 1701–99 equals the 18th Century) will not be mastered unless it is specifically taught' (Thornton and Vukelich 1988: 74).

Another important point to emerge in recent research is the unevenness of children's historical thinking. A survey of Year 7 pupils' understanding of dating systems, basic time vocabulary and ability to use 'century' accurately revealed wide variations, and pronounced 'school effects' in the results. Overall, 64 per cent of pupils were able to identify which century they were living in, but in some schools this dipped to under 50 per cent. Only 14 per cent could explain correctly the reason 'why we call it 1994/5' and less than half of the sample were able to consistently manipulate 'century' accurately. Many pupils could offer no definition of the word 'chronology', and most of those that did offer a definition simply equated it with 'time'. In spite of the fact that Latin is not widely taught in state schools, more children knew that the term AD stood for Anno Domini (not always correctly spelt), than what AD meant (50 per cent to 37 per cent). In some schools that scored highly on the test overall, no pupils knew what an anachronism was or could give an example of one; in other, low-scoring schools, significant numbers of pupils answered these questions correctly. In interviews with the history teachers who taught the pupils, teachers generally expressed surprise at some of the gaps in their pupils' grasp of time vocabulary and dating systems. Reasons suggested for the gaps were that it was not part of the '45 boxes' that then constituted the attainment targets for history, that it had been covered but not retained, that it had been covered at primary school, or that they had simply taken it for granted that pupils would know about centuries, BC and AD, and words such as 'reign' and 'decade' (Haydn 1999). It should be remembered that the survey was conducted before the 1995 revision of the history curriculum, which made the teaching of time vocabulary explicit in the attainment targets.

An examination of 'first-generation' National Curriculum era history Key Stage 3 textbooks reveals that, with the exception of the Shuter and Child book *Skills in History I*, the teaching of basic time concepts was almost entirely neglected. Some secondary teachers went back to the ageing SCHP 'What is History?' materials on chronology to fill this gap. More recent textbooks have rectified this omission, and a range of suggestions for activities to develop pupils' understanding of time can be found on the National Grid for Learning. A suggested structure for the development of secondary pupils' understanding of time, and exemplar exercises, are also given in *Learning to Teach History in the Secondary School* (Haydn *et al.* 1997: 86–93). An interesting survey of secondary pupils' understanding of time can be found in the Booth and Husbands paper (1993), 'Assessment of history at Key Stage 3'.

How can children's understanding of time be developed?

There are various indicators, both in investigative research and in publications on classroom practice, towards effective ways of developing children's understanding of chronology through teaching.

Visual evidence seems to be a very effective trigger to a child displaying understanding of time. West (1981a), Lynn (1993), Harnett (1993) and Stow (1998) have all used pictures as a stimulus for discussion about time. In a visually rich 'information age' it makes sense to capitalise on children's awareness of stereotypical images of period. They seem to be able, at a young age, to codify through costume the relative periods that pictures belong to. Initially this is done by drawing a distinction between new and old, often on the basis of false dichotomies between colour and black and white. This misconception can persist up until the age of eight or nine in some children, but gradually over this time children seem to become more able to find exceptions to this 'rule'. Teaching strategies that specifically address this misconception might include deliberately giving children pictures to sort that include contemporary black and white images and older colour pictures. The subsequent discussions can highlight the misunderstanding. As they grow older their understanding becomes less linked to stereotypes, although other misconceptions may arise. Some children are easily confused by anachronistic features: for example, in pictures of a Tudor mansion the presence of a car causes confusion. Others can show confusion between time and place, apparently imagining that Victorian penny-farthing riders come from 'another country'.

There are many ways of building up the child's visual 'library' of associations with period and understanding of sequence. Morris (1992) gives excellent suggestions to develop a child's ability to interpret portraits, while Blyth (1994) and Cooper (1995c) emphasise the particular value of visual sources for developing knowledge of differences between the present and the past at Key Stage 1. Andretti (1993) further emphasises the value of artefacts as a multi-sensory stimulus to develop children's sense of chronology and sequence. Buildings and the use of the historic environment are other essential aspects of widening the child's concept of period. Architectural styles, as evident in building materials, shapes, styles of windows and doors, and even types of building, can be focused on through visits to sites and the use of architectural timelines.

The timeline is often recommended to be the recurrent visual marker of time in primary school. Thornton and Vukelich (1988) point out that there is little empirical evidence to support its apparent universality. Friedman (1982) does, however, list 'image coding' as one of three ways in which children actively process their thinking about time, and the timeline could be an example of this.

Timelines are frequently proposed in the literature, and have become a strong aspect of preferred practice. Hoodless (1996) has a number of recommendations about progression with the use of these: beginning with early-years children, who may use zigzag books, personal lifelines and even three-dimensional lifelines in the classroom, the timeline progresses to three strands of local, national and international developments across or within periods. In line with children's mathematical development, it is recommended that the numerical complexity of the calibrations also increases with the children's age. Children can also construct small-scale timelines within periods to help sequence events. To ensure continuity and progression, they should be used throughout a child's primary schooling, with increasing complexity. More complex timelines can also be of use in secondary history, not least to develop children's awareness of 'deep time' and 'duration' – the fact that history did not start with the birth of Christ or the Roman invasion of Britain, and that change occurs at varying rates.

ICT (Information and Communication Technology) resources can be helpful in this area, whether through use of the timeline on the Encarta CD-ROM, or websites such as *A Walk through Time* (http://www.globalcommunity.org/wtt/), which gives a vivid and succinct overview of the 4,600 million years since the Earth's formation as a counter to the idea that we are about to enter the third millennium. Another site gives a good example of an anachronism, on a page that shows Eric Cantona's role in the Battle of Hastings (http://anfield.mersey-world.com/pics/cartoons/eric.jpg). The word processor can also aid the development and execution of sequencing exercises (see Chapter 8).

There is some debate over the appropriate ages at which children should be taught about various periods. Oakden and Sturt were sure that children should only deal with the 'picturesque and descriptive' aspects of history, as they could not cope under the age of eleven with dates and periods (Oakden and Sturt 1922: 335) . It has been shown how this notion has subsequently been challenged. Following the important work of West (1981a), the model for the National Curriculum (DfEE 1995) focuses Key Stage 1 children on the child's own and family past, and a period beyond living memory. The model is essentially a Piagetian one, in that it begins with the child and the known world, and moves away to look at previous generations. Most schools, in line with many of the main educational publishers in this area (for example Longman, Ginn, Wayland and A&C Black), introduce children in Year 1 or 2 to the late 1800s and early 1900s as a period beyond living memory. This is chosen presumably as a natural extension to studying the older generations of a child's family. However, it could be argued that, in trying to give children a growing sense of 'the past', it might be more effective to look at a distant period. In being introduced to the Romans at Key Stage 1, children could look at a period of time where almost everything would appear markedly different from today. It could also be argued that images from Roman times are quite familiar to children at that age, through exposure to the media and the heritage industry. Certainly, many of the Year 2 children in Stow's (1998) study readily identified Roman costume and architecture, while showing some confusion between images from the 1940s, and the Tudor and Victorian periods. In numerical terms, an understanding of the time of the Romans would be beyond Key Stage 1 children, but then they are not comfortable with numbers over one hundred at that age in any case. What might be clearer to them, in this instance, is the distinction between the past and the present.

There is room for debate too about the order in which periods should be taught at Key Stage 2. Many educational publishers (Longman, Heinemann, Collins, etc.) have aimed their material at the teaching of units in chronological order. However, there is no research evidence to suggest that this is a more effective way of fixing the sequence of periods in a child's mind than teaching them in reverse order, or in no particular order. Contrary to popular belief the National Curriculum (1991 and 1995) has never stipulated the order in which they are taught. Some schools may have chosen to follow a model that mirrors more closely children's arithmetical development. This starts with the study of Britain since 1930, and moves backwards through time. Provided that units are related to children's previous areas of study and existing understanding of time, and that a broad picture is developed through the whole Key Stage, the order of study may be immaterial. It seems absurd, in any case, to suggest that the Tudors 'follow' the Vikings in any meaningful way, when there is a gap of more than 400 years between these eras. At secondary level, it is important to make connections between the strands of history that run across the core study units, such as the changing role and influence of the Church, or the changing balance of power between monarch and Parliament. Here, graphs can be an important aid to overview, for instance as a line to trace the changes in the monarch's power between 1066 and 1688 or beyond. Recent guidance on the importance of outlines and overviews has been helpful in terms of stressing the importance of 'putting the bits of the picture together again' (Riley 1997: 20–2). In addition to the gradual building up of an overarching chronology of the past there are occasions, particularly in secondary history, where children need to possess a range of accurate and clearly grasped 'micro-chronologies' – in the sense of an understanding of the precise order of events in a historical crisis – if they are to construct an accurate explanation of events such as the Munich Crisis, the outbreak of the Second World War, or the Franco-Prussian War. This is a necessary but not sufficient condition for a coherent explanation. The chronology must obviously be complemented by an understanding of why things happened, and the relations between events. Putting events in order is only part of the equation.

Research indicates that a range of methods should be used to scaffold children's thinking about time. Cooper (1995c) indicates various ways in which children's understanding of clock and calendar time should be developed, and many of these methods echo Friedman's three models of children's cognitive processing of time (see Friedman 1982). These are:

- verbal lists, whereby children may recite (mentally or aloud) lists of members of a time set – this could include days of the week, months of the year and numbers of days in months ('Thirty days hath September'), and would in times past have included lists of kings and queens of England ('Willy, Willy, Harry, Steve … ');
- associative networks, used for storing characteristic features of units of time – examples could include weather associated with years of a child's life, or characteristics of costume, architecture or artefacts associated with particular periods;
- image coding: a child might use a circle or a line as a representation of a series of units of time or events – at Key Stage 1, birthday wheels or trains are effective examples of this model, and timelines (as discussed earlier) can be justified in these terms.

The least fashionable of these at Key Stage 2 would be verbal lists. The idea of memorising lists of kings and queens or learning dates by rote is a baby that has long ago been thrown out with the bath water. At first this removal of rote learning was an important aspect of making the study of history more developmentally appropriate at a primary level, and more intellectually honest. The over-emphasis on 'knowledge without understanding' was criticised as recently as 1992–3 by OFSTED. However, Thornton and Vukelich (1988) have speculated whether there is not some value in the mechanical learning of some aspects of time. It could be argued now that as an addition to a broad development of an understanding of time, through the use of timelines and detailed learning about historical periods, the rote learning of some dates or the sequence of periods might have a place. Wood notes that awareness of 'a few key dates' can be helpful in giving pupils landmarks to be used in negotiating the past (Wood 1995: 12). Perhaps there are some areas of history, like times tables in maths, which need practice and repetition, so that pupils grasp and retain the 'rule' about centuries, or about counting backwards for BC. (A secondary Post-Graduate Certificate in Education (PGCE) student noted in an assignment that the rote learning of dates could also be used as a sanction against deviant behaviour in the history classroom.)

An aspect of teaching about time that all researchers and authors can agree on is the centrality of language development in the acquisition of an understanding of time. Jahoda (1963), Fraisse (1982), Harner (1982) and Friedman (1982) all stress its role as the overt symbol of understanding. West (1981a) reported in his Dudley study that children's skills in sequencing were most significantly dependent on language ability. Wood (1995) described the concept of time as being inextricably linked with language issues. Cooper describes language as 'the tool for unlocking the past' through which children can refine concepts. It is essential therefore that activities devised to develop children's understanding of time have a clear emphasis on discussion and a defined core of vocabulary (Cooper 1995c: 14). A more systematic approach to the development of time vocabulary has recently been adopted in many secondary schools, with 'target words' for the term being placed prominently as part of classroom display. A variation of this is the display of a calendar that gives alternatives to the prevalent Christian one, so that children begin to grasp that calendars are human constructs, and that it is not 1999 AD (or whenever) everywhere in the world.

What for history teachers are the key implications of these issues?

A summary list of points can be drawn up from the questions raised above, which could form the basis of a discussion with colleagues, or a check-list for the teaching of chronology across a primary or secondary school or within a class:

- a rigid, age-related scale of the development of children's understanding of time in history is inappropriate: children progress along this scale at different ages and pace;
- some children at Key Stage 1 may possess quite sophisticated knowledge of chronology; some in secondary schools may not yet have grasped very basic time concepts, such as which century they are living in, or what AD means. We should not make assumptions about pupils' understanding of time or assume ceilings about what children can achieve in this area: careful monitoring is necessary;
- systematic teaching about chronology level does influence the rate of development of children's understanding;
- to understand chronological systems children need to be familiar with a range of terms, and to develop confidence in using these through modelling, instruction and discussion;
- misconceptions and stereotypical ideas about time need to be specifically addressed and challenged, but can form the basis for useful starting points in discussion;
- dates and period labels can be learned mechanically, alongside developing understanding of sequence, intervals of time and duration;
- the order in which periods of history are taught is not as important as the need to relate periods to a wider time frame;
- early-years children may find it easier to distinguish the distant past than the recent past when comparing it to the present;
- visual representations of time should be used consistently throughout the primary years, but with increasing complexity;
- visual evidence (including artefacts and buildings) is a powerful way of developing children's associative networks in relation to period or age;
- all children have some familiarity with images of the past, which can be built on and widened through teaching. It can be helpful to draw on and try to engage with the ideas about time that they bring with them to the classroom;

- children's understanding of chronology can be most effectively developed through a range of methods, but methods that show some consistency through a child's school career;
- given the variety of experience of history that children encounter in the primary school, it can be helpful to do an audit of where pupils are in their understanding of chronology when they start secondary history;
- sequencing work needs to be complemented by discussion of the relationship between the events, people or artefacts sequenced if we are to develop historical understanding effectively;
- teachers need to keep in mind the various strands of pupils' progress in time; the building up of a framework or mental map of the unfolding of the past, the development of an understanding of time-related vocabulary, and an understanding of dating systems, so that children can make consistent progress in all these areas;
- teaching children about time needs to be sustained as well as systematic – there is a need to go back to aspects of time to check that understanding has been retained.

What is vital is that, at a time when the amount of history taught in primary schools seems set to diminish, this key aspect of historical understanding is still given prominence. The concept of historical time and its associated skills and links to other concepts is one of the most essential aspects of understanding for the primary child to take forward into secondary education.

In addition to being a fundamentally important part of the discipline of the subject, providing coherence and one of its key organising principles, there are other reasons for according time and thought to the teaching of chronology in the history classroom. It is comparatively easy to measure pupil progression in some elements of chronology – for instance vocabulary acquisition, understanding of AD and BC, the ability to manipulate centuries accurately, or place periods of history in order. This can be an aid to pupil (and teacher) motivation. There is also evidence to suggest that, although the introduction of a National Curriculum for history has led to a much more consistent exposure to history for pupils (Bage 1993), some aspects of teaching children about time have been neglected or have not been effective, and that there are some 'black holes' in terms of children's basic understandings about time. In the light of research findings, which revealed that 13 per cent of British adults were unable to locate the UK on a map of the world, Rex Walford warned of the danger of not providing pupils with essential knowledge about the world; 'We make wonderful claims for what we do in education, but sometimes the essential underpinning just isn't there' (the *Independent*, 29 February 1988). It would be 'a good thing' if all children leaving school possessed a solid vocabulary of time terms, a sound grasp of dating systems, and well developed frameworks of how we got from 'olden times' to where and how we are now. The earlier they acquire these skills and understandings, and the further they develop them, the better. All history teachers need to give careful thought to the effectiveness of their approaches to teaching children about time, so that, in the next millennium, there will be far fewer children who do not know what century they are living in.

Further reading

Claire, H. (1996) *Reclaiming Our Pasts: Equality and Diversity in the Primary History Curriculum*, Stoke-on Trent: Trentham Books.

This excellent book deals with the balance implicit within the curriculum, and the need to provide a variety of cultural, ethnic and social perspectives in teaching history at Key Stages 1 and 2. There are useful examples of timelines for each Study Unit, which offer an inclusive perspective on those periods.

Cooper, H. (1995) *The Teaching of History in Primary Schools: Implementing the Revised National Curriculum*, second edn, London: David Fulton.

Hilary Cooper provides (pp. 22–6) a typically informative survey of research in the area of historical time, including some less well-known studies. There are many other references in the book to developing chronological understanding.

Haydn, T., Arthur, J. and Hunt M. (1997) *Learning to Teach History in the Secondary School*, London: Routledge, pp. 86–93.

Attempts to provide a coherent structure for the development of pupils' understanding, and includes examples of exercises that might be used in the classroom to complement timeline activities.

Wood, S. (1995) 'Developing an understanding of time – Sequencing issues', *Teaching History* 79, April: 11–14.

A succinct and practical guide to helping pupils forward in their understanding of time, including some consideration of the importance of narrative in this process.

8 Information and communications technology in the history classroom

Terry Haydn

> It doesn't really matter whether or not a majority of history teachers use IT in their classrooms. What does matter is that history is part of the curriculum and that it is taught well.
>
> (An assertion made at a recent history workshop, quoted in Dickinson 1998)

> In future, there will be two sorts of teacher, the IT literate, and the retired.
>
> (Cochrane 1995)

> Computers are useless. They can only give you answers.
>
> (Pablo Picasso, quoted in the *Daily Telegraph*, 11 April 1996)

Introduction

Is it possible to reconcile these statements? The development of new technology over the past twenty years has implications that all history teachers need to consider, but it is possible that the pace of technological development (together with a range of curriculum, assessment and inspection initiatives in education) has been so rapid that teachers have found it difficult to find time to reflect fully on how best to incorporate new applications into their teaching.

There is now considerable pressure on teachers in the UK to use computers in their teaching. There is talk of 'zero tolerance of non-IT literate teachers' (see, for example, Cohen 1999), and anxiety that insufficient use of ICT will jeopardise OFSTED inspection judgements. In spite of this pressure, it is difficult not to feel that, in the long term, history teachers will only use ICT in their day-to-day teaching if they are confident that it will improve pupil learning in history. Will they use it when no one is looking? What can it do to improve teaching and learning in history?

Why ICT is an issue in history teaching

There is a disparity between the hopes and claims made for the educational use of ICT by many politicians and policy-makers, and the more measured and cautious response of those who work closer to the classroom. The seductive image of the ICT-rich classroom with media archive, independent learning pods, 'virtual professor' link, multimedia writing bay, laptop bank and data projector (see, for instance, Bright 1997; Carvel 1998; Davitt 1999) does not correspond to the reality of the contemporary history classroom, but the use of new technology in the history classroom is not just a question of the level of technological provision. Many history teachers would acknowledge that there is a gap between the potential of new technology to enhance teaching and learning in history, and current use, but much more thought needs to be directed towards *exactly what can be done* with the wide range of new technology applications in the history classroom. Voice-type software is a technological miracle, but not yet an educational one (none of our 300 or so most recent Post-Graduate Certificate in Education (PGCE) students have seen it used in a classroom context). Video and electronic conferencing can produce impressive 'set-piece' showcase demonstrations, but some institutions that have the technological capacity to use it find that it is often underused or neglected. The 'infrastructure' of ideas for using it is, at the moment, insufficiently developed for it to have had a substantial impact on day-to-day classroom practice. Some history departments make extensive use of ICT, but this is not yet the norm.

The new technology application that has had the most powerful impact on the history classroom in recent years is the use of the video recorder/television. Over 90 per cent of history teachers in the UK use it as a regular part of their classroom practice (Sharp 1995). It can be used for a variety of teaching purposes, is easy and flexible to use in terms of fitting it into a lesson, and the teacher only needs one video and large-screen television to work with the whole class. To complement the 'hardware', there is a wide range of schools broadcasts, with accompanying teacher's notes that provide detailed information on how teachers might use the programmes. Many history teachers have developed an 'archive' of dozens, or even hundreds, of video extracts that have been tried, tested and refined, and assimilated into classroom practice. In addition to the range of 'software' (programmes) and ease of use, the large television screen provides the opportunity to present emotionally powerful and vivid images and accounts that may well be seared on to a child's memory for years. It is perhaps not surprising that a recent (very) small-scale survey found that when asked what they wanted for their classroom, three times as many teachers said they would like a video recorder rather than a computer (Evans 1997).

If computers are so wonderful, why isn't everyone using them, what has the video recorder/television got that computers lack, and what can the computer do in the history classroom that the video recorder and television cannot?

The use of computers in the history classroom is an important issue in history education because, in spite of the enthusiasm of politicians and those who sell technology to schools, computers have not yet had a widespread transformative effect on the history classroom, in the way that television and video have. A key question is how to harness the potential of ICT to deliver what is pedagogically useful in day-to-day history teaching, rather than what is technologically impressive in terms of 'what can be done'. Davitt's assertion that 'data projectors will become an essential school resource – you connect the computer to the projector and hey presto, Encarta wallpaper' does not answer the question of whether Encarta wallpaper will help to enhance pupils' achievements in history (Davitt 1999).

Getting beyond 'the usual suspects'

In addition to establishing precisely what various ICT applications have to offer the history teacher, it is important to have a sound understanding of the barriers that prevent history teachers from using ICT. It is also important to get beyond 'the usual suspects' inhibiting the use of ICT, where circumstances have changed, so that policy is not predicated on outdated information and inaccurate assumptions.

Amongst the myths that still circulate are that history teachers' Luddism and technological inadequacy are at the heart of the problem, and that teachers are 'a hurdle to be overcome' (DfEE, quoted in Cohen 1999). Although in the early 1990s there was some evidence to suggest that there was a degree of 'ideological' resistance to the use of computers amongst some history student teachers and their mentors (Easdown 1994), more recent research suggests that most student teachers have sound technical capability in ICT, and a positive attitude to exploring the possible uses of ICT in the history classroom. (Haydn and Macaskill 1995; Mellar and Jackson 1994). Things have moved on since Downes's finding that many history student teachers did not use computers because 'the thought did not occur' (Downes 1993). Feedback from history student teachers, and history teachers undertaking INSET courses, suggests that most, far from being dismissive of new technology, are interested to explore these avenues for enhancing the teaching of their subject, but find lack of time to explore these agendas and limited access to computers to be major obstacles.

In spite of the increase in the number of computers in secondary schools, I visit very few history departments where there are several computers in every history classroom (or even one in each classroom), where there is departmental access to the Internet, or which possess large monitors or conversion leads that would facilitate whole-class teaching with a single computer. The move towards networked ICT suites may well have reduced access to computers, given the problems that exist in schools where many departments have to fight for access to a handful of dedicated ICT rooms. The development of ICT activities that do not require access to ICT suites, and the purchase of large monitors, or conversion leads to make use of television screens, would help in this respect.

A recent survey of the student teachers and history departments I work with suggested that lack of technical confidence and expertise, and 'ideological' resistance to the use of ICT in history were not major factors in the use of ICT. Although access issues remain an important factor inhibiting the day-to-day use of ICT in history lessons, closely followed by 'lack of confidence/knowledge of what to *do* with computers in history lessons', the most prevalent factor cited was 'lack of time to plan how to integrate the use of computers into lessons'.

One former student teacher from the course wrote apologetically, 'One thing I have neglected so far to a large extent is ICT. I hate to admit this, but it's really difficult to find the time to plan a worthwhile lesson using it. That's one of my goals for next term.' As Naughton (1999) remarked, 'When we die, "so much information, so little time" will be found engraved on our hearts.' The most precious resource in education at the moment is teacher (and student teacher) time, given the demands of responding to various forms of audit, target setting, the National Curriculum for Initial Teacher Education (ITE), and over twenty current DfEE initiatives.

One obvious way forward is for the development and dissemination of 'worked examples', tailored to fit in with core areas of the history curriculum. The NCET/Historical Association's recent materials on word processing and data handling are a good example of this approach (NCET/Historical Association 1997). The National Grid for Learning, and similar subscription sites such as the Historical Association's *History Online* and Research Machines' *Living Library*, would seem to be ideal solutions to this problem. Michael Barber's exhortation to use the DfEE's website, 'designed to provide practical guidance and examples of good practice on raising standards in a format that is attractive, accessible and useful to busy teachers', would seem to be a good example of the use of ICT to prevent teachers from having to re-invent educational wheels (*The Times Educational Supplement*, 2 October 1998). Barber added that 'the standards site will be ready for you, when you are ready for it'. This elicited a response (from a practising teacher) who 'had been ready for it since January when nothing much was happening on it – and quite a waste of time it was logging in month after month to see no content' (*The Times Educational Supplement*, 16 October 1998).

I mention this to reinforce the important point that such initiatives must be accompanied by an infrastructure of worked examples, and tried and tested materials, before they are trumpeted as a triumph of educational technology. In terms of materials to support teaching and learning in history, the National Grid for Learning could best be described as 'patchy' – some excellent resources from the Public Records Office (http://pro.gov.uk/education/snapshots), but an awful lot of 'black holes'. Similarly, a major subscription site with a promising button to 'Secondary History Resource Packs Archive' revealed that there was as yet nothing in the archive. One of the factors hampering rapid development of such 'gateway' agencies is that many of the teachers (and teacher educators) who are best placed to contribute to the development of the National Grid for Learning are struggling to respond to the deluge of initiatives and audits of policy works and administrators. The DfEE should bear in mind that teachers are part of the solution, not the problem. Teachers should bear in mind that things can change rapidly with ICT, and within months the National Grid for Learning and other gateway sites might be full of invaluable resources and practical ideas for integrating ICT into the history classroom.

Several years ago, there were many history teachers and student teachers who lacked confidence, expertise and belief in the use of computers to improve teaching and learning in history. Now, however, problems of access, time and the limited development of eminently practicable, tried and tested examples of ICT activities are the most significant barriers to the exploitation of new technology in the history classroom. This is why major extension of the DfEE scheme to provide laptop computers to teachers might well be the quickest and most effective way of accelerating the effective deployment of ICT in the classroom. It would give teachers access to new applications twenty-four hours a day, and give them the time to explore their potential for classroom application in a way that short in-service training sessions cannot match. The BECTA (British Educational Communications and Technology Agency)/Historical Association booklet describing the work of history departments that have made successful use of ICT would also be a useful guide to 'what works' in history and ICT (BECTA/Historical Association 1998).

The advantages and limitations of ICT in the history classroom: the importance of instructional design over technological advance

In spite of the unrestrained enthusiasm of politicians and ICT fundamentalists for increasing the use of computers in the classroom, there is not yet a substantial body of research evidence to affirm the 'value added' learning benefits of ICT applications. There does appear to be a growing body of evidence to suggest that pupils enjoy using computers, that it improves their attitudes to school, and that they feel that they 'learn better' using ICT (see, for instance, Askar *et al.* 1992; Papert 1993). This is not an inconsequential advantage, given the scale of disaffection and disengagement from learning in secondary schools in the UK, and it is a finding that might be noted by secondary history departments concerned with post-14 take-up of history. It does not, however, extend to a proof that using ICT will raise standards of achievement in history, or other subjects. Citing the work of Clark (1983; 1994), and Kozma (1991; 1994), Owston argues that 'after more than 50 years of research on instructional media, no consistent significant effects from any medium on learning have been demonstrated' (Owston 1997: 29). If anything, recent research has tended to point out the limitations of new technology rather than its advantages over traditional educational methods, particularly in terms of shortening pupils' attention span (Oppenheimer 1997; Brosnan 1998; Healy 1998). Kay points out that computers are not good for reading extended prose: 'the tendency is to show pictures, diagrams and short "bumper-sticker" sentences, because that is what displays do well' (1995: 152). This has particular implications for history, where it is helpful for pupils to be provided with a narrative, to help to put sources into some form of context. Kay uses the term 'junk learning' to describe the dangers of ICT-based learning that is founded on the idea of the information superhighway as a vehicle for pumping information into pupils, and of education as 'a bitter pill that can be made palatable only by sugar coating' (1995: 148).

I mention these findings not to argue against the use of ICT in the history classroom, but to make the point that the most urgent priorities should be improvements to the instructional design of history software, the development of an archive of practical classroom applications and resources, and time for teachers to consider how to integrate ICT into their teaching.

Adjusting to the information-rich history classroom

One of the most important implications of recent developments in ICT for the history teacher is the increase in the amount of information available to both teacher and pupils:

> Until the last few years, a characteristic of schooling in general, and history education in particular, has been that it occurs in an information-impover-ished environment. Of all the information pertinent to a historical issue, a very small percentage has typically been available to students.
>
> (Copeland 1997: xiii)

In accessing the Trimdon Grange mining disaster of 1882 whilst searching the National Grid for Learning in a history classroom, Tony Blair echoes Cope-land's enthusiasm for this facet of ICT. 'It's going to bring libraries and archives right into the classroom. The children can access virtually anything they want. They love it – a whole new world for them' (the *Guardian*, 7 November 1998).

Consideration of this facet of ICT needs to bear in mind the distinction between history as an academic discipline, and history as a school subject, as well as the overlap between the two. In the past it was suggested that as infor-mation technology was 'a useful tool for the historian ... it should be employed as historians need it: to store, retrieve and analyse information' (DES 1988). For the historian, the increased accessibility of information is an almost unqualified advantage (although even for the professional historian it can make the quan-tity of information available almost unmanageable). In an information-poor society, one of the problems for the historian was to find out what happened. In an information-rich society, the problem is how to cope with all the informa-tion available and assess its trustworthiness, utility and significance in answering a particular question. One of the key purposes of school history is to help young people to handle information intelligently: 'History now is about learning to manage complex subjects and manipulate data' (Rollison 1998). One of the keys to realising the potential of ICT to enhance teaching and learning history is to understand the difference between what ICT offers the historian, and what it has to offer history teachers and pupils in schools. For pupils, the key asset is not access to vast amounts of information, but the facility to organise and manage the information, with a view to making sense of it. The ability to access and retrieve information is a comparatively low-order skill in the history classroom (even in terms of the ability to conduct Internet searches). The key to developing pupils' historical understanding is their ability to analyse and deploy information after they have accessed it.

When considered in this light, the exponential increase in historical information available for pupils to access is not an unalloyed benefit. As Counsell (1998a) points out, just giving pupils 'more stuff' won't in itself help them forward in learning. Counsell's advocacy of ICT in the history classroom is partly based on the premise that a key problem that pupils face in history is that it is so vast and unmanageable. Many pupils are already drowning in information. Giving them more information may be the last thing that they need. ICT can help pupils to organise, manage and make sense of the deluge of information they encounter in the history classroom, but the applications that will help them to do this are at the blunt edge of new technology, such as word processing and data handling, rather than the 'cutting-edge' showpiece applications that have elicited the enthusiasm of those who work at some distance from the history classroom.

Interactivity, new technology and the history classroom

One of the most commonly cited adjectives applied to the use of ICT in education is that it promotes 'interactive' learning. Bill Gates (1995) defines interactivity as meaning that 'a title is organised in such a way that the person controls what he or she sees or hears'. Although interactive uses of ICT are starting to emerge now that attention is starting to focus on instructional design and pupil activities, there is a degree of irony in the use of this term. Computers have been used in the history classroom to do (laborious) transcription from hand-written text, for the uncritical and often unread downloading of pictures and text, and for gazing at, and browsing through, the images on screen, in the same way that people flick through magazines – a fairly passive engagement with learning, rather than deep interaction with content. As Taylor points out:

> If they think it's all to do with trial and error, jumping from one thing to another, pressing this button, that button, that's not learning, that's not getting the knowledge into their minds in an integrated way that they can make use of, that's just mucking about.
>
> (Taylor 1996)

Here is Blair again, on CD-ROMs and interactivity:

> Even the most determined technophobe can't help but get excited about the way that CD-roms bring information to life. ... The other important point about CD-roms of course is that they are interactive. Learning is no longer a matter of passively receiving information; you can become actively involved in the process yourself, answering quizzes, manipulating images, summoning up pictures or music and pasting together your own notebook of words, images and sounds on screen.
>
> (Blair 1995)

Whilst agreeing with Blair's comments on the attractive and colourful presentation of information, the definition of interactivity that follows bears little correlation to how children learn in history and how they tend to use CD-ROMs in practice. The observation of Sparrowhawk (1995) of over 200 primary children using CD-ROMs found that over 160 of them used it for either casual and undirected browsing, or for downloading pictures. This is interactivity at the level of the television remote-control button. Is it possible to have a debate or an argument with a history CD-ROM? Can it disturb pupils' preconceptions, generate new ideas, or change pupils' minds beyond the level of accumulation of factual detail? Madian argues that the multimedia format can actually discourage students from thinking deeply about content: 'The medium has managed to make the trivial more attractive, but the medium has not encouraged in-depth research and thinking' (1995: 16).

Schick's definition of interactivity offers a clearer insight into what is needed if ICT applications are to improve children's learning in history:

> The term 'interactive' involves two related issues: control and response. ... In practice, both control and response basically mean that the user does something to the machine – provokes another screen. What should also happen is that the machine does something to the user – provokes another idea. It is here that much educational software fails. However flashy the graphics, or 'non linear' the organisation, such software is essentially static. ... Something is needed to draw the user into the activity.
>
> (Schick 1995: 12)

Whatever the ICT application, there are two important principles that underpin the effective use of new technology in developing pupils' historical understanding. The first is that pupils must be asked to do something with the information they are presented with, rather than simply being provided with access to an increased volume of historical information. The second is that there should be some valid historical purpose to the activities that pupils are engaged in, rather than meretricious comprehension, matching and representation exercises. This can be in the form of asking students to make connections and demonstrate understandings with other areas or aspects or historical information, or presenting them with a choice between two or more alternatives and asking them to make intelligent choices between them, based on the principles underpinning history as a discipline.

> We must consider what cognitive skills are involved in the interaction, and what questions the user takes away from the interaction. ... We must not simply move the user from 'Place A' (where the user begins) to 'Place B' (where the program ends) but beyond the immediate topic to provide information the user can apply to other problems, to strengthen cognitive skills for processing new data, or to ask questions which challenge the user to think differently about the past. ... The vital interaction should take place

in the student's mind. Without this the potential for learning diminishes significantly.

(Schick 1995: 10)

Key applications and ways forward in ICT and history

Some ICT applications have little or no relevance to the history classroom (for instance, data-logging), others have some potential, but are limited in scope (concept keyboard, or digital camera). What follows is a consideration of ICT applications that appear to have particular potential for enhancing teaching and learning in the history classroom.

The word processor

Because it is not at the 'cutting edge' of new technology, and because it has often been used in schools simply to do transcription of hand-written notes for presentation purposes, the word processor has perhaps been the most under-valued of ICT applications for the history teacher. Only recently has its utility as a tool for editing and organising historical information been widely developed for use in the history classroom, whether to simply sort information into manageable categories for pupils to analyse, or to help pupils forward in constructing accounts and explanations. It can also be used to devise sequencing activities of different levels of complexity, to improve children's grasp of chronology, and to develop pupils' analytical and discursive writing.

> It can search, annotate, organise, classify, draft, redraft and save that funda-mental of the historian, the written word. When we consider those processes, and the implicit difficulties they represent for so many of our students, the true power of the word processor becomes clear. It is not a typewriter, it is an awesome tool for handling information in written form.
>
> (Walsh 1998: 6)

The ability to select text and highlight it in different ways, to move and delete, or to make tables and columns, enables pupils to separate and organise information relevant to a specific question, to discard the irrelevant, to put things in order of time or significance, to quickly refine and revise judgements, make connections, spot overlaps and also put together various elements of an explanation into a piece of extended writing. As Hassell points out, word processors can help children:

> to think more strategically, and analyse what happened, to isolate the important issues and put them in order of chronology or impact … to help them to focus not so much on the words as the patterns and relationships involved. It improves their ability to ask questions, manipulate data and start coming up with interpretations.
>
> (Hassell 1999: 17)

It is also one of the areas where there are the beginnings on an archive of worked examples to model how it can be integrated into lessons. The NCET/Historical Association package, *History Using IT: Improving Students' Writing in History Using Word Processing* (NCET/Historical Association 1997) has now sold well over a thousand copies, and has recently been complemented by a further range of examples and suggestions in the recent ICT issue of *Teaching History* that was given over entirely to ICT issues (Walsh 1998). As nearly all schools now possess word-processing packages, and most teachers already have the basic word-processing skills to execute the exercises, history-based text manipulation tasks may represent the quickest, cheapest and easiest ways for history departments who have not yet made great strides in ICT to 'get started' in ICT.

Data handling

In terms of their level of technological sophistication, many data-handling progams are quite primitive, compared to the high specification multimedia packages that are now available. Data-handling programs are a good demonstration of the proposition that there is no necessary correlation between the sophistication of technology, and its potential for enhancing learning in history; it is one of the areas where there is most obviously a valid overlap between the activities of the professional historian and the opportunities to provide pupils with worthwhile and genuinely historical tasks. They provide a clear link with Key Element 3 of the present National Curriculum for history: historical enquiry. In conducting historical enquiries using data-handling activities, pupils are required to look for significant patterns in the past, explore and test hypotheses, and learn to formulate their own questions and hypotheses. There are already a wide range of datafiles and database packages available, which come with suggestions for classroom use, and, as with word processing, most schools now have data-handling packages, so that, once history teachers have learned to use the program, they and their pupils can devise their own datafiles, as a cost-free resource. It is now possible to purchase massive datafiles on CD-ROM, such as a database on soldiers killed in the First World War ('Naval and Military Press'), or much simpler and smaller databases (see, for instance 'Mentor', by Appian Way Software) that offer a collection of sources on a particular historical topic, which can be accessed in different ways, and which come with eminently 'do-able' classroom enquiries. In addition to the facility databases offer for the development of pupils' skills of numeracy, through work on ratio, percentages and averages, more complex databases such as the HiDES (Historical Document Expert System) 'A' level programs (Research Programmes International) allow students to investigate and analyse the validity of various explanations of historical events. It is this ability to 'problematise' the past that gives such scope for the development of higher-order thinking skills in history. The facility of the program to analyse the adequacy of students' responses and indicate omissions and misinterpretations makes the program more genuinely interactive (using Schick's definition of the term) than many of the quizzes and games provided by history CD-ROMs. As with word processing, the NCET/Historical Association's package on data handling (1998) provides a range of worked examples, complete with disks and structured pupil activities, for secondary history departments wishing to develop this facet of ICT. Of all ICT applications, the manipulation and analysis of historical information which data-handling activities involve, offers pupils activities that are consistently focused on the development of historical skills and understanding. This includes, when used skilfully, the important aspects of understanding the limits and problems posed by the information available, and the problem of what questions to ask of it.

CD-ROMs

CD-ROMs can do incredible things compared to sticks of chalk and black-boards, but I suspect I am not the only history teacher to have accumulated an increasing range of history CD-ROMs that have not been fully exploited in teaching. They offer the advantage of colourful and graphical presentation of historical sources, and enormous volumes of information, but history teachers still have to think how to translate that into a purposeful and genuinely histor-ical lesson activity. (Can you remember many things that you learned through using a CD-ROM?) History student teachers placed CD-ROMs fairly low on the list of ICT applications they had used or seen used in the classroom (Haydn 1999).

Although there are several sources for obtaining reviews of history CD-ROMs (http://www.becta.org.uk, http://teem.co.uk), the problem is not just that history teachers are not sure of which ones to purchase, but also one of finding time to think what to do with them in the classroom, given the vast amounts of information that they contain. One big step forward in this respect is the devel-opment of history CD-ROMs that have been written with a range of historical investigations and enquiries built into them, together with a teacher's hand-book, such as the British Library's *Making of the United Kingdom* (British Library 1998). History CD-ROMs are now giving more thought to instructional design and classroom use. A key step forward here is the presentation of alternatives that pupils are asked to explore and make judgements on – was the English Civil War like a game of cricket, or like the recent war in Bosnia? (Walsh and Brookfield 1998). Pupils are given sources *and a narrative*, and are asked to make sense of the problems posed by a carefully chosen range of sources. Other history CD-ROMs have made great strides forward in terms of their potential for asking pupils to think about the past as problematic, and in terms of genuine 'interactivity', but are crying out for an accompanying large monitor, so that they can be used as part of interactive whole class teaching. *The Troubled Century* (YITM 1997) asks pupils to make judgements on the motives of protag-onists in key twentieth-century crises, and then suggests what (all!) 'real' historians think. Even the deficiencies of ICT software can be exploited by the history teacher to make points about interpretation and perspective. It should be stressed that there are also history CD-ROMs that are sufficiently dire that they could be used as a deterrent against poor behaviour in the history classroom.

CD-ROMs are an increasingly rich source of good teaching activities in history, but access problems continue to limit their use. CD-ROMs that are accompanied by a well thought-out handbook of suggestions for use, and which take account of 'throughput' of pupils, given the not uncommon scenario of one computer per classroom, are likely to gather less dust than those that leave the teacher to think about what to do with them. General reviews of history CD-ROMs are less helpful than the dissemination of practical and eminently manageable ideas for classroom use. The National Grid for Learning would be an ideal vehicle for dissemination. The TEEM website (Teachers Evaluating Educational Software, at http://www.teem.org.uk) offers case histories of how educational software has been used in class, where it has succeeded or failed, and its impact on pupils' learning, but as with the National Grid for Learning it is not yet fully developed.

The Internet and communications technology

As recently as two years ago the Internet was a source of some exasperation, disappointment and time-wasting for many history student teachers. The percentage of high-quality and relevant sites often did not repay the time invested in wandering round Cyberspace for ideas and resources. Attractive sounding 'virtual tours' of history museums that promised almost as much as a pupil visit, turned out to be just a few pictures, and, even when relevant resources were located, they needed time-consuming adaptation for classroom use.

More recently, increasing numbers of history student teachers are routinely using web-based materials as part of their classroom teaching.

One of the major factors in this turnaround is the development of history 'portals' or 'gateway' sites, where someone else has done the trawling through the morass of Cyberspace to find resources that are appropriate for the history classroom. In addition to being a source of classroom teaching resources, the sheer interest of many of these sites is helpful for developing students' (and teachers') subject knowledge, and reminding them of why they were interested in history in the first place; a useful antidote to much of the administratively imposed reading they are subjected to. In addition to subscription sites, such as Research Machines' 'Living Library' (http://www.eduweb.co.uk/), AngliaCampus (http://www.angliacampus.com) and the forthcoming Historical Association's 'History Online' (http://www.historyonline.co.uk), there are free sites such as the BBC (bbc.co.uk/education/history/), Channel 4 (http://schools.channel4.com) and the History Channel (http://www.thehistorychannel.co.uk). There are also education sites, like 'the Cybrary of the Holocaust' (http://www.remember.org), and publishers' free sites (see, for instance, http://www.spartacus.schoolnet.co.uk/eduwebsites.htm), as well as sites on many historical topics that attempt to draw together web resources on that topic, such as the Vietnam War (http://chss.

montclair.edu/english/furr/vietnam.html) and the Norman Conquest (http://www.hc.cc.tx.us/library/histnc.htm). Many school history department websites have excellent collections of Internet sites and resources, in addition to examples of pupils' work, and guidance on how to avoid inefficient use of ICT (see, for instance, the Great Sankey High School's History Department site at http://www. users/globalnet.co.uk/~sgood/).

Other developments that have enhanced the Internet's potential for improving learning in history are the linking of web sites to history CD-ROMs, and structured investigations based on Internet materials, such as the History Courseware Consortium's *Core Resources for Historians*, which can help to bridge the gap between 'A' level and undergraduate history (History Courseware Consortium 1998). Many sites have made progress in providing more meaningful forms of 'interactivity' in the sense of requiring some engagement and initiative in thought by the reader, and sites such as the Chatback Trust (http://atschool.eduweb.co.uk/chatback/) provide a valuable alternative to 'straight' oral history by providing commentaries from those involved in twentieth-century historical events. Applications such as Pagemill, Webwhacker and Web Wizard have also made it easier to edit web pages for classroom use, keep the links to related sites and put web resources onto CD-ROM, all of which extend the potential for work on interpretations and the synthesising and comparison of sources.

Above all, the Internet and communications software transform our ability to receive and disseminate information – precisely what is required to spread ideas about good practice in other aspects of ICT. This does not necessarily mean a revolution in the number of 'all singing, all dancing' network room ICT spectaculars, but, rather, the more efficient execution of prosaic but helpful tasks, such as getting hold of individual exam questions, and the mark schemes and examiners' reports on them (already possible for core subjects with some exam boards), and getting hold of teachers' notes on schools broadcasts (a free service on some channels). Together with the use of e-mail, intranets such as 'First Class', and electronic conferencing, the Internet offers the opportunity for history teachers to communicate with each other much more effectively. In mainland Europe, a substantial number of history teachers already use electronic communication to keep up with developments in their subject (Beaber 1998). This could provide the same benefits for the teaching of history as 'open sourcing' has for software development in general (Raymond 1998).

The medium is not the message

There are many other ICT applications that can enhance learning in history, including multimedia authoring packages, simulations, concept keyboards, timeline programs, 'Clicker Plus' and other Special Educational Needs software. The near future may well bring software for assessing essays (see the *Daily Telegraph*, 17 April 1998), diagnosing strengths and weaknesses, and independent learning packages that might provide a more effective way of covering for absent colleagues (see *The Times Educational Supplement*, 15 May 1998). The applications described in the previous section represent four of the applications that, at the present moment in time, might offer the best ways forward of capitalising on the potential of ICT to improve learning in history and make computers part of the day-to-day learning tools of history teachers and their pupils. This will only happen if thought is focused on pedagogy, classroom application, and the development of children's historical understanding. One of the positive aspects of the new National Curriculum for ICT in Initial Teacher Education is the clear emphasis on subject application, rather than technological proficiency (DfEE 1998a).

To return to the three quotations at the start of this chapter; computers are clearly not useless, but we need to think carefully about why their impact has as yet been limited in many history departments. Asking the right questions of what ICT can and can't do will be more helpful than any amount of inchoate enthusiasm, pressure and testing to make teachers use computers. These questions are:

- How can we ensure that history teachers get time to fully explore how to build ICT into classroom use?
- How can we best disseminate the experience of history departments who are already making extensive and successful use of ICT?
- How would it be best to invest in ICT in the history classroom – laptops for teachers, more large monitors in history classrooms, improved Internet access or more in-service training?

An inability to make full use of new technology will not render history teachers useless and fit only to be professionally 'culled', as Cochrane suggests, but like many other groups in society, history teachers need to think about how ICT might help them to do their job more effectively. At the very least, it seems a reasonable proposition to suggest that failure to consider the use of ICT will result in lost opportunities for engaging pupils in history and enhancing their learning. Good teachers are always looking for ways to improve their teaching, and are able to adapt and change to meet new challenges and opportunities, but let's not pretend that computers are an unproblematic educational miracle. History education ought to play an important role in helping young people to handle information intelligently, and the nature of ICT means that it should play a major part in this objective, but we're not there yet, and it will need clear thinking and good communication if we are to maximise the potential of ICT for teaching and learning in history. Part of this clear thinking is an understanding that history education is not just about filling up pupils' hard-disk space; it is also about helping them to develop more powerful and intelligent information processors.

Further reading

BECTA/Historical Association (1998) *Defining Effectiveness in History Using IT: Approaches to Successful Practice*, Coventry: BECTA.

Martin, A., Smart, L. and Yeomans, D. (ed.) (1996) *Information Technology and the Teaching of History*, Amsterdam: Harwood.

Teaching History (1998) 93, November. Special issue devoted to ICT.

9   History teaching, literacy and special educational needs

Wendy Cunnah

The two key issues of relevancy and complexity are major considerations for the history teacher challenged with meeting the needs of a wide range of pupils in the inclusive classrooms of the future. This chapter examines why history is perceived to be a difficult subject, by making reference to the nature of the discipline and the application of learning and special-needs theory and research. The impact of such theory and research on classroom practice is analysed within the context of changing legislation on Special Educational Needs (SEN) and the National Curriculum. Finally the chapter examines the challenges posed for history teachers in the inclusive environment of the schools of the future.

History for adults, the able or all?

Thirty years ago, predominant views of the nature of history and how best to teach it were exacerbated by a 'medical' interpretation of the nature of learning difficulties. As a consequence of these views, history was viewed as an academic discipline that presented insurmountable difficulties for pupils in relation to historical ideas, historical evidence and motivation (Husbands 1996: 8). In 1967 the Plowden report stated that 'History … is an adult subject. How then can it be studied by children without it being so simplified that it is falsified?' (Central Advisory Council for Education 1967: 25–6, cited in Sylvester 1994: 14).

Such scepticism concerning the ability of young pupils to cope with history was based on Piagetian theories of learning, which suggest that children think differently from adults and older adolescents. Consequently, children's intellectual development progresses through stages and it is not until they reach adolescence (about the age of eleven) that they are capable of 'formal operational thought' (Piaget 1962). As a result of such thinking it was thought that some pupils were limited in their ability to understand the more complex and abstract aspects of history, so that the accumulation of facts was all that could reasonably be expected from them. Consequently, history teaching was dominated by 'the great tradition' where the role of the school history teacher was to help pupils learn a body of knowledge about the past (McAleavy 1998: 11).

History teachers influenced by a Piagetian framework of cognitive psychology were also subject to contemporary legislation and philosophy in relation to pupils with SEN. Until the Warnock report (DES 1978b) the application of the 1944 Education Act meant that pupils with learning, sensory and physical difficulties were categorised according to their 'disability' and consequently conceptualised within a model that focused on their own deficiencies (Lindsay and Thompson 1997: 5). External factors like the quality of teaching received were not seen as a direct cause of difficulty. The medical terminology 'disability' that was applied to such pupils meant that they were seen as requiring educational 'treatment', hence the focus of learning for such pupils was a narrow skill-based curriculum. Consequently, it was felt that there was little place for the study of an academic subject like history, which many researchers felt was inappropriate for mainstream pupils. Wilson commented that 'History ... cannot be taught to these (ESN-s) [educationally sub-normal] children because they function at an early level of development' (Wilson 1985: 4).

However, in the 1970s advocates of a 'New History' emerged, who associated many of the problems in history with the type of content taught and the didactic 'memorising of facts' style of teaching and learning prevalent in the subject. In 1972 the SCHP advocated that pupils 'do' history in the same way as historians rather than 'receive' it as a body of knowledge. As such, it adopted a Brunerian approach to learning theory, which emphasised that 'Any subject can be taught effectively in some intellectually honest form to any child at any stage of development' (Bruner 1960: 13). It questioned the view based on Piagetian thinking that considered some young pupils as incapable of formal operational thinking.

Contemporary research into the learning of history demonstrated that pupils can form abstract concepts like independence, conquest, colonialism and capitalism (Booth 1978, cited in Culpin 1994: 135). Also, pupils who are taught differently in history may well make progress very differently (Shemilt 1987). This research suggested that the kind of thinking required for the study of history is possible if appropriate teaching strategies are employed and that it is often teachers' failure to recognise the challenges related to the study of history, rather than the limitations of pupil thinking, that restricts progress in worthwhile school history (Dickinson and Lee 1984a). Consequently, the question that began to emerge was not 'should we teach history?' but 'how should we teach history?'

Alongside these changing views about the nature of pupil learning in history, a radical transformation of the way in which pupils with SEN were viewed and educated was taking place. The Warnock report inspired new thinking and led to a radically different approach to special-needs education. The report stated that, with 20 per cent of pupils likely to experience some form of SEN at some stage in their school career, SEN would become an essential ingredient of all teaching, not just that in special schools. The medical term 'disability' was discarded in favour of 'learning difficulty', as the specific focus should be on the 'needs' of a child, not any inherent 'disability'. Consequently, a 'needs' rather than a 'deficiency' model of SEN emerged where the onus was on the classroom teacher to meet the needs of such pupils because, although the purpose of educa-tion is the same for all pupils, individuals require different help in order to achieve the same goals (DES 1978b).

The implications of the Warnock report were crucial for classroom teachers: with the vast majority of pupils with SEN being educated in mainstream class-rooms, pupils would necessarily be educated with their peers and, consequently, follow a similar curriculum to them. Not only was special needs changing its focus from problems 'within child' to the responsibility of classroom teachers to meet individual needs, but learning theory was providing evidence that pupils could grasp complex historical concepts at a young age if taught in an appro-priate manner. The implications of such changing philosophy were immense for teaching and learning in history, and their impact was enhanced by the intro-duction of National Curriculum history.

The National Curriculum's requirement that pupils are entitled to a broad, balanced, relevant and differentiated curriculum, and should have access to that curriculum, again emphasised the need to provide for the needs of all children. The Education Act of 1993 introduced *The Code of Practice on the Identification and Assessment of Special Education Needs*, which stated that most pupils should have their needs met in the mainstream without a statutory assessment or statement (DfE 1994). Thus, the responsibility for addressing needs lies with the school and, more specifically, the classroom teacher. Clearly such radical changes led to some apprehension amongst teachers who felt ill-equipped to teach the complex knowl-edge, skills and concepts of history to pupils with SEN, and many teachers found the National Curriculum more appropriate for able pupils and relatively inappro-priate for teaching the less able (Phillips 1993: 346–7).

However, the revised National Curriculum History Order reduced content and provided a much more flexible framework within which teachers could operate; it emphasised that the subject should be made accessible to 'the great majority of pupils in the Key Stage, in ways appropriate to their abilities' (DfE 1995: 1). The following section examines how history teachers have used this flexibility to adopt a variety of teaching and learning approaches and strategies to meet the needs of all pupils.

Differentiation: resolving the mismatch?

An effective model of SEN must take account of both 'within child' and 'envi-ronmental' factors, and the ways in which they interact, because it is the 'relative influence of each factor which is important' (Lindsay and Thompson 1997: 10). Consequently, presenting the same history curriculum content to all children may result in some pupils being faced with work that is too easy or too difficult, so teachers should differentiate curriculum content and use a variety of teaching strategies in order to overcome some of these difficulties. Differentiation can be defined as the process of matching activities to pupil need; that is, adapting the curriculum, where inappropriate, to suit the needs of particular groups or individuals. Some see this approach as an attempt to devise strategies that overcome difficulties related to a mismatch between the characteristics of some children and the curricular arrangements made for them. Hence support is directed towards helping the child to meet the needs of the system or modifying the system to accommodate a range of pupils (Ainscow 1998: 8–9).

The two most popular approaches to differentiation have been by task or outcome. Differentiation by task involves the teacher preparing different tasks to suit the needs of individuals; for example, in a history lesson based on source investigation, some pupils may be provided with fewer sources, less complex and demanding written sources or more pictorial sources than more able pupils studying the same topic. Differentiation by outcome involves the use of open-ended activities that provide pupils with the opportunity to respond in different ways; for example, in an extended writing task more able pupils would be expected to write with greater detail, analysis, depth and complexity than other pupils completing the same task. These approaches are not mutually exclusive, as teachers may use a combination of both approaches because 'Every instance of differentiation by outcome depends on the setting of an appropriate task, and every attempt to differentiate by task will inevitably lead to different outcomes' (Ainscow 1998: 8–9).

However, while the design of particular activities is important in ensuring the needs of individuals are met, of greater importance to successful differentiation is the 'skill with which the teacher manages the classroom and learning', so that the focus should be on the establishment of an orderly, hard-working environment, on informal circulation and intervention to prevent difficulties, the quality of whole-class teaching and using support staff effectively (McAleavy 1994: 154). Consequently, differentiation is concerned with effective teaching for all rather than the more mechanistic issues related to worksheet or question design. Crucially, it is 'lively, imaginative and flexible teaching' that enables pupils to 'think and talk through their way to forming concepts' (Booth 1978, cited in Culpin 1994: 135).

Hence, the challenge for history teachers is to move away from the 'differentiated worksheet model' that still exists in some schools, and which is based on 'task' and 'outcome', as differentiation by outcome leads to a reinforcement of low expectations of pupils with SEN and the same is true of differentiation by task as pupils realise that they have the easy task (O'Brien 1998: 150). Crucially, it does not challenge teachers to examine the learning environment as a whole, or the actual process of learning. Clearly the implication is that the adaptation of a worksheet is an inappropriate and inadequate view, as a programme of learning based on worksheets is 'laborious for the teacher' and 'unlikely to excite and motivate pupils' (NCC 1993c: 70). Successful differentiation includes a full range of teaching approaches that allow the opportunity to meet the range of pupil needs, including effective formal teaching that inclusively involves and engages all pupils. Such an approach may include a well told story or the use of effective questioning techniques that provide access and structure to history work. Other approaches should include pair-work, group-work, discussion, debate, local studies, role-play, use of audio-visual aids, ICT and drama (Curriculum Council for Wales 1991, 1993). Teachers also need to be aware of the limitations of some resources, particularly textbooks, and be prepared to use a range of different resources to suit the needs of a variety of pupil abilities.

Thus, it is essential to beware of using National Curriculum terminology like 'access' and 'differentiation' as 'technicist concepts', which suggest that the curriculum is a finite thing that can be 'processed and regulated like a machine' (Thomas *et al.* 1998: 36). Such an approach cannot make the curriculum accessible, but what is needed is an inclusive approach that increases opportunities for all children to learn. Successful differentiation can only occur when teachers, first, believe that all children can learn and, second, are willing to provide an environment of mutual responsiveness in which high expectations and reward for achievement exist. Furthermore, the effectiveness of differentiation depends on the willingness of teachers to continue their own learning through continued professional development and critical reflection on their own classroom practice. Thus, the challenge is for teachers to question what they are doing and why they are doing it .

Thinking through difficulties: facing the challenge

Some suggest that the decline in history has come about because of student perceptions of the difficulty of the subject (Lomas 1998: 6). Consequently, it is essential to adopt a perspective that considers the limitations of the history curriculum in relation to the difficulties it presents, rather than focusing on 'within child' limitations. The result of such an approach implies that changes introduced to help low achievers will actually benefit *all* pupils. It follows from such an argument that if teachers are to plan for differentiation then they should be aware of the difficulties presented by the subject, and able to manage strategies that recognise pupil strengths and capabilities, in order to ensure provision for educational development (Harrison 1997: 141).

One of the most important factors here is literacy as 'high standards in history and in literacy are necessarily intertwined' (Hoodless 1998: 1). Language is the 'symbolic medium through which we can communicate our understanding of abstractions, of which the past is a part' so teaching and learning of history is heavily dependent on language skills, particularly because history is retained, recorded and transmitted through the use of language:

> At any level, speaking, listening, reading, reference skills and writing frequently all play a part in the process of historical enquiry, the use of sources, historical thought and understanding and in the communication of historical findings. Indeed, it would be difficult to develop in children the process skills of history without the extensive use of this entire range of language skills.
>
> (Hoodless 1998: 2)

Vygotsky highlighted the role of language as 'mediator' in the thinking process; he believed that human development is 'intrinsically social and educational' and that 'children undergo profound changes in their understanding by engaging in joint activity and conversation with others' (cited in Harrison 1997: 145). Pupils' progression and development in historical knowledge, understanding and skills is essentially related to their ability to use language (SCAA 1997b: 1). Consequently, the spoken word is the foundation upon which literacy skills are built, so that progress in writing skills is dependent upon language learned first through speaking.

The nature of language can be part of the process of constructing historical understandings of the past; the problem is that historians often use language that is not literal or apparent and in ways that produce obstacles for the learner. Consider the use of the concept of 'Church' without adequate teacher explanation and the resultant image of the local Baptist chapel that would spring to immediate mind for some pupils. Thoughtless use of the term 'political party' may conjure up images of politicians at a disco for some pupils! Clearly teachers need to be aware of the dangers of making the subject more abstract than needed. Also, the language of time is part of the organising principle of history (that is, terms like millennium, century and decade) but pupils are confronted by the limitations of their own experience of time so that 'Teacher talk and the way teachers use talk is of crucial importance to the way pupils learn' (Husbands 1996: 34–5).

Teachers therefore need to provide pupils with opportunities to understand aspects of language; pupil talk is also important as it gives pupils the opportunity to explore language. Hence, the need for using exploratory talk to facilitate learning, enabling pupils to deal with new knowledge and to develop their ideas, so that they can progress from oral to written language skills (Curtis and Bardwell 1994: 170). History is an excellent context for developing such discussion skills, for example sharing and exchanging views in a question and answer setting or a more formal debate. It is essential that all pupils have the opportunity to participate in such discussions (Curriculum Council for Wales 1993: 15). Another effective approach to a 'talk-centred' approach is group-work, as pupils taught in an interactive group-work setting use much more analytical language than those taught in a teacher-dominated approach (Wray 1990). This may include pupils working in small groups to identify different interpretations of an event or reaching some consensus; for example, as part of continuing work on the English Civil War, pupils could be asked to decide whether Cromwell deserved the title 'democrat' or 'dictator'. Thus, task-focused group-work gives pupils the opportunity of 'doing, thinking, visualising, feeling and verbalising' and it is the interaction of these processes that is essential to the learning process as they enable pupils to 'shape meaning' and to develop the concepts and the language to express them (Curtis and Bardwell 1994:173). Role-play is another means of helping pupils to understand different perspectives of the past and to communicate historical understanding. Small groups of pupils could examine the circumstances surrounding the execution of Charles I. They could then, in role, explore the range of political and religious ideas and attitudes related to this event.

However, it is very difficult to develop interpretative understandings of history where 'transmission-derived' teaching approaches dominate or where history is 'preconstructed by the textbook or the teacher' (Husbands 1996: 34–5). While there is 'immense potential value' in speaking for pupil learning most classrooms are dominated by teacher talk (Farmer and Knight 1995: 66). This implies the need for teachers to be sensitive to the way pupils speak and how they use language themselves so that the classroom becomes a place for using language to explain ideas, rather than simply to describe outcomes. This is so that the emphasis is on having and exploring ideas about the past, because 'Words, for both teachers and pupils, are the most potentially powerful tool we have in thinking about history' (Husbands 1996: 97).

Hoodless analyses the difficulties associated with reading and writing in history thus: 'the conceptual demands upon the reader of historical writing are frequently very great, requiring an understanding of a bygone age in which different values and assumptions underlay interactions and events' (Hoodless 1998: 5). Pupils also experience difficulties related to awareness of time and manipulation of time in literature, and to the technical demands of reading documents and history texts with high readability levels. It is clear that, in a subject like history, reading difficulties may result in pupils being restricted in the range of historical work that they can undertake. However, history does provide opportunities for pupils to develop their communication skills if texts are made accessible; for example, pupils can be given a set of techniques to enable them to focus on key issues including highlighting text, sequencing activities, cloze procedure and representing information (NCC 1993c: 73). If it is true that in this 'National Year of Reading' up to 20 per cent of pupils fail to read with confidence and the result is failure, frustration and disaffection (Townsend 1998: 129–33), as 'writing is closely related to reading – the two activities reinforce each other' (DfEE 1997 and 1998: 5), the consequences for history teaching are significant.

The study of history is heavily dependent on written language skills as it 'relies heavily on handling, understanding and interpreting evidence, much of which is written' (Curtis and Bardwell 1994: 167).

Key Element 5 of the current History Order states that 'Pupils should be taught: to communicate with increasing independence in a variety of ways, including extended writing, visual and oral presentations' (DfE 1995). Pupils are therefore required to communicate the results of their historical study orally, visually and in writing, so the need for language skills is very significant. History teachers have often responded to the assumption that history is difficult for low attainers by emphasising oral history, visual sources, and historical sources that depend on less written language skills for pupils with SEN. However, oral history and visual sources are no less complex than written sources in relation to the historical concepts they contain, so it is inappropriate to provide different types of history for different needs, as the aims and objectives of the history curriculum should be common regardless of the ability of pupils (Curtis and Bardwell 1994: 167).

Although all types of writing have their place in history education, if pupils are to make progress in the critical historical thinking required at Key Stage 3 and GCSE, analytical and discursive writing is essential. It is because analytical and discursive writing is difficult that many teachers believe that lower attainers cannot construct written analyses or explanations and are consequently doomed to fail (Counsell 1997: 7). Many of the difficulties pupils experience with extended writing are related to their inability to 'join up' their thinking (Byrom 1997: 7). The factors that present challenges to all pupils are related to memory and concentration, which result in lower-ability pupils losing sight of the question being asked. These are particularly difficult for pupils with SEN and often lead to such pupils' writing deteriorating into 'indiscriminate copying or a drift into irrelevance' (Byrom 1997: 7). This is because they do not have the necessary memory and concentration to consider several ideas and sources and 'join up' their thinking concerning them (Counsell 1997: 13–16). Pupils with SEN also find it difficult to select relevant and appropriate material for an enquiry or to describe, analyse or explain because they have not been taught the need to sort; they also have difficulties moving from the general to the particular and vice versa so that using evidence to substantiate a position is difficult. Also, 'the language of discourse' is often not available to low attainers and they find linking ideas problematic because they do not have adequate language to demonstrate the relationship of one idea to another – they have to be empowered to do this (Byrom 1997: 7).

Pupils can be effectively empowered to confront the organisational problems of any enquiry. Each enquiry should act as a springboard towards extended writing, encouraging pupils to find relevance and order (Byrom 1997). Hence, it is essential that topics are taught and learned in a way in which pupils are given the opportunity to progressively develop their historical knowledge and skills, thus extending confidence and building structures that ensure access to challenging tasks. Some pupils are unsure of where to start and how to start in relation to structured, written argument, so that they find sentence and overall text structure difficult; one solution is providing a scaffold or writing frame around which pupils can build their own line of argument (Mulholland 1998: 17). In addition to problems with structure, children also have problems with style so sentence starters or paragraph starters help pupils find the right language with which to link up their ideas; for example, in examining the cause of Henry VIII's break with Rome, pupils could be given sentence starters encouraging them to write paragraphs related to religious, political, personal and financial reasons for the event. A final paragraph would allow pupils to express their view on the relative importance of each cause. Such an approach allows pupils to analyse different types of causes and gives the opportunity for more able pupils to make links and connections between different types of causes or examine the nature of long and short-term causes. Thus, differentiation in history should take place through an inclusive process of scaffolding that provides support for the more able through activities that enrich knowledge and conceptual understanding, or create a more complex organisational framework (Byrom 1977: 7).

It is clear that pupils' perceived difficulties in history, with reference to the amount of reading and writing involved, highlight the need for writing that has purpose and structure, and which leads on to more analytical work (Lomas 1998: 6). This can be done through building discussion and sharing of ideas into written work. The work of Lewis and Wray (1994) endorses such an approach to using writing frames in order to enable pupils to think about appropriate discourse structure. Pupils can be taught such structures in such a way as to develop independent writing skills (Bereiter and Scardamalia 1987, cited in Mulholland 1998: 19).

In summary, it is only through history teachers analysing difficulties that they can begin to develop creative approaches to helping pupils to achieve higher levels of performance and so that pupils can write analytically and critically, whatever their ability, if the appropriate help is provided. Once difficulties pupils face have been identified it is possible to design strategies to overcome them, by providing pupils with the necessary 'scaffolding' to enable them to succeed at complex historical writing activities (Counsell 1997: 17–20). Hence, with appropriate strategies pupils can be moved on to examine more complex abstract terms, and effective teaching approaches make difficult terms accessible for low attainers and also challenge the more able to write more analytical accounts.

Clearly history presents many challenges to teachers and pupils alike. However, it is evident that research has shown that teachers who are aware of these difficulties and are able to adopt a reflective and dynamic approach to intervention are the most likely to improve learning for all pupils in their classes, whether low or exceptionally high achievers. In the inclusive schools and classrooms of the future such an approach can be the only way forward if we are to avoid a return to a 'deficit' conceptualisation of learning difficulty.

Challenges for aspiring history teachers

History is a subject which is accessible and has relevance for all pupils, including those who have learning difficulties. It has the potential to enrich the curriculum and provide many interesting contexts in which learning can take place (Carpenter *et al.* 1996: 73).

Such a positive view of school-based history poses many challenges for the history teacher in relation to inclusive practice and the future of history as a lively, relevant and challenging aspect of the curriculum. First, it is clearly essential that pupils who are labelled as 'different' receive provision based on need, and not on learning difficulty. This forces history teachers to examine the whole learning environment in the schools and history classrooms of the future. Hence, the need to focus on what is wrong with the school, rather than what is wrong with the child, as it is only a 'needs focus' that will allow this to take place and 'describe a positive route into the learning and teaching process' (Ainscow 1998: 70–5). Thus, the need to move away from a perspective that explains educational differences in terms of individual characteristics of pupils, whether that be disability, social background or psychological attributes. Related to this is the need to ensure that differentiation does not degenerate into a negative and devaluing process, where inequality and injustice prevail, for those labelled as 'different'. A positive view of 'difference' recognises 'what is relevant to an individual's learning development and needs' (Norwich 1994: 293).

Second, and related to the above, is the need for history teachers to be aware of the difficulties presented by the subject for all pupils, particularly in the area of literacy. Also, that they are prepared to adopt teaching strategies and approaches that provide the necessary 'scaffolding' to enable all pupils to make progress in history. Such an approach should include:

- an awareness of the language demands of the subject and the ways in which teacher and pupil talk can provide access routes into written language skills;
- an acknowledgement that low achievers can grasp demanding concepts if concrete everyday examples are used, which relate to their own experiences and provide a bridge into understanding historical events;
- the availability of a range of teaching and learning strategies that motivate, develop discussion skills and provide a dynamic and interactive teaching environment;
- the development of specific structures and writing frames to enable all pupils to write analytically and discursively;
- a belief that all pupils can make progress in history if taught in an appropriate manner.

Third, if we are to meet the needs of all pupils in an inclusive environment then 'we need to adopt reflective and dynamic approaches to intervention' (Bayliss 1998: 76). Three principles underpinning successful learning in history are identified by Byrom as motivation, rigour and appropriate pace, so that 'the inspirational teacher must be empowered with the wow! factor to prepare pupils for an inspirational historical journey', and the well told story, read with 'lively exaggerated intonation', is an essential ingredient for memorable understanding and making history accessible for low attainers (Byrom 1998a: 1). Imaginative, creative, motivating strategies represent good history teaching for all children, not just those with SEN. There is no simple formula for the most appropriate approach to teaching history to pupils with SEN. The key issue is not necessarily training or experience, but effective history teaching, which inspires and motivates all pupils in the history classroom. The crucial issue is a focus on curricular organisation and practice as provided for all pupils, rather than a specific focus on the few. 'The task means continually seeking to improve overall conditions for learning with difficulties acting as indicators of how improvements might be achieved' (Ainscow 1998: 9). Teachers adopting such an approach are likely to encourage enquiry as a means of achieving improvement.

Fourth, the creation of history classrooms that can foster the learning of all children will only occur when teachers become more reflective and critical practitioners, capable and empowered to investigate aspects of their practice with a view to making improvements (Ainscow 1998: 11). Clearly, history teachers need to learn themselves, so there is a need for commitment to professional development. Classrooms are the most vital resource for 'on-the-job INSET', as reflection on classroom interactions enables teachers to learn from them, teachers learning to ask what they are doing and why (O'Brien 1998: 150). Consequently:

> progress towards the creation of schools that can foster the learning of all children will only occur where teachers become more reflective and critical practitioners, capable of and empowered to investigate aspects of their practice with a view to making improvements. Only in this way can they overcome the limitations and dangers of deficit thinking.
>
> (Ainscow 1998: 11–12)

Fifth, history teaching is more demanding than ever before and the increasing diversity of the school population presents varying challenges to teachers, so that 'Teachers' continuing professional development is essential to meet the ever-changing needs of students in today's schools' (Swafford 1998: 54). The development of an inclusive curriculum is doomed to failure without increased training for staff, some of whom may find 'the critical mass of the inclusive curriculum' too much (O'Brien 1998: 151).

Finally, other socio-political issues place barriers to the road to full inclusion. Schools judged according to league tables may view pupils with learning difficulties as a threat and 'A society that places such market-force ideology as the highest aspiration of its education system reinforces an image of disability and learning difficulty as pitiful and hopeless' (O'Brien 1998: 151).

Principles of exclusivity will not give way to inclusive and democratic practice. If the conclusions of Lomas (1998: 9) are correct, and low attainers are the least likely to study history post-14, history teachers must consider how to make history accessible, interesting and challenging for all because:

> History ... is a lively, challenging, indeed thrilling subject which deserves – and indeed I would say has – to be at the centre of any well balanced curriculum ... the primary purpose of education is to produce well-rounded and sensitive human beings. If that is indeed our belief history must be central to the education of our children.
>
> (Davies 1998: 5)

Questions

1   Differentiation can be viewed as a positive approach that aims to adapt the whole learning experience to meet the needs of pupils and so enhance learning. However, it can be viewed as a negative enforcement of 'difference' as pupils are necessarily treated unequally and consequently devalued. Consider the merits and challenges associated with such an approach to meeting the needs of pupils with SEN.

2   Consider the view that schools can only move towards a culture in which the learning of all children is improved when teachers become reflective and critical practitioners. What are the implications for history teachers and how can such an attitude impact positively on the history classroom?

3   Davies claims that 'History is essential; nothing less' (Davies 1998: 5) because education should be concerned not only about training pupils in specific skills, but also about their fulfilment as human beings and contribution to society. Can history realistically achieve these aims for all pupils, regardless of ability?

4   To what extent can current practice and philosophy in relation to SEN be viewed as a 'deficit' conceptualisation of learning difficulty?

Further reading

Clark, C., Dyson, A. and Millward, A. (eds) (1998) *Theorising Special Education*, London: Routledge.
   This is an invaluable analysis of the impact of SEN theory and research on classroom practice.

Counsell, C. (1997) *Analytical and Discursive Writing at Key Stage 3*, London: Historical Association.
   This is an excellent summary of practical approaches to structuring written work in history in order to provide access and progression.

Evidence Interpretation (1998) *Teaching History* 91.
   The entire edition is of immense value for examining effective approaches to teaching history in the context of appropriate research and theory.

Hoodless, P. (1998) *History and English in the Primary School: Exploiting the Links*, London: Routledge.
   A useful and thorough examination of the way in which history is inextricably linked with literacy.

10 Thinking and feeling

Pupils' preconceptions about the past and historical understanding

Chris Husbands and Anna Pendry

Introduction

> I don't know what I would have done because after all Mary was related to her and I wouldn't kill my cousin even if she was plotting against me. I would have tried to do something to stop her but if I hadn't of been able to stop her I would of been dead so I don't know. I might of called a family and friends meeting to see what they thought I should do in this situation.

Stacey, a Year 8 pupil wrote this in response to a task set on the execution of Mary, Queen of Scots. The class had re-enacted the trial of Mary, and had concluded, like Elizabeth in 1587, that she should be executed. For homework, the teacher had asked the class to explain in writing why Elizabeth had reached this conclusion, and then asked them to explain what, in Elizabeth's place, they would have done. Stacey has *tried* to explain what she makes of a task that is in many ways beyond her comprehension; thus, the deliberations on Mary, Queen of Scots become, in Stacey's account, rather like the tribulations of a soap opera cast: Mary and Elizabeth were cousins and this, perhaps more than the high politics of religion and the Spanish threat, shape the narrative for Stacey, giving her a point of reference against which to measure her own thinking.

In this chapter we want to explore the relationships between the work pupils produce, the tasks they are set, and just one aspect of the preconceptions they have that are relevant to their study of the past. We do so drawing on work, again on the Tudors, produced by Year 8 pupils. First, we present two pieces of work written by 12-year-old pupils on religious changes in sixteenth-century England. We analyse the work, and then consider the relationship between the work completed and the classroom tasks that were set. Finally, we draw together the ideas from the pupils' work and the classroom context to highlight implications for classroom practice.

Pupil writing and historical understanding: sixteenth-century religion

Example 1: Kate

I'm telling you this so you can realise what life was like for us between 1540 and 1580. Henry was Catholic so all the churches were all bright and grand. Henry wanted to divorce Ann Boleyn but as he was a Catholic he couldn't so he turned Protestant and turned all the churches into cheap, empty buildings. Also he could divorce Ann Boleyn and when he managed this he then turned back to Catholic and changed all the churches into Catholic churches again putting everything back in and making them bright and grand again.

Under Edward the church goes Protestant and English churches were plain

When Henry died Edward his son became King. When Edward became King he turned Protestant. He then changed all the churches Protestant so that they all went bare and poor again. He also changed the Holy Book to English and it was not easy to learn believe me.

Not many people wanted to be Protestant because they were Catholic. When Edward turned Protestant he got rid of all the crosses and anything to do with Christ or Jesus.

Mary turns Church back to Catholic

When Mary became Queen she was Catholic so because she was Queen she had the power to then change the Protestant churches back into Catholic churches where all the writing in the Holy Book turned back into Latin and it was easier to read. The churches turned grand and bright and everyone who betrayed her was killed.

Inside the church we had to get rid of the table and put an altar in instead. We had to get rid of the normal glass windows and put in stained glass windows, we had to get rid of the Royal Arms, put the statues back in again and then we had to put a statue of the Virgin Mary back in again.

Queen Elizabeth and the Church of England

When Mary died Elizabeth became Queen. She would then burn everyone who betrayed her or her Court. The churches then went plain again.

Conclusion

> From this I have learned that different kings and Queens have different ideas on religion and churches and what they expect to find in their churches. Some liked to have the church nice and bright but others thought that the churches should not be bright but should be plain because of what they follow.

Kate has tried hard to do what she was asked, and plot the religious changes in the sixteenth century. She has included a great deal of factual information, much of which is accurate and is correctly sequenced in chronological order. Her writing has a deliberate structure and she has divided it up in a way that demonstrates her awareness of important aspects of extended writing. She word processed her work, and to give it a touch of authenticity used an 'olde English' font: a real attempt to present her work well. But she has found it impossible to put herself into the past: she tries at the outset, essentially through the use of the first person, but finds it impossible to sustain – even at the level of syntax. Although she has evidenced a basic grasp of contextual material, she has not been able to demonstrate historical *understanding*. The sixteenth-century world is too remote, and her own approach too immature for her work, despite its merits, to carry conviction.

Example 2: James

> I am going to tell you about the religious changes in my lifetime. First, when I was but a child in the reign of great King Henry to now under the power of her Majesty Elizabeth, chosen by God she was.

> Now when I was but five years old, was when it all began. It is very faint and I can vaguely remember it. The news spread quick that the king has broken from Rome and he had sent his men to destroy the local monastrie. It was a terrible sight, all the wonderful statues being smashed and the jewels, gold and silver being taken away. Monks were dragged away and punished for supporting the Pope. Animals and food were taken away, within a few days all was left was an empty shell.

> Later that year my father bought a copy of the Bible, all in English it was. I can remember it cost him a whole weeks pay to get that back.

> Just 8 years later our king died leaving his son Edward to the throne. Edward was Protestant and he made many changes, and I can remember them well. First he made all the services in English so they could be under-stood also we had to pray in English as well. Priest could marry and no longer had to wear fancy clothes. This really got up the nose of many Catholics you know. Edward also painted over murals and removed all the

decoration in our local church this caused uproar. Then after just 6 years he died.

That year the church turned back to Catholic after the crowning of his sister Mary. I can remember also the burnings, anyone who remained Protestant was killed. Many were burned in our village. I watched one of those burnings, it remains vivid in my mind. Everyone stood watching as a man with a lighted faggot stepped up in the middle stood two villagers strapped to the post. The man with faggot stooped down and lit the fire. Cries of pain issued from the villagers, the smoke was thick and smelt of burning flesh as it rose. Many of their friends stood by the fire feeding on to it more wood to make them burn quicker and ease them of their pain as guards pushed them back. What a terrible sight it was to behold and I hope I shall never see such a thing again.

My father had to destroy his Bible only to regret that he didn't hide it away because only 5 years later Mary died and our great Queen Elizabeth was put on the throne.

During the next few years the church changed a lot and our new church was formed, Elizabeth wanted no more deaths over religion so she made a compromise that she was the dictator so some strong Catholics believed that the Pope was still head of the church in England. She made the church so the Catholic decoration remained with the Protestant things in the church but the services were now in English. Over the last few years there has been a lot of change but remember those kings and queens have only joined religion that helped them most.

James's work, more sophisticated than Kate's, exhibits a number of strengths. He is able to deploy some important writing conventions: the piece uses paragraphs and there are a variety of sentence structures. The piece has an overall structure. The opening sentence indicates the scope of the piece, and the final paragraph attempts a summary. These strengths are important, and will help James to organise more complex writing about history, and other subjects, later in his school career. There is also some attempt at genre writing: he adopts some phrasings and writing conventions that are deliberately chosen to create an impression that this piece is not written in the last years of the twentieth century. For a 12-year-old, he is able to marshal a considerable amount of accurate information. It is correctly sequenced, and there is, underlying the piece, a sense of historical *process*. There are cross-references between historical events. Finally, and importantly, James has clearly done what he was asked to do: he has created an account by trying to put himself into it, and he has tried to reconstruct a *sense* of what the events witnessed *meant*. In one way this sense of the historical perspective is at the core of the enterprise of teaching history;

however, as we shall see, one of the problems even for James, as for Kate, is that the act of 'putting themselves into' their work is problematic.

Pupils' understandings and preconceptions: an analysis

All these pupils – Stacey, James and Kate – are struggling to make sense of complex material, which, recent research suggests, presents significant cognitive demands (Ashby, Dickinson and Lee 1996): they are exploring change over a time-scale longer than their own lives and in a remote time. They are exploring political and religious ideas that, to the twentieth-century mind, appear abstruse. Each of them in different ways is defeated by the conceptual difficulty of the task. James is confused by the Elizabethan Settlement, but, equally, misunderstands the Marian Counter-Reformation. At root, like Kate, he seems not to understand the significance of religion for early modern people.

The struggle to generate genuine historical understanding in the classroom has been addressed by teachers and academics over the last twenty years (Barker 1978; Booth 1983, 1987; Shawyer *et al.* 1988; Husbands 1996), but, of course, it is the complexity of historical detail that is the key to the past: these were difficult tasks about a difficult period. All three pupils we considered have a reasonable sense of the informational context, and two of them attempted to construct extended accounts of aspects of the period. However, they find the ideas here extremely difficult. One reason for this lies in the genuine difficulty that pupils have in getting to grips with political and religious history: the interplay of abstract ideas and complex narratives make this sort of history especially challenging. A second reason lies in the extent to which the political and religious historical issues are also overlain by what we might call *affective* and *personal* issues rather than *cognitive* issues. By *affective* issues we mean those elements of educational development that are concerned with the feelings, beliefs, attitudes and emotions of students (Pring 1984; Lang 1995; Heimlich 1988). In their attempts to write *historical* accounts, Stacey, James and Kate structure relationships and attitudes around the personal, family and emotional worlds that they know. These worlds are different from the personal and emotional worlds of the past *both* because people in the past thought differently from us, and also because the pupils are children asked to get to grips with the mind-set of adults. There is a tendency here, and for all pupils, to back-project modern family, domestic and emotional relationships on to the past. This comes out in some of the obvious anachronisms, but also in the attempt to make sense of the past at more than an informational level. In this sense they are working against the grain of historical thinking: they grasp a sense of 'what' happened but not of the different mind-set that shaped what people think.

One of the consequences of this is the way in which the three pupils here, but especially Kate and James, attempt to structure their account – to organise it around a beginning, a middle and an end with internal coherence and a sense of 'tidiness'. Of course, every historical account, from the simplest story-book to the most sophisticated analysis, imposes on the past an order that it lacked. Gordon

Leff once pointed out that the concept of the 'Roman Empire' was not recognised by those who experienced it (see Lowenthal 1981). But these accounts establish too direct a link between high politics and provincial experience.

Pupils' historical ideas and classroom tasks

Clearly, the task required these pupils to deal with complex and abstract historical issues: for a twentieth-century adolescent there are few things more daunting than sixteenth-century religious disputes, and few historical tasks more complex than the discussion of intricate patterns of ideological and cultural change. In practice, there is some evidence that the lesson made provision for these difficulties. The work was produced by an upper-ability set of 12-year-old pupils in an English comprehensive school, following a series of lessons on religious change. Earlier work had introduced the Henrician Reformation through textbook study, a video and short-answer worksheets. Before the pupils began this piece of work there was extensive whole-class discussion. The pupils report an easy, relaxed classroom in which human and social relationships are good and teacher and pupil exchange ideas informally. Pupil errors are dealt with in a low-key way and pupils seem not to be concerned that their initial contributions might be wrong. The class teacher describes his style as 'discursive narrative': there is highly interactive classroom practice, with long whole-class discussion, in which the characteristic form is that the teacher advances a hypothesis ('I want them to see the way these things hang together and to understand the way I see it') or, which is similar, advances a narrative – a version of the past. This active teaching, advancing and connecting ideas is, for this teacher, the way in which pupils can be encouraged both to make connections between complex ideas and to understand the need for extended historical thinking and writing. Discussing the classroom work, the teacher was 'pleased' that pupils had picked up some of his own ideas about why religious change took the form it did, and also about particular significances, and that they had embellished and developed them. His written comments on the pupils' work – not reproduced here – prize above other things 'good observation': the well-made point, and the individual idea within an overall structure. It is also clear that he saw one of the purposes of this task as being the opportunity for an upper-band group to develop their writing style: it was intended to be a piece of extended writing, drawing on ideas discussed in class and books consulted out of class. Again, his discussion of the work prized those places where a turn of phrase suggests that they have thought about the Tudor context – for example, James's reference to Elizabeth as *chosen by God she was*, as compared to another pupil who wrote in twentieth-century vernacular. Most pupils in the group responded well to the task – one boy wrote twenty-five pages! But the task was not simply presented as an essay task: pupils were given a simple writing frame, and there was extensive discussion of strategies for addressing the task (see Counsell 1997; Wray and Lewis 1996).

Had these pupils been asked to simply write a narrative piece of extended writing about the religious changes in the sixteenth century they all would have done it well – and some, like James, very well indeed. But they have been asked to do more: to make sense of and communicate the motivations, experiences, reactions and actions of a range of grown-up people in the past. There is a double challenge here for young history learners: to understand not only the past but also *adults* behaviour in the past.

History teachers have typically used the concept of *empathy* to fill this gap. Ten years ago there was a considerable debate about empathy as a domain of historical thinking. Where some commentators argued that empathy placed too much emphasis on the undisciplined imagination (Skidelsky 1987), researchers developed a model of empathy that could be understood in terms of a progression from everyday to differentiated empathetic thinking (e.g. SREB 1986; Portal 1987). A key concern was that, if pupils were to 'enter into some informed appreciation of the predicaments or points of view of other people in the past' (HMI 1985: 3), they needed opportunities to acquire detailed contextual knowledge about the past, from a range of perspectives, and the capacity to project themselves imaginatively into past situations, the outcomes of which could not be known at the time. Despite its contentious nature this concept has been valuable – but it serves only to fill part of the gap created by the double challenge of needing to understand both the past and adult behaviour in it. In itself it says nothing about the 'adult' element of this challenge, and it is here that young learners' affective and emotional maturity will be important: their existing ways of making sense of the world they inhabit as young people. To some extent this is clearly an issue of maturation but to see it only in these terms suggests that young people cannot be expected to engage in genuine historical thinking. It is to fall into the Piagetian fallacy that historical understanding depends on the acquisition of certain patterns of thinking. What emerges from the accounts of Stacey, Kate and James is not that they are *cognitively* incapable of engaging with difficult historical ideas, but that their *affective* understandings need to be addressed to enhance their genuine historical understanding. An alternative would be to explore what is now known about learning and development to see in what ways teachers can, in the classroom, extend pupils' capacity to make sense of the adult world of the past.

Linking classroom history, the pupil and her ideas

Stacey, James and Kate are learning history. If, in L.P. Hartley's over-quoted phrase, 'the past is a foreign country', they have a guide-book and a phrase-book but they are not yet fluent speakers of its language. Like all learners, they need to negotiate a settlement between what they already understand about their world – the human and emotional world they bring into the classroom – the material that their teachers require them to master, and the tasks and products that provide vehicles for this mastery. As their teachers, we want this negotiation to be on certain terms: we wish their grasp of the historical information base to be secure, and to allow them to avoid grosser errors. We wish them to develop a secure cognitive grasp of the substantive concepts of historical knowl-edge that operationalise their grasp of the content. Curriculum development over the last twenty years has emphasised this aspect of the pedagogy of the subject. We might wish, also, that their work displays some sense of historicity – of the way in which people in the past spoke and behaved, and this is both a linguistic and affective set of issues. But we also need to place at the centre of our provision for their learning an understanding that as pupil-learners their emotional and affective grasp of the world is immature and insecure, and, through the learning we arrange, provide opportunities for them to develop their human understandings.

Over the last twenty years, Vygotskyian ideas have had a powerful, if often implicit, influence on classroom practice (Wood 1988). Vygotsky was a Russian psychologist whose research on learning led him to argue for the importance of the nature of the interaction between teacher (adult) and learner (pupil) or discussion between learners in developing understanding. Vygotsky argued that in order for learning to be successful, teaching needs to identify, and then operate within, what he called the learner's *zone of proximal development* (Vygotsky 1978). Vygotskyian ideas have encouraged moves towards an interactive teaching methodology, where through questioning and structured task-setting teachers identify learners' *zone of proximal development* and plan learning activi-ties that encourage development. Good teachers provide 'scaffolds' that support learners' cognitive advancement (Bruner 1974, 1986; Wood 1988; Cooper and McIntyre 1996). In recent years, academic and professional work on pupil writing has similarly emphasised the need for teachers to 'scaffold' pupil writing through the construction of writing frames, which enable pupils to manipulate complex ideas within a provided structure (Wray and Lewis 1996). Our discus-sion of these pupils' work suggests that scaffolding in the classroom and in pupil writing is a necessary but not sufficient component of classroom practice if effective learning is to follow.

Of equal significance are classroom strategies that enable pupils to unpack the emotional and affective complexity of learning about the past. For Stacey, as for the others, the past and its grown-ups remain mystifying in spite of teachers' attempts to organise and structure their work. Teacher expertise consists in mediating relationships in the classroom between historical material, classroom pedagogy and the instinctive human, emotional and affective under-standings their pupils bring.

Work in history education may have under-estimated the extent to which children's capacity to respond to historical tasks is affected by issues of emotional and affective maturation, and not just by the level of their cognitive development. Nonetheless, there is a well-established research tradition which suggests that learners' ability to make sense of new knowledge and under-standing is closely dependent on their *a priori knowledge or understanding* (Anderson 1977; Wood 1988).

Some adults, and some historical contexts, may be more accessible for learners than others – and the more that the adults are removed, especially by virtue of their position of power within any society, from the experiences and emotions of young people, the more opaque may be their worlds. In these circumstances, teacher skills and strategies in mediating learning are at a premium. The nature of the task or activity demanded of pupils will be significant. Inviting pupils to 'imagine that they are … ' or to 'put themselves in the place of … ' are phrases that actively encourage pupils to *be themselves* in the past, with all that that means in terms of making sense of that past. At best they will be able to recreate the historical context but will then 'act' as they are, drawing on their existing emotions and explanatory frameworks. Pupils' capacity and inventiveness in doing this should not be underestimated. Their written and oral work is full of examples, so that world wars – to name just one type of historical event – are explained in terms of 'getting even', a common enough pursuit for adolescents. Constructions of the past in these sorts of terms can be effectively challenged though productive classroom talk, and especially pupil-to-pupil talk (Ashby and Lee 1987; Norman 1992) in enabling pupils to articulate, examine, challenge and develop their own ideas. Teacher talk is equally important where teachers engage in *dialogue* with pupils rather than *exposition*, in Vygotskian terms where teachers act as the 'knowledgeable other' who can tease out the dimensions and perspectives that are missed by the pupils who all inhabit a young world. Effective dialogic questioning and especially sequences of higher-order questions enable teachers to feed in information and questions that force pupils to consider an issue in different terms, such as 'What would have been on Elizabeth's mind? … Remember she's the Queen … What would be the problems for someone in her sort of position?'

This type of approach resonates with recent professional work. Clear focus on developing pupil *thinking* is a common concern, for example, of the analysis by Andrew Wrenn (1998) of the ways in which GCSE pupils developed a sophisticated and mature understanding of war memorials, the work of Dale Banham (1998) on the importance of structuring writing in order to promote sophistication in understanding and the arguments of Chris Husbands (1996) for the centrality of talk in supporting thinking. Written work can play a part, with increasingly 'adult' understanding achieved through drafting and redrafting, in which initial ideas are tested out against increasing amounts of evidence. Although the use of contemporary analogies is fraught with difficulties and the potential for confusing red herrings, we recognise their value in helping pupils recognise, for example, issues of partiality in the historical record. It may be that they can be of use here too – exploring contemporary responses to high politics, for example. These approaches, mostly concerned with talking, are hardly radical and nor do they represent any departure from accepted practice in good history classrooms. But they are concerned with a focus that has not been evident in much that has been written recently about history teaching, and which may have slipped out of sight in classrooms. If children are to think historically they need to make sense of not just the past but also the adult people in it, and listening to pupils and looking at their everyday work reveals that this is an aspect of their understanding and development in which they need our support. Without such support, they are likely to continue to be overly influenced by their existing ways of thinking.

Acknowledgements

Thanks to Trevor Bennett (Head of Humanities, Reepham High School), Bill Lowe (Deputy Headteacher, Coundon Court School and Community College) and their Year 8 pupils for material and lessons on which this chapter is based.

Questions

1   Consider classroom situations in which learners must move between, or integrate, cognitive understandings about history and affective understandings of the way people think and feel. What different classroom strategies can you identify that support learners in addressing the relationship?
2   In what different ways can language support the development of thought and feeling in the history classroom? What are the implications for teachers?
3   What *preliminary* stages underpin the construction of an effective written historical account by (a) 11-year-olds, (b) 14-year-olds, and (c) 18-year-olds?

Further reading

Bruner, J.S. (1986) *Actual Minds, Possible Worlds*, Cambridge, MA: Harvard University Press.
  Bruner's book draws together many of his insights into the nature and process of learning, and reminds readers of the importance of thinking and, therefore, of the need for educators to identify and develop the world-view of their pupils.
Husbands, C. (1996) *What is History Teaching?: Language, Ideas and Meaning in Learning about the Past*, Buckingham: Open University Press.
  Husbands draws together debates about language, thinking and the nature of history as a subject. He argues for a systematic approach to the nature of history as an interpretative discipline in which language and thought inter-relate.
Mercer, D. and Edwards, N. (1994) *Common Knowledge*, Buckingham: Open University Press.
  This is an immensely important book. Drawing on exceptionally detailed classroom observation of teachers and learners, it outlines ways in which understanding emerges as a result of communicative interaction between teachers and pupils. This negotiation is neither straightforward nor unproblematic, because the negotiation of shared meaning involves a balance between presenting and sharing knowledge, between building understandings and resolving misunderstandings.

Part II

Broader educational issues and history

11 Citizenship and the teaching and learning of history

Ian Davies

Introduction

> History is a priceless preparation for citizenship.
>
> (DES 1990a: 2)

National Curriculum documentation has explicitly stated that citizenship education is a key aim for history teachers and students. Recent developments suggest that the profile of citizenship has been heightened and its significance for history education been more strongly emphasised. It is vitally important for all history teachers to respond to these imperatives. An attempt is made in this chapter to draw attention to key issues that teachers may need to consider. First, there is a discussion of the shifting status and meaning of citizenship education and in particular how it is linked to the key features of history education. Second, the challenges associated with implementing education for citizenship through history, that so far have meant that little has been achieved in classrooms as a result of explicit efforts by teachers and children, are discussed. And, finally, there is a discussion of possible ways forward.

It is necessary at the outset to make clear in general terms the meaning of citizenship that will later be discussed in more detail. According to Heater and Oliver:

> Individuals are citizens when they practise civic virtue and good citizenship, enjoy but do not exploit their civil and political rights, contribute to and receive social and economic benefits, do not allow any sense of national identity to justify discrimination or stereotyping of others, experience senses of non-exclusive multiple citizenship, and by their example, teach citizenship to others.
>
> (Heater and Oliver 1994: 8)

In considering what the above means for the work of teachers and pupils Heater has explained that 'a citizen is a person furnished with knowledge of public affairs, instilled with attitudes of civic virtue, and equipped with skills to participate in the political arena' (Heater 1990: 336). Given the above ambitious set of aims for education for citizenship there are at least three broad questions that need to be resolved. How can the previous low level of attention devoted to citizenship education be changed without overburdening teachers? How can civic engagement be developed from its current very low base without promoting an agenda that could be criticised for having an undesirably narrow political focus, and which would lead to accusations of indoctrination? And how can the value of a broad-brush approach to citizenship education that recognises the essential nature of morality, communities, identity, and so very many other issues be used without losing intellectual coherence? These questions are fundamental and policy related. They are, to some extent, preliminary to those vital pedagogical questions that relate to issues such as what content works best for different pupils, what levels of pupil thinking exist, and how can work in this field be assessed. Current efforts to develop citizenship education are to be welcomed, but in aiming 'at no less than a change in the political culture of this country both nationally and locally' (QCA 1998c: 7) the scale of the task must not be underestimated.

The status and meaning of education for citizenship

This section of the chapter has two main parts: it reflects on the extent to which history and citizenship are regarded as legitimate high-status areas; and it explores the meaning of citizenship and how it might relate to history education.

It is easy to point to high-status global research on citizenship (Torney-Purta 1996; IBE 1997); projects on education for European citizenship (Osler, Rathenow and Starkey 1996; Davies and Sobisch 1997); and Government-supported action within England and Wales, and at times more broadly within the UK (e.g. NCC 1990; Speaker's Commission 1990; QCA 1998c). Very many organisations are playing an active role (e.g. the Citizenship Foundation; the Council for Education in World Citizenship; the Values Education Council; the Politics Association). The communitarianism that is so popular within the ranks of the Labour government is acknowledged generally in the way ministers draw from authors such as Etzioni (1995), and in particular by David Blunkett's aim to develop citizenship education.

However, there is often more heat than light in these assertions, and more debate by academics and politicians than action in classrooms. When, in the past, the profile of education for citizenship has been raised it has usually been associated with a perceived sense of crisis (Stradling 1987). In recent decades citizenship education (in various guises) has been called upon as a weapon to fight the growth of political extremism in the 1970s; to overcome economic inefficiency (as the New Right strove to introduce economic diversity and an entrepreneurial spirit within a substantive moral framework) in the 1980s; and to tackle moral decline, fragmented communities and rising crime, particularly among young people, in the 1990s.

The status of history is similarly low. Although the rhetoric is highly charged as participants fight for the 'big prize' of controlling the past (Crawford 1995; Phillips 1998a), the battle, perhaps, is vicious in practice (as Henry Kissinger once said about university politics) precisely because there is so little at stake. History has for some considerable time been 'in danger' (Price 1968). The Dearing review saw no reason why history should be compulsory for pupils beyond the age of fourteen, and the announcement in early 1998 by the Labour government that primary schools were required to spend more time on numeracy and literacy clearly meant that history will no longer be a compulsory element in Key Stages 1 and 2 (for pupils aged five to eleven). The recently launched campaign by the Historical Association to save history seems very necessary, well timed and depressingly familiar. The grand rhetoric associated with both history education and education for citizenship is not matched by action by teachers in schools.

The two areas are also very similar in terms of meaning and purpose. In describing the trends in the meaning of education for citizenship and history education it should be noted that the potential for overlap between the two areas is very great indeed. Dewey, in his key work of *Democracy and Education*, believed that education utilises 'the past for a resource in a developing future' (Dewey 1966: 93). Oakeshott defined political education as 'knowledge as profound as we can make it of our tradition of political behaviour' (Oakeshott 1956: 16). Heater even went so far as to say that history and politics are 'virtually identical subjects' (Heater 1974: 1). So, while the general purpose of both areas seems remarkably similar, complementary trends can also be seen in the way the areas have been characterised. For citizenship education, prior to the 1960s, if anything was done explicitly it was in the form of factual knowledge about institutions transmitted to high-status students. By the end of the 1970s political literacy (Crick and Porter 1978) was gaining support from key figures (e.g. Slater and Hennessey 1978). It stressed that political education should be issue-focused, a broad concept of politics was to be used, procedural rather than substantive values were to be important and there was to be a concern with skills and not just knowledge or attitudes. Global education came to the fore during the 1980s and is perhaps an umbrella heading for a long list of adjectival educations: peace education, gender education, human-rights education, development education. Ideas for citizenship education arising from within the Home Office of Douglas Hurd and his junior minister at that time, John Patten (who would later become Secretary of State for Education), were initially seen as being more to do with obligations rather than rights. It developed from a concern about a declining Welfare State, a rising crime rate and a concentration on economics and consumerism rather than politics that led to the perceived need for more volunteering, particularly by younger people. There is now the possibility that citizenship education is becoming something that is rather more professionally based under the leadership of Bernard Crick, who was the principal figure in the political education movement of the 1970s. His committee has established a three-pronged approach of social and moral respon-sibility, community involvement and political literacy (QCA 1998c).

This brief summary should not be taken as a complete outline of the nature of education for citizenship. The above gives a particular view of citizenship (focusing more on politics, for example, and less explicitly on moral behaviour). It does not give a full account of the many different models that exist. Rauner (1997) has concentrated on post-national conceptions of citizenship; McLaughlin (1992) gives a model related to four key aspects of identity, virtue, political involvement and social prerequisites; and Sears (1996) gives activist and élitist conceptions. Those who have reviewed a range of models give different perspectives: Gross and Dynneson (1991) identify twelve and Heater (1990) five. For the latter, for example, the area is characterised by a combina-tion of identity and civic virtue, as well as social, civil and political citizenship. It would be possible for teachers to consider these ideas to help their thinking about citizenship. The ideas may also be useful as a framework for the sort of classroom activities that are considered later in this chapter.

In history education there has been a well-documented shift from the teaching about 'great white dead men' through to debates, for example, on the interaction between knowledge and skills. There are five areas in which a remarkable similarity between the meaning of the fields of history education and citizenship education can be seen. There has been in both areas a shift in knowledge from institutions and Politics with a capital 'P' to a concern with issue-based politics in everyday life, and a wider-lens approach through a focus on political, economic, social and cultural matters in history. There are ongoing debates in both areas concerning appropriate contexts that see work taking place on local, regional, national and global citizenships and histories. The debate on skills in both areas shifts from a narrow concentration on remem-bering information to a recognition of the importance of critical thinking. Preferred dispositions of pupils who have studied in both areas are discussed in terms of the promotion of a commitment to a tolerant, pluralistic democratic society, and so the same debates about the limits to that pluralism within a more or less relativist or universalist context can be seen. Finally, both areas see the resonance of real-world involvement by struggling over the extent to which pupils can be involved in debating or becoming practically involved in contem-porary issues. For history the debate was made explicit by Kenneth Clarke's twenty-year rule, which disallowed discussion of recent historical events. In citi-zenship education it is not hard to find evidence-free (and rather ridiculous) allegations concerning young people who are said to be exploited by teachers who are attempting to indoctrinate them (see Scruton 1985).

Implementing citizenship education through history: the problems

The challenges of developing citizenship education need not overwhelm us. Rather, the clearer identification of these tasks will make implementation more likely. It is possible to create valuable professional work.

That said, it cannot be denied that citizenship education through history is tremendously challenging. There are ambitious and, perhaps, contradictory goals. There is a chasm between the thinking of the theorists and that of teachers when the nature of citizenship is discussed. The models referred to above that have been produced by academics mean little to classroom teachers (Davies, Gregory and Riley 1997). Those involved in citizenship education need to talk with each other. The substance of what is to be implemented needs to be considered. It would be inappropriate to insist on the teaching of one form of citizenship but it cannot be acceptable for the current confusion to continue in which there seems at points to be no distinction made between key terms such as 'awareness' and 'citizenship'; 'person' and 'citizen'; 'identity' and 'nationality'. There is the unhelpful perception that politics is an adult activity.

The method chosen for implementing citizenship will always be problematic. The four nations of the UK did not in the past require a common citizenship in the same way as other countries so there is a lack of a tradition of citizenship education. Schools are seen as being unable to teach democracy by example. Teachers have not been trained for citizenship education and there are few associated career paths. The current range of advisory committees (e.g. personal, social and health education; sustainable development education; creative and cultural education; and spiritual, moral, social and cultural development) may overlap unhelpfully. It may be possible that Crick's three-pronged approach (social and moral behaviour; community involvement; political literacy) will be seen as something that is driven more by the need to operate within parameters set by politicians rather than emerging from work with teachers or from an examination of thinking about the meaning of citizenship. In this situation it may be possible that the most controversial of the three areas (political literacy) will be neglected altogether. It is vital to ensure that too many additional burdens are not placed on teachers. However, the commitment to 'specific learning outcomes for each key stage, rather than detailed programmes of study' (QCA 1998c: 22) may lead, in an area that has always hitherto escaped proper evaluation or assessment, to very little being done in practice.

The value of various approaches to education for citizenship should never be ignored: citizenship education through the ethos of the school; as a part of a modular personal and social education programme (PSE); through specific projects that may take place within the school such as a mock general election or in the community as part of efforts to help others can all be positive. However, the particular difficulties associated with working through an academic subject need to be explored. Recent work by Whitty, Rowe and Appleton (1994) show some of the very serious problems in making cross-curricular themes work:

- Some teachers feel that themes get in the way of their real work.
- Pupils at times do not know what it is that teachers are trying to do.
- Vital discussion work is often seen as a low-status non-work activity.
- So-called 'real' examples are often not genuinely from pupils' experience.

- Some subjects use 'hooks' as a preparation for pupils to understand key concepts. Pupils cannot distinguish between 'hook' and 'substance'.

When history teachers are asked to tackle education for citizenship the above problems are immediately recognisable (Davies 1997). Advocates of history often support education for citizenship but there has never been a co-ordinated effort to present relevant knowledge in an integrated and positive way. Rather, citizenship is seen at best as a goal. The quotation that began this chapter ('History is a priceless preparation for citizenship') is a good example of this gap between the characterisations of the two areas. As a result of this key difference there is often an absence of an explicit focus on politics by history teachers. Recent research seems to suggest that some history teachers may misunderstand key aspects of political learning. Even those that talk initially about the centrality of teaching citizenship through history are in fact more concerned to teach aspects of the past or to explore the nature of being human, and see citizenship as only one relatively small part of their role (Bousted and Davies 1996). For many history teachers, work on, for example, human rights as a key citizenship issue is to be kept firmly in its subordinate place. In explaining the reluctance to include such an approach one teacher involved in a project to promote citizenship though history explained:

> You see that would have led me too far away from the history really. ... There is potential ... but it's not history really. ... I mean it's not building up kind of raw ideas of historical change or causation or attitudes.

There is a need for history teachers to do more than provide an academic narrative. It is true that history teaching now explores very many vitally important issues and the need to teach, for example, an understanding of causation as shown in the above quotation is not to be questioned. However, there may exist at present a desire to understand a particular sort of narrative that avoids the posing of important questions. It would be possible for work in history classrooms to explore education for European citizenship by focusing on such issues as the existence of core European values at different points; or the degree to which Europe has become more or less integrated; or by considering issues arising from the cases that have come before the European Court of Justice. But these questions and methods tend not to be used because they are in some way deemed not to be history. Finally, there is a pressing need to recognise that teachers are perfectly capable of providing activities for pupils at an appropriate level of complexity. This rather obvious point needs to be emphasised. There is some slight evidence to suggest that, unless lesson materials are based on a teacher's own academic discipline and constructed in such a way as to show congruence with existing practice, plans will be rejected as being too difficult for pupils. Citizenship, of course, is no more difficult than any other topic. It is not acceptable that the hugely complex Roman Empire has somehow become undeniably suitable for 11-year-olds; work on dinosaurs (hardly a matter that is within concrete everyday experience) is largely for pupils aged below nine. We need not be bound by the simplistic thinking that has led to these accepted ways of working, and we should develop a way of teaching and learning about citizenship that is appropriate for pupils.

Implementing education for citizenship through history: a way forward?

There are a number of general ways forward. For example: by giving the area high status; increasing the focus on citizenship during initial and in-service teacher education; co-ordinating the various committees and advisory bodies that are active in this area through their work on academic subjects, values or community service; commissioning research that would tell us more than the very little we currently know about the way pupils think when considering the key issues related to citizenship. There are also examples of action that can be taken generally in schools that may not necessarily or directly involve the history staff (e.g. ensuring that the personal and social education programme does not show an imbalance towards the interpersonal and neglect the other necessary elements). It is possible that good political education combined with explicit articulation of issues relating to citizenship ultimately leads to good history teaching. As well as being professionally based and obviously purposeful and useful, this will help raise the status of history in schools.

Specifically, there are a number of very straightforward ways in which the history teacher can take a strong lead in the development of education for citizenship. The most obvious step is perhaps merely to ensure that appropriate content is being offered and (very importantly) that pupils are made aware, in an appropriate manner, of the purpose of this content. Earlier examples exist of how this can be done with previous formulations of citizenship education (Davies and John 1995) and the task is as straightforward with the current advice from the Crick committee (DfEE 1998: 52). Social and moral responsibility could, for example, be illustrated through a case study of the life of Anne Frank with questions being posed about the actions that were taken, could have been taken and should have been taken in particular historical circumstances. Community involvement could be illustrated through a local history project that required, for example, the gathering of evidence about the changing purpose and function of a local site that may be deemed to be worthy of redevelopment or preservation. The views of local people today could be used as a means of developing insight into the changing value (sentimental, financial and other) we place on the remains of the past. Political literacy could be illustrated very easily through an examination of the growth of political rights at particular points. Studies of the French and Russian revolutions are already very common in schools and would need little alteration to make the purpose of the work clear for developing an understanding of, for example, rights and responsibilities within a democratic society.

The four key frameworks within the Crick report (QCA 1998c): key concepts; values and dispositions; skills and aptitudes; and knowledge and understanding are illustrated below.

Key concepts

A specific example of work that could relate to the area 'Co-operation and conflict' is the cold war. That is already a vital feature of National Curriculum and GCSE work.

Contributions to conceptual understanding by history teachers can be identified in four areas. First, general political concepts (as outlined by Crick 1978) can be successfully understood through a study of history. In the SHP medicine part of the GCSE syllabus, for example, power can be explored through the Roman ability to provide public health facilities; welfare by the modern National Health Service; order by the development of the relatively stable Egyptian civilisation.

Second, pupils can gain a greater understanding of the concepts that underpin democratic machinery. The introduction and impact of factory legislation figures largely in the National Curriculum. The impact of the reform acts of 1832, 1867, 1884 and 1918 are similarly regarded as basic ground to cover. Of course, I am not suggesting that historical study will always automatically teach pupils about democratic institutions today, but it seems obvious that the examination of historical issues encourages the establishment of an increasing conceptual awareness that may be transferred between different periods of the past or to the present.

Third, particular political beliefs and ideologies can be understood. Mention has already been made of the Second World War and it would not be at all difficult to teach a series of lessons around the themes of communism, fascism and totalitarianism. The First World War can be used to develop debates around the issue of conscientious objectors. The life of Gandhi is a useful way into debates about State power and passive resistance.

Fourth, and perhaps most importantly, pupils need to know more about what could be termed the procedural concepts of history and again political material provides a very useful motivating influence. History teachers wish their pupils not to be satisfied with simple ideas such as placing emphasis on a single causal factor in an explanation of an event. Rather, there is a need to show interlocking factors in webs of causation with a consideration of unintended and intended consequences, as well as the difference between short-term and long-term issues. Work on interpretations of history seems to hold particular potential for developing insights relating to citizenship education. If pupils can come to understand that different judgements have been developed at particular points in history, then it may be possible not only to develop greater tolerance but also to recognise the forces that act upon citizens as they create specific forms of society. Many of these features are commonly included in assessment schemes for GCSE and other history courses as well as within the National Curriculum. Furthermore, it would be a major step forward if there could be an elaboration of the procedural concepts of citizenship. This would mean that citizenship would go from being an aim that was targeted by history teachers to a process in which investigations could take place to establish what it means to be a citizen. The issues involved in such a suggestion cannot be explored in depth here but guidance does exist for how further work might be undertaken (Cloonan and Davies 1998).

Values and dispositions

A specific example of the area 'commitment to equal opportunities and gender equality' is the changing roles of women, or, more narrowly focused work, on the suffragettes.

The nature of the current work on values suggests that some caution is needed before history teachers simply assume that appropriate values can be easily promoted. While some wish to promote substantive values (e.g. Bloom 1987), others regard procedural values to be more important or argue for some sort of middle way between these different positions (Jonathan 1993). Although it seems unlikely that the postmodernists have exerted much influence upon history teachers it should not be assumed that this area does not contain challenges (Davies 1996). Whilst, generally, postmodernism is a dangerous and illogical collection of diverse (and perverse) positions it should be recognised that some of its unintended consequences may be positive if space is created for the development of more critical approaches to 'official histories' (Phillips 1998b).

Skills and aptitudes

A specific example of pupils' need to 'adopt a critical approach to evidence' is surely not needed. This sort of aim is already absolutely central to the work of the history teacher. There is, however, a need to go further to ensure that politics is perceived as something that affects pupils' everyday lives and allows them to begin to develop the active skills necessary for the full enjoyment of their democratic capabilities. The skills and aptitudes noted by the Crick committee cover both cognitive and active aspects of citizenship. There is currently no research evidence available that would demonstrate that there is a simple link between active political skills and history teaching. There may though be a case for arguing that the development of cognitive historical and political skills lays the foundations for the acquisition of other skills. Further, the use of role-plays, simulations, field-work and other techniques used in history classrooms suggest that much can be done to develop an ability to present a reasoned case, orally as well as in writing, to undertake efforts at support mobilisation, and to evaluate the success of campaigns that have established specific targets. Or, as the committee recommend, 'identify, respond to and influence social, moral and political situations' (QCA 1998c: 44).

Knowledge and understanding

A specific example of 'human-rights issues' is slavery (although care would need to be taken to ensure that positive role models are developed rather than presenting particular groups in stereotypical fashion as victims). The fact that knowledge and understanding has been placed last in the list of four sections is useful. Simple information about the past or about civics should not drive the curriculum. The focus on this part of the recommendations on topical and contemporary issues is very important and can allow for the good work of history teachers to be recognised. Said comments:

> Even as we must fully comprehend the pastness of the past, there is no just way in which the past can be quarantined from the present. Past and present inform each other, each implies the other, and in the totally ideal sense implied by Eliot, each coexists with the other.
>
> (Said 1993: 2)

The wave of commemorations that are a feature of school as well as national and international life can be used positively for educational purposes. A proper sense of citizenship includes knowing about the links between the past and present.

Conclusion

It is a cause of professional concern that the links between history education and citizenship education have in real terms been neglected. The outpouring of rhetoric is a poor substitute for a few good lessons on a regular basis in all our schools. If evidence is sought for a democratic deficit the absence of such work is all that is needed. A democracy that chooses to teach history to those who will not be historians, science to those who will not be scientists and refuses to teach citizenship explicitly and professionally to those who will be (or, are already) citizens is a democracy in name only. The simple proposition that political matters will always be in evidence in schools leads to the pressing need for something to be done. The way forward is uncertain but attention to a number of features may be helpful. First, we need to aim to raise the status of work on education for citizenship by supporting current official efforts that, while certainly not perfect, may lead to the establishment of some consensus within a broad framework about its importance and its nature. Second, we need to look for a meaningful structure in which citizenship can be taught and learned in schools. This will mean giving a heavy responsibility to the history teacher, but also to others in what will hopefully lead to some sort of co-ordinated effort rather than unnecessary duplication or the development of unbalanced programmes. By doing this we must ensure that the 'harder' and potentially less acceptable elements of citizenship are not neglected. Finally, we need to find a way of making, in classroom terms, citizenship to be less of a goal and more of a process, by establishing procedural concepts that will allow for vital work to be targeted directly.

Questions

1   What are the key elements of citizenship education that need to be promoted in a democracy?
2   Why has citizenship education not yet become an explicit part of our educational work?
3   What would a good lesson on citizenship look like? What aims would it have; what subject matter would be used; and what teaching style would be appropriate?
4   How can citizenship education be assessed?

Further reading

Davies, I. and Sobisch, A. (eds) (1997) *Developing European Citizens*, Sheffield: Sheffield Hallam University Press.
Raises questions about the extent to which we are European citizens and gives examples of educational projects that promote better understanding and action towards the goal of European citizenship.

Dewey, J. (1966) *Democracy and Education*, London: Free Press/Macmillan.
A classic statement about the nature and purpose of education in a democratic society.

Heater, D. and Oliver, D., (1994) *The Foundations of Citizenship*, London: Harvester Wheatsheaf.
Probably the best and most accessible overview of the key issues that relate to citizenship.

Marshall, T.H. (1963) *Citizenship and Social Class*, London: Macmillan.
A classic statement by a sociologist who gave an overview of the development of citizenship. He emphasised that citizenship has a number of different elements that were developed at different times. Civil aspects became important in the eighteenth century; political aspects in the nineteenth century; and social aspects during the twentieth century. Marshall has been regarded as influential by those recently seeking to reform the curriculum (especially the Speaker's Commission of 1990 and the NCC in 1990, and to some extent the Crick committee).

Pike, G. and Selby, D. (1989) *Global Teacher, Global Learner*, London: Hodder & Stoughton.
There are many different conceptions of citizenship. It may be useful to look at a way of approaching citizenship education that emphasises the global and moves much further than others away from constitutions and institutions. Lynch, J. (1992) *Education for Citizenship in a Multicultural Society*, London: Cassell is similarly interesting although, unlike Pike and Selby, does not include ideas for practical work in classrooms.

Reeher, G. and Cammarano, J. (1997) *Education for Citizenship: Ideas and Innovations in Political Learning*.
A good overview of practical work including service learning.

12 'History for the nation'

Multiculturalism and the teaching of history

Ian Grosvenor

Introduction

This chapter takes as its focus the question of historical content and what should be included in the narrative of the nation with which pupils engage in schools. It begins by asking, 'What are the implications for education and history of the pluralist nature of British society?' It then considers how this pluralist nature is reflected in the National Curriculum and how an inclusive narrative of the nation might be developed. This is followed by a discussion of some of the pedagogical issues posed by the teaching of such a narrative and it ends with a consideration of the role of the history teacher in this process.

What is the multicultural challenge?

'The traditional curriculum', as the American, Paula Rothenburg has observed, 'teaches all of us to see the world through the eyes of the privileged, white, European males and to adopt their interests and perspectives as our own.' It is a curriculum that 'effectively defines this point of view as "reality" rather than a point of view itself, and then assures us that it alone is "neutral" and "objective"'. The traditional curriculum defines 'difference' as 'deficiency' and, by building racism, sexism, heterosexism, and class privilege into its very definition of reality, 'it implies the current distribution of wealth and power in society ... reflects the natural order of things' (Rothenburg 1991: B3). Rothenburg's definition of the traditional curriculum represents a succinct summary of the significant challenges that multiculturalism poses for the educational curriculum in modern industrial democracies, but it also implicitly draws attention to the central issue of power in society. Multiculturalism constitutes a challenge to the status quo.

So, to advocate a multicultural approach to education is to challenge both received knowledge and authority. Thus, in Britain in the late 1980s campaigners for multicultural education were castigated as being ideologically unsound, culpable and at variance with traditional values and beliefs, while the Conservative educational reform programme, which was in part a response to the perceived advance of the 'multicultural agenda' in schools, was presented as a way of securing traditional values and beliefs (Grosvenor 1997).

Similarly, to argue for multicultural approaches in history, for the recognition of gender, 'race', ethnicity and class, and the inclusion of a plurality of voices and viewpoints in historical narratives of the nation, is to court controversy (Phillips 1998a). History is the most political of subjects, able to arouse the most fierce partisan voices, and the call for multicultural and anti-racist history to be included in the National Curriculum for England and Wales generated fierce debate amongst historians, history teachers and in the press. For example, under the headline 'Raised voices in a very British battle', *The Times Educational Supplement* reported details of an 'intense debate' at Ruskin College, Oxford on 'History, the Nation and Schools' in which 'conservatives wanted to socialise children and restore a national identity, radicals challenged xenophobia and stereotyping, and liberals urged respect for cultural variety'. Such positions may not have been as mutually exclusive or as incompatible as they appeared, but the possibility of consensus was denied because 'of a deeply entrenched reluctance on the part of the right to give any ground at all' (*The Times Educational Supplement*, 25 May 1990).

History is always about selection 'and everybody makes the selection differently, based on their values, and what they think is important' (Zinn 1993: 8). *The Final Report of the History Working Group. History for Ages 5 to 16* (1990), which had prompted the Ruskin debate, recognised that one of the purposes of school history is:

> To contribute to pupils' knowledge and understanding of other countries and other cultures in the modern world. Education in British society should be rooted in toleration and respect for cultural variety. Studying history of other societies from their own perspectives and for their own sake counteracts tendencies to insularity, without devaluing British achievements, values and traditions.
>
> (DES 1990a: 1)

As a consequence of this stated concern for cultural pluralism the Working Group demanded that the history of non-Western societies should be studied in Key Stages 2 and 3. However, it was British history and 'British achievements, values and traditions' which dominated the curriculum that emerged for schools, with nearly 50 per cent of the content to be studied relating to the history of England, Scotland, Wales and Northern Ireland from Roman times to the present day. This 'selection' was determined by the Working Group's view of the role of history in a multicultural society: 'an ethnically diverse population strengthens rather than weakens the argument for including a substantial element of British history within the school curriculum' (DES 1990a: 184). This position was reaffirmed in the history non-statutory guidance issued in 1991 to accompany the Statutory Order, and that the aim of school history was 'to help pupils develop a sense of identity through learning about the development of Britain, Europe and the world' (NCC 1991: B1). Taken together, these two statements clearly indicate that what was valued and seen as important in terms of determining the content of history for the nation was a concern for promoting national unity, and that in this process the teaching of British history was held to be critical for identity formation in an 'ethnically diverse' society. This position was reaffirmed by the Dearing History Review Group who reported in 1995.

The history non-statutory guidance did include a brief section on 'equal opportunities and multicultural education': 'National Curriculum history requires pupils to be taught about the cultural and ethnic diversity of past societies. ... Through history pupils acquire understanding and respect for other cultures and values'. It also suggested that: 'pupils might study how women were portrayed in late nineteenth century literature and art ... or explore why textbooks contain few references to the role of black troops in World War I not to mention World War II' (NCC 1991: C18).

Nevertheless, the content of the British history units, as Martin Booth observed, gave a clear message: 'British history is essentially about the white indigenous people and is the whiggish story of the political and economic improvement of the great British people.' In short, the narrative of the nation it offered was 'the story of the dominant white majority' (Booth 1993: 79).

What is the current situation in schools?

OFSTED reports indicate that a concern for multicultural issues is not a strong feature of current schooling in England and Wales:

> 'About half our schools were giving at least a satisfactory degree of attention to the ethnic, cultural and social diversity of the societies studied' (OFSTED 1993).
> 'Understanding of different cultural traditions ... in only a few schools was there any systematic attempt at exploiting the potential of subjects' (OFSTED 1995a).
> 'Schools need to broaden their approach to history, in particular by giving more attention to more distant places and times' (OFSTED 1996a).
> 'Most schools, particularly primary schools, make insufficient provisions for pupils' cultural development' (OFSTED 1996a).
> 'Pupils' cultural development is satisfactory in most respects, but in many schools awareness of the contribution made by other cultures to British multicultural society is too low' (OFSTED 1997).

The situation may actually be worse than the reports suggest as OFSTED itself is inconsistent in its reporting. For example, the OFSTED History report, *History: A Review of Inspection Findings 1993–94* (1995), makes no reference whatsoever to ethnic or cultural diversity. The 1996 *Subjects and Standards Report, Secondary Schools* is similarly quiet. Furthermore, the Black and Asian

Studies Association (BASA), who have been very critical of OFSTED's apparent lack of concern for 'ethnic, cultural and religious diversity', reported in 1998 that 'no specific assessment is made of inspectors' knowledge of and interest in the diversity and richness of other cultures and pupils' own cultural traditions'. Finally, a research study of predominantly White secondary schools in Bedfordshire, Essex, Norfolk and Suffolk in 1998–9 fully supports BASA's concerns about multiculturalism in schools. The research found that many teachers had little or no idea of what defines an ethnic minority, what racism is or how to teach about it, and teachers admitted that their pupils left school 'ill-prepared for life in a multicultural society' (*The Times Educational Supplement*, 26 February 1999).

The significance of this data about multiculturalism in schools can best be understood by placing it in a broader social and political context. Britain has a population of 55 million. Of these, 47 million live in England, 5 million live in Scotland and 3 million in Wales. Five per cent of British people are from non-White ethnic minorities, of whom 50 per cent are South Asian and 30 per cent are Afro-Caribbean. Irish-born people in Britain number 840,000, with 640,000 from the Republic and 200,000 from Northern Ireland. The population of Jewish origin is 300,000. In Greater London 20 per cent of the population is of ethnic minority background. In Britain a third of ethnic minority people are under sixteen, compared with just a fifth of White people. The different age patterns of the British population show that in twenty years' time members of ethnic minorities will represent about one in ten of the population. Black and White children start school with similar levels of attainment, but Pakistani, Bangladeshi and Black pupils are only half as likely to obtain five or more good GCSEs as White pupils. Ethnic-minority groups have higher staying-on rates in post-16 education than the White majority, but at the same time Black children in some areas of England are fifteen times more likely to be excluded from school than their White counterparts. Between January 1991 and February 1999 twenty-five people died in Britain as a result of racist attacks. In 1988 the number of 'racial' incidents reported to the police was 4383. By 1996 this figure had risen to 12,222. The Home Office estimate that only 10 per cent of racist incidents are reported to the police (Runnymede Trust 1998; Social Exclusion Unit 1998; *The Times Educational Supplement*, 11 December 1998; *Guardian*, 24 February 1999).

It is clear from the above that as the nation enters the twenty-first century it cannot be described, if indeed it ever could, as politically and culturally indivis- ible. Britain is multicultural, multilingual and multifaith. Children have access to a range of cultural, linguistic and faith identities. What are the origins of this state of the nation? In terms of history for the nation are there different histo- ries, different narratives, and different voices hidden within the British history areas of study? Are these histories ones that offer a counter to 'the story of the dominant white majority'? These are voices that, if recognised, would form part of an inclusive history for the nation.

Can an inclusive 'history for the nation' be developed within the National Curriculum?

Kenneth Baker, Secretary of State for Education, told the Society of Education Officers in January 1987 that 'Pupils' should have:

> a well-developed sense of our national past. They need to have some feeling for the flow of events that have led to where we are, how our present political and social fabric and attitudes have their roots in the English Reformation, the Reform Bills, the Tolpuddle martyrs and the Suffragette Movement, and how our national security, our place in the world, was shaped by Waterloo and El Alamein. The selection is crucial. My concern is that so much of the selection is unbalanced and *that pupils leave school without an adequate mental map of those things which have led us to where we are now.*
>
> > (*The Times Educational Supplement*, 30 January 1987; my emphasis)

Baker selected half-a-dozen 'crucial' events that he felt were central to 'a well-developed sense of our national past'. But how developed is our knowledge of our own history? Are the events he selected solely concerned with the 'White indigenous' population? Or, to put it another way, are there other histories attached to these events that directly relate to the origins of multicultural, multilingual, multifaith Britain? To take each of Baker's crucial events in turn:

The English Reformation

(Area of study: Key Stage 2, 'Life in Tudor Times'; Key Stage 3, 'The Making of the United Kingdom'.) A Black trumpeter was employed by the courts of Henry VII and later by Henry VIII and is recorded as being present at the Westminster Tournament of 1511, which was held to celebrate the birth of a son to Catherine of Aragon (Greater London Council 1986: 6–7).

The Reform Bills/the Tolpuddle martyrs

(Area of Study: Key Stage 3, 'Britain 1750–*circa* 1900'.) Rajah Ram Mohan Roy was a philosopher, reformer, poet and a journalist who was resident in Britain between 1830 and 1833. He acted as ambassador for the Mogul Emperor, Akhbar Shah, associated with English political radicals, was a friend of both Jeremy Bentham and Mary Carpenter, and was lionised by London society. He died on a visit to Bristol in 1833 (Carpenter 1866; Fryer 1984: 262–3; Grosvenor and Chapman 1987: 4).

William Davidson, Robert Wedderburn and William Cuffay were three Black men who were prominent amongst the radical working-class movement of the nineteenth century and, like the Todlpuddle martyrs, were punished for their activities. Davidson was hung and then beheaded on 1 May 1820 for his part in the Cato Street plan to blow up the House of Commons (Fryer 1984: 214–20) Wedderburn, who condemned the Peterloo Massacre as 'an act of Murder, committed by the Magistrates and Yeomen', was jailed for sedition and blasphemy in 1820 (Fryer 1984: 220–7). Cuffay was one of the leaders of the Chartist movement and was transported to Tasmania for life in 1848 (Saville 1982: 78). Other 'men of colour' who were associated with the Chartist movement include David Anthony Duffy and Benjamin Prophitt (Fryer 1984: 239).

The Suffragette Movement

(Area of Study: Key Stage 2, 'The Victorians'; Key Stage 3, 'Britain 1750–*circa* 1900'. In addition, the non-British area of study Key Stage 3, 'The Twentieth-Century World'.) A single image from 1911, the summer in which King George V was crowned, captures a moment on the mass Women's Coronation Procession organised by the Women's Social and Political Union and shows five Indian suffragettes shoulder to shoulder, advancing the cause of 'votes for women' (Atkinson 1988: 31).

Waterloo

(Area of Study: Key Stage 1, 'Famous Men and Women, including Personalities Drawn from British History'; Key Stage 3, 'Britain 1750–*circa* 1900'.) The British armed forces in the eighteenth and nineteenth centuries employed Black soldiers and seamen. For example, John 'Jack Punch' Perkins, of Jamaica, was a celebrated commander in the Georgian navy (Marcus 1975: 81). In C.W. Sharpe's painting, *The Death of Nelson* (1805), Walker Art Gallery, Liverpool, several Black seamen, including one cast in the heroic role of identifying the source of the fatal shot, are portrayed. This same scene, along with representations of other Black seamen, is featured around the base of Nelson's Column in Trafalgar Square. A Black soldier is included in an engraving depicting the jubilation of Chelsea pensioners on hearing the news of the victory at Waterloo, the land victory that matched the sea victory at Trafalgar.

El Alamein

(Area of Study: Key Stage 1, 'Famous Men and Women, including Personalities Drawn from British History; Key Stage 2, 'Britain since 1930'. In addition, the non-British area of study Key Stage 3, 'The Twentieth-Century World'.)

Black and Asian soldiers from all over the world served with the British forces in the Second World War. Black soldiers were among a company of specialist air landing troops of the Oxfordshire and Buckinghamshire Regiment who were involved in capturing a canal and a river bridge between Ouistreham and Caen on the night of 5–6 June 1944. These soldiers were the first Allied troops to land on D-Day (Ambrose 1984: 66). Britain's Black population also shared in the crises and hardships experienced on the home front. So, for example, in Birmingham in 1939 air-raid wardens reporting on difficulties encountered in using equipment identified particular problems experienced by Sikh men in the city because of their religious beliefs (Grosvenor and Chapman 1987: 19). Evacuation was also a shared experience as the following two extracts from evacuees reveal:

> I was made welcome by George and Flo Harding, a childless couple. Flo was a Jamaican, married to an Englishman, and as both loved children it was a good and happy home. ...
>
> We lived in a lovely house just outside Preston with a farm and we were given a pony and a donkey. There were very few black people in Darwen and none at all outside Preston.
>
> (Wicks 1988: 97, 128)

Photographic evidence, interestingly included in an assessment pack circulated to infant schools by the School Examinations Assessment Council in 1993, also captures the shared experience of evacuation. The image shows eight children, three Black and four White, arriving labelled, carrying gas masks and luggage at Eastbourne on 1 September 1939 (SEAC 1993a).

* * *

It should be readily apparent from the above examples that 'our island story' is more complex than might at first be assumed. The evidence for the making of multicultural, multilingual, multifaith Britain can be found in archives, museums and art galleries, and in community memories. However, this evidence is not regularly incorporated into historians' narratives of the nation (Grosvenor 1997: 153, 186–200; Sherwood 1998: 14–20). In other words, some histories in our national past have been ignored. Therefore, it follows that the historical narrative of the nation that currently is shared with pupils in history classrooms is 'unbalanced' and that pupils *are* leaving 'school without an adequate mental map of those things which have led us to where we are now'.

Since the early 1980s there have been significant advances in the development of British Black and Asian historical studies, and the past presences and experiences of different communities have begun to be recorded and analysed. However, it is by no means inevitable that this process will be accompanied by an end to the marginalisation or exclusion of Black experiences in historical narratives of Britain's past. First, what is currently being documented and written is generally described as 'Black history'. This compartmentalisation has the effect of reinforcing the marginal status of Black historical experiences. It legitimises the lines of difference: separate histories for separate fixed spheres of interest (Kerridge 1998). Second, 'Black history' has been characterised by right-wing educationalists and political pundits as part of a broader concern with Black Studies, which is viewed as being narrowly conceived, ideologically motivated and therefore unsound (Partington 1986). These are views strongly proclaimed by the publishers of Roy Kerridge's *The Story of Black History* (1998):

> Do we need to rewrite the curriculum, to found a 'blackacademe', in order to make blacks visible in the books as they are in the streets of modern Britain? If so, what should be changed? Which bits of history must be censored out, which newly included, and which rewritten so as to change the emphasis or even change the facts? These questions are not academic; on the contrary, they lie at the heart of a new intellectual endeavour, which is to produce a black-centred curriculum, and to overthrow the cultural hegemony of 'racist Britain'.
>
> (Kerridge 1998)

Third, publishers appear reluctant to acknowledge and incorporate this 'new' history into school textbooks. The Black and Asian Studies Association (BASA), for example, undertook a survey of National Curriculum history textbooks in use in schools and found many relating to the 'Roman Empire', 'Britain 1750–1900' and 'Victorian Britain' unsatisfactory in terms of their coverage of the presence and contributions of Black peoples to the history of Britain (Sherwood 1998). Fourth, where the history of the Black presence does appear in history texts it is generally perceived through the prism of racism, where Black and Asian people are associated only with problems and violence. In general accounts of Britain since 1945 the history of the Black presence has its own individual chronology: 1948, 1958, 1962, 1981 – years associated with 'problems'. So, for example, in Arthur Marwick's *British Society Since 1945* (1982), Guy Arnold's *Britain since 1945* (1989), Kenneth Morgan's *The People's Peace: British History 1945–1989* (1990) and David Child's *Britain since 1945* (1992) a history is offered in which Black people appear on the page as 'immigrants', as the cause of 'race' riots in the 1950s and as leading actors in inner-city riots in the 1980s. Thus, in these texts, beyond racism and revolt, Black people were not part of Britain's history since 1945. Black experiences lay 'outside of history'; that is, outside of received notions of Britain's past. Finally, those who have the power to influence curriculum content in schools 'the Dept [*sic*] of Education, its quangos, the Publishers' Association' have chosen in the 1990s to ignore campaigns for change and have led Marika Sherwood, Secretary of BASA, to conclude 'there is as little hope for a more inclusive curriculum under New Labour as there was under the Conservatives' (BASA, *Newsletter* 23, 1999: 34).

In the 1990 debate at Ruskin mentioned earlier, Stuart Hall predicted that the 'British muddle will leave a lot of windows open through which progressive teachers will continue to march'. Raphael Samuel made a similar point: 'Debate will not be settled by ministerial memo but what happens in the classroom' (*The Times Educational Supplement*, 25 May 1990). In short, an inclusive history for the nation will be dependent upon teachers' creativity in identifying relevant material, 'seeking-out' hidden histories and incorporating them into their schemes of work. The scope for teachers to develop such an inclusive history for the nation is enormous under the new National Curriculum.

Is 'history for the nation' just about content?

In a BBC discussion between leading British historians on the theme of 'the history of nations' Patrick Collinson observed that:

> [History is] a contested subject – I think it should be contested – and I think everything should be contested in the classroom. ... I have a daughter who teaches in a big comprehensive in North London, with an extremely varied population ... lots of Irish children, lots of Afro-Caribbean children, and lots of children from the sub-continent. And it [history] is contested and it is discussed, and so it should be.
>
> (Hennessy *et al.* 1991: 14)

History for the nation is not just about the selection of content; it is also about the pedagogy of the classroom. The how of teaching is just as critical as the what. Indeed, for some advocates of multiculturalism, pedagogy has been seen as the forgotten dimension (Davey 1983; Richards 1986; Troyna and Selman 1989; Carrington and Short 1989).

HMI in 1985 identified history in a multicultural society as a 'controversial, even politically sensitive' issue, but believed that the 'procedures' of history were objective and thereby preserved 'professional and academic integrity' (DES 1985a: 29). These 'procedures' – the use of evidence, the distinguishing between fact and opinion, the identification of contradictions, the recognition of bias and propaganda, the consideration of views and interpretations of the past – the History Working Group believed should if pursued in the classroom 'assist in identifying, and thus combating, racial and other forms of prejudice and stereotypical thinking' (DES 1990a: 184). Such thinking was also very much in evidence in the non-statutory guidance:

> Through history pupils ... should ... develop the quality of open-minded-ness which questions assumptions and demands evidence for points of view. ... As pupils' ability to understand interpretations of history develops, they will be able to explore conflicting viewpoints and thus challenge racial or other forms of prejudice and other stereotyping ... [and through] the skilful handling of sensitive issues, teachers of history can help pupils develop tolerance and mutual understanding.
>
> (NCC 1991: C18, 19, 26)

However, just as the circulation of 'new' knowledge about the history of the Black presence does not necessarily result in the incorporation of this knowledge into history textbooks, so a concern for a pedagogy, which attends to historical skills, linked to appropriate content, will not necessarily produce rational thinking or greater toleration and understanding in pupils (Brandt 1986; Figueroa 1993).

What can teachers do to encourage objectivity? To take one teaching strategy identified by Collinson, effective classroom discussion is dependent upon the fostering of a positive learning environment. Pupils are more likely to explore issues sensitively and rationally if a supportive and friendly environment is available for them to discuss their ideas without being ridiculed or judged. This observation is particularly true in relation to teaching about racism, as Alfred Davey has written:

> Purging the textbooks of black stereotypes, boosting the minority groups in the teaching materials and adjusting the curriculum to accommodate cultural diversity, will have little impact on how children treat each other, if teachers make rules without explanation, if they command needlessly and assume their authority to be established by convention.
>
> (Davey 1983: 181)

The classroom ethos should be one of collaboration and co-operation rather than one where didacticism and an asymmetrical relationship between pupil and teacher is the norm. Discussion will not just happen in the history classroom; it has to be planned and led.

The area of historical vocabulary can create some unforeseen difficulties. Commonplace historical vocabulary, such as 'civilisation', 'massacre', 'crusade', 'peasant', 'host community', 'progress' and 'discovery', can be value-laden through the process of association. Such vocabulary should not be avoided, but as Farmer and Knight cautioned:

> people's cultural backgrounds, whether shaped by class or by race and religion, exert a profound influence on the range of concepts, understandings and assumptions that they bring to their school history. Failure to appreciate this can lead to history that deals in misconceptions – teachers taking it for granted that children see the world in a white middle class way. We are not taking a strong line that these differences are such there is no common ground, but we are saying that they are significant enough for us to think twice when teaching history.
>
> (Farmer and Knight 1995: 34)

Not withstanding such considerations teachers have to be prepared for negative pupil responses, such as those identified by Sally Tomlinson among White pupils in the 1980s. She categorised six types of negative views of ethnic minorities articulated by White pupils in schools: Exclusionary, Ethnocentric, Imperial regret, Scapegoating, Repatriation and Racial Strife (Tomlinson 1990: 45–6). In addition, Lewis and Theoharis have warned that teaching about 'race' and multicultural history can make pupils 'angry, depressed, demoralised, even scared' (Lewis and Theoharis 1996: 45). Teachers have to recognise that racism continues to shape the lives of many Black and Asian children (Grosvenor 1999).

Conclusion

This chapter, with its advocacy of an inclusive history for the nation and its critique, albeit brief, of the assimilationist nature of the National Curriculum, of the common cultural heritage approach of the history curriculum and of the narrow sense of British identity consequently promoted, represents a reading of the past. Evidence has been consulted and an interpretation presented. It is a reading of the past very much at odds with the views of, for example, Roy Kerridge. In this context, it is useful to complete the Howard Zinn quote cited earlier: 'all history is subjective, all history represents a point of view ... [and] since it's not possible to be objective, you should be honest about that' (Zinn 1993: 8). History, as Collinson reminds us, is 'a contested subject', and this chapter has been written in this vein, but what about the teacher's role in this process?

Questions

History teachers have authority over the past in their classrooms; they determine, within the contraints of the National Curriculum, which voices of the past are heard. In this context:

1   How can the history teacher avoid the accusation, whether from left or right, of bias and indoctrination?
2   What role should the history teacher adopt when controversial issues are discussed in the classroom: the 'devil's advocate', the 'impartial chairperson', or the 'declared interest role'?
3   If teachers do not reveal their value positions, where do pupils get their value judgements and suggested behaviour from?

Further reading

Three key texts that will aid the teacher to seek out the history of the Black presence in Britain are Peter Fryer's *Staying Power. The History of Black People in Britain* (1984), Rozina Vizram's *Ayah's, Lascars and Princes* (1986) and the Greater London Council publication, *A History of the Black Presence in London* (1986). The *Black and Asian Studies Newsletter* (three times a year from BASA, c/o ICS, 28 Russell Square, London WC1B 5DS) provides regular updates on new texts and conferences, as well as articles on the making of multicultural Britain. Finally, Roy Kerridge's *The Story of Black History* (1998) offers a counter-reading to the arguments offered in this chapter.

13 Primary school history in Europe

A staple diet or a hot potato?

Hilary Cooper

How important is history in the primary curriculum?

How unique is the achievement of the National Curriculum for history in England and Wales? How hard should we fight to retain and defend it in our primary schools and why? This chapter will be of interest to those who wish to evaluate the English National Curriculum for history, particularly for Key Stages 1 and 2, from a European perspective, to consider whether it has any contribution to make to curriculum development in other countries, and if so how they could contribute to this process.

The National Curriculum (DfE 1991) required that all pupils from the age of five to fourteen should engage in genuine historical enquiry using a range of sources: written and oral sources, museums, buildings, sites, photographs and graveyard studies. Research has shown that young children can learn to discuss such sources (Cooper 1991, 1995a, 1995b); can consider alternative viewpoints and suggest reasons for behaviour (Knight 1989a, 1989b); and can consider causes and effects of changes (Lee *et al.* 1996a, 1996b, 1996c), all in increasingly complex ways.

Yet in most educational systems history is not formally taught as a subject before the age of eleven or twelve (Stradling 1995: 21). Even then it rarely takes as its starting point pupils' existing knowledge. History educators at a meeting in Strasbourg in 1995 agreed that:

> Enquiries have shown that young people in most countries obtain their notions of history from out of school sources, in particular the mass media, peer groups, the family, rather than from what is taught in school. History teaching therefore has to take account of out of school notions, prejudices, knowledge and understanding of pupils and build upon them, rather than impose concepts which are not understood.
>
> (Council of Europe Council for Cultural Co-operation 1995: 5.3)

Yet research has shown that, by the age of twelve, most pupils have conventional and fixed viewpoints about the past and do not find school history interesting or feel that it has any influence on their lives (Borries 1994). It seems then that by the age of twelve many children have developed rigid, stereotypical ideas about the past from sources outside school. These are not challenged by the school history curriculum, which is didactic and factual, not discursive.

This chapter focuses on a small-scale study investigating what 6-year-old and 10-year-old children, in a range of European countries, know about the past from outside of school sources before they begin formal history education. It considers whether it would be possible for their teachers to build on this knowledge and help their pupils to reflect on it and critically evaluate it as part of the history curriculum in school.

An investigation of what young children in a range of European countries know about the past and how they acquired that knowledge

What did the project aim to find out and why?

First, young children are inevitably aware of the past from an early age and this is an important aspect of developing their sense of identity. Stories and images form our childhood imagination, aspirations and wisdom. They shape our sense of the past, of our place in it, and of ourselves.

> Identity is a complex concept which covers: language, religion, a shared memory and a sense of history – sometimes even of historical grievance and injustice. It is rich in symbolism: heroes, battles lost and won, national anthems, songs, poetry, paintings, memorials and street names.
>
> (Stobart 1996)

However, the sense of identity developed through such sources can also encourage bias and xenophobia if not filtered through education: through discussion about where they come from, and why; and about the meaning and perspectives they convey. Young children rarely spontaneously ask questions to unravel apparent illogicalities (Donaldson 1978). The history curriculum, which has evolved in England through fierce political debate, aims to include such 'unofficial' images of the past, and to discuss them within an educational context (Phillips 1998a).

For forty years the Council of Europe has organised conferences and seminars to discuss the possibility of teaching history that draws on family and local sources, and which encourages pupils to think critically about issues of immediate relevance and interest to them. However, these debates have been concerned with secondary education and have had little impact on classroom practice (Slater 1995).

The first suggestion, that sources such as local and family history, and museums might be integrated into history teaching for *young* pupils, seems to have arisen at a Council of Europe meeting for experts in research in history education in Strasbourg in 1995. This meeting was, interestingly, chaired by a primary history specialist. Participants were asked to consider whether it is possible to match school history with the cognitive development of pupils, and, by implication, whether history education could begin at an earlier age than is generally assumed. It was agreed that young children may well be able to begin to learn historical thinking skills if teachers select materials and activities that interest them and that they can understand.

There is evidence that young pupils can learn to ask questions about historical sources, make inferences, argue their points of view, and listen to those of their peers, even when no adult is present to guide the discussion (Cooper 1993). Yet the classroom ethos that makes such discussion possible is a culturally embedded achievement. In many countries it is outside teachers' experience and the potential is not generally self-evident. At a conference in Paris delegates listened politely to a paper describing an empirical study of English 8-year-olds' ability to discuss historical sources, but seemed to think it a little eccentric (Cooper 1998: 230–4). The ensuing discussion concluded with the view, '*Madame, ce n'est pas possible!*' And at a conference at the Georg Eckert Institute (Braunschweig Conference 1998) the response of one participant to the study described in this chapter was, 'of course young children are interested in these things. They are interested in everything. But how can that help us to teach history in schools?' Yet 'the massed battalions of European History students are between 5 and 15. History teaching has a responsibility to lever their misunderstanding and diminish their ignorance of the world in which they live, and particularly of the New Europe (Slater 1995: 19).

A discussion in 1996 between a group of 5-year-olds in the former East Germany, who had been born just before the Berlin Wall was pulled down, illustrates their partially understood knowledge of remaining traces of the recent past in their immediate locality, their attempts to reason about it and make sense of it, and their wish to know more.

'My mummy told me there used to be a wall so nobody could go away. So everybody had to stay at home. There was a war on.'

'I think the wall was there to keep the dogs out.'

'No, it was so that they knew where East Germany was.'

'I saw the wall at Brandenburg Square.'

'I saw it at Alexander Square.'

'Before people had to go all the way round when they wanted to go home because the wall was in the way. ... You could only go on the Baltic because the wall was right up to the Baltic.'

(*Die Zeit*, 4 October 1996)

Methodology

The project aimed to investigate what a small sample of 6- and 10-year-old children in a range of European countries knew about the past and how they acquired that knowledge (Cooper *et al.* 1997). The countries involved in the project were selected because they represent a broad spectrum of recent political history and geographical diversity, and also because each of the four English researchers had personal links with an educational researcher in one of the countries: in Bucharest, Romania; Rovaniemi, Finland; Rotterdam, Holland; and Athens, Greece.

The researcher in each country selected a school that was considered 'typical'. The sample consisted of twelve children in England and in each of the other four countries involved (three boys and three girls aged six, and three boys and three girls aged ten). Those selected were considered by their teachers to be children of average ability who would enjoy taking part in the project.

Each group of 6-year-olds and of 10-year-olds worked with the researcher who spoke their mother tongue to make a concept map of the past. The English colleague was an observer. This activity was introduced in an informal way using a standard introduction:

> 'I expect you know what the word "history" means. It means what we know and understand about the past. This may mean a long, long time ago, or not very long ago.
>
> 'Can you tell me how we can find out about the past?' (At this point the researcher writes down the list of sources of information by the children, giving a code to each one. The children may well add to this initial list as the activity gets under way.)
>
> 'We are doing this activity with children of your age in several countries. You are representing X (name of country).
>
> 'I want you to play this game. You see it says HISTORY in the middle of this BIG sheet of paper. I want you all to take turns to tell me something you know about the past and how you know it. I'll give you each a pen in a different colour and we'll see who can remember most things. If you want, I'll write what you say for you, with your coloured pen. Who's going to start ... ?'

There was no time limit. The children (or the researcher) wrote down each statement and a symbol to indicate how the child said they knew that information. The researcher intervened only for the following reasons: for organisational purposes (to ensure turn-taking); to clarify what was said; to ask 'how do you know that?'; and to keep the process going until ideas were exhausted.

This open question was considered more appropriate than any initial attempt to categorise information (for example through sequencing cards or discussing images or concepts), because the aim was to find out what images of the past children have that might inform their learning in school, because of the variety of variables that influence metacognition in history, and also because extensive translation would be difficult.

The findings

An overview of the concept maps showed that the younger children were aware of many aspects of the past over a vast time-span and the older children mentioned even more topics (see Figures 13.1 and 13.2). However, the understanding of both age groups often seemed to be piecemeal and confused. Here are some examples:

- Information of varying status was juxtaposed as equally significant: 'The Second World War, Elvis Presley, old movies.' (*The Flintstones* stimulated as much animated discussion as a creation story.)

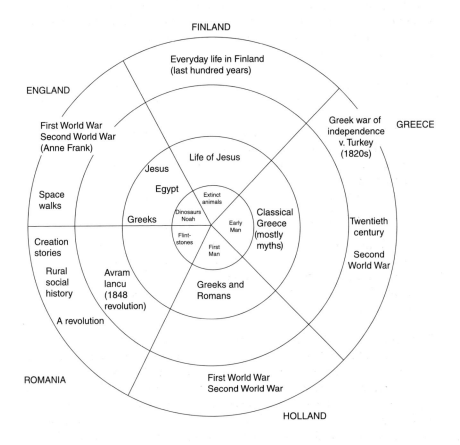

Figure 13.1 Topics referred to by 6-year-olds
Source: Cooper *et al.* 1997.

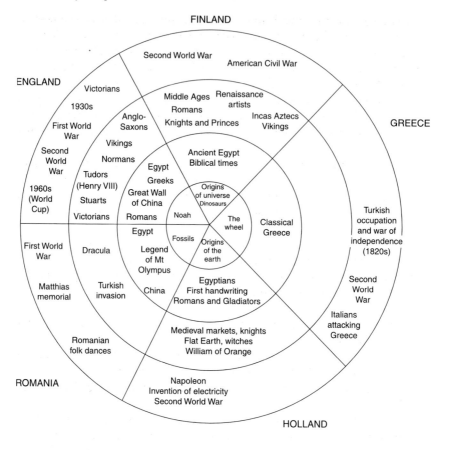

Figure 13.2 Topics referred to by 10-year-olds

Source: Cooper *et al.* 1997.

- Vivid images were remembered but not understood: 'I went to the seaside. I saw old boats, stone elephants; they were old, they were broken.'
- Gobbets of information were recorded: 'Lord Elgin stole our marbles'; 'Napoleon – he destroyed the nose of the sphinx'; 'England won the World Cup in 1966.'
- 6-year-olds demonstrated their acute awareness of silences: 'I don't talk to my grandparents. They don't have time, and even if they did they wouldn't talk about history'; 'They don't let me watch TV at all'; 'Only cartoons. They don't let me watch anything else.'
- Sometimes there is awareness of a half-understood past: 'My dad told me at the Art Museum there was a war a long time ago. He did not participate but he knows it because you can see the bullet traces in the walls'; 'There were revolutions too. Near my flats there is a church. When they built the

flats they built the church too. It's only in that area that people used to make wars. But the church collapsed and now there's only the cross left.'

- There is evidence too that 6-year-olds *want* to understand: 'We want to understand, because we don't understand'; 'I'm fond of history. I intend to see only historical films and read books about history.'

- Throughout there is evidence of story. There are school readers: 'I've got a history of Romania at home. I read it step by step. I started learning to read on it. When there was a great war in the history of Romania – I remember that. ... '

- And there are references to bed-time stories: 'I like the Legends of Olympus, heroes and gods'; 'I know the story of Mesterual Manole [Balkan Legend].' There are references too to chats with grandma: 'My grandma from Cluj told me about Avram Iancu [1848 revolutionary figure].'

To investigate their initial questions about how the children knew about the past, and the period and geographical areas the children knew most about, the English researchers collated the information from the concept maps made by each age group in each country in the following categories:

- Sources of information: museums; books; film/TV; family; locality/places visited; schools; art galleries.
- Chronology: prehistory; ancient – AD 500; medieval (AD 500–1500); modern (AD 1500–1900); recent (the twentieth century).
- Geography: local history; national history; European history; global history.

Table 13.1, for example, shows references made by the 6- and 10-year-olds in Romania to museum visits, one of the categories within sources of information.

In order to make some comparisons between sources of information, chronological periods and geographical areas referred to across age groups and countries, the number of responses in each category was recorded and ranked in order for each country. These rankings may be of interest as discussion points, but it is important to remember that because of the sample size they are not significant. Tables 13.2 and 13.3 show historical periods referred to, as an illustration of this process.

A synopsis of the findings is given in Table 13.4; it should be noted that there were national variations. This table shows that the younger children knew most about the past from museums and their families, and referred most often to the recent past, and from a national perspective. (Global references were to creation myths, dinosaurs and early Man.) The older children, by contrast, knew most from formal sources, knew most about ancient history and least about the modern world, but also frequently referred to events from their national history.

Although only very tentative implications can be drawn from such a small study, it raises a number of questions (see p. 171).

Table 13.1 Analysis of concept maps for Eminescu High School, Bucharest: historical
sources referred to (1) Museums

6-year-olds	10-year-olds
Historical sources referred to and contexts	

6-year-olds	10-year-olds
I went to the Antipa Museum where I saw dinosaurs and the Farmers' Museum and I also went to the Botanical Gardens.	At the Antipa Museum (Bucharest Natural History Museum) I saw many models of people from the past: how they hunted; how they dressed; the weapons they used.
At the Antipa Museum there were bugs with wings, and butterflies too.	And the fact that people derived from monkeys.
Mother told me about the Dinosaur Museum.	When there was rain and lightning people discovered fire, because it gave them heat. Then they started walking in a vertical position, making weapons of bone, stone, metal.
I've got a book about it and a video tape.	Fire protected them from animals; they built houses in the woods and in the rocks.
	To make fire they hit two stones, sparks came out and they set something on fire; and they tamed animals, first the dog, then the cat, and many others.
	After discovering fire they started cooking meat; they realised it was better.
I visited a museum where I saw old telephones, small racing cars, carriages too, but that had no wheels … they put them on iron supports. They also built some stone bases outside to pull.	I haven't been to the History Museum of Romania but I've been to the Army Museum. Father's in the military. I saw weapons, the way soldiers in ancient times and more recent times were dressed, the prince's swords, and by the way what they found in kings' tombs. They found mirrors, pots, glass, precious wooden thrones. Pharaohs wore mortuary masks, the best known being the Sphinx, according to which the pyramid was also built.
Three or four years ago I went to Moscow. I went to a Museum in Moscow. I can't remember what I saw.	
I went to a Satellite Museum in Constanta. I looked at the satellites and other planets. I realised it was history.	

Source: Taken from Cooper *et al.* 1997.

Table 13.2 Analysis of historical period referred to by 6-year-olds

Country	The prehistoric world		The ancient world		The medieval world (AD 500–1500)		The modern world (AD 1500–1900)		The twentieth-century world (AD 1900–97)	
	Rank order	No. of responses	Rank order	No. of responses	Rank order	No. of responses	Rank order	No. of responses	Rank order	No. of responses
England	3=	1	2	7	5	0	3=	1	1	8
Finland	3	3	4	2	5	0	1=	15	1=	15
Greece	4	3	1	13	5	0	2	8	3	7
Holland	4	1	3	3	5	0	1=	6	1=	6
Romania	2	4	4=	0	3	2	4=	0	1	6
Total response		12		25		2		30		42
National rank order	4		3		5		2		1	

Source: Taken from Cooper et al. 1997.

Table 13.3 Analysis of historical period referred to by 10-year-olds

Country	The prehistoric world		The ancient world		The medieval world (AD 500–1500)		The modern world (AD 1500–1900)		The twentieth-century world (1900–97)	
	Rank order	No. of responses	Rank order	No. of responses	Rank order	No. of responses	Rank order	No. of responses	Rank Order	No. of Responses
England	5	2	3	4	4	3	2	5	1	6
Finland	4=	3	2=	7	2=	7	1	8	4=	3
Greece	3=	2	1	37	3=	2	2	10	3=	2
Holland	3=	4	1=	5	3=	4	1=	5	5	3
Romania	2	6	1	8	3	4	4	3	5	2
Total response		17		61		20		31		16
National rank order	4		1		3		2		5	

Source: Taken from Cooper et al. 1997.

Table 13.4 Synopsis of findings: number of responses in each category across all national
groups

	6–7-year-olds		10–11-year-olds	
Sources				
Museums	1	School	1	
Family	2	Books	2	
Books	5	Visits	6	
Visits	6			
Periods				
1990–7	1	Ancient world	1	
500–1500	5	1900–97	5	
Areas				
Global	1	National		
National	2	Global	2	
Local	4	Local	4	

Source: Taken from Cooper *et al.* 1997.

Note: National rank order refers to the rank order of the named category of responses across all
national groups.

- If young children are curious about the recent past and national events that
  they learn about (through their families) but only partially understand, and
  if the 10-year-olds' main source of information is books, how can schools be
  supported in using parents and their locality, in ways that build on children's questions and avoid bias and prejudice?
- If 10-year-olds know most about the ancient worlds, and little about Europe
  and their own region, is twentieth-century history being avoided, and if so
  does this matter?
- If children seldom mention the medieval period is this because it precedes
  the Nation-State?

What issues arise from the project?

First, the project surprised the researchers by demonstrating the range of
contexts in which the 6-year-olds referred to the past. The Greek researcher
said of the Greek children, 'I was amazed by the extent to which the younger
children had been influenced by their families.' The Romanian researcher said

that she was 'positively surprised' about 'the children's remarks that they do not understand and wanted to understand'.

Since the younger pupils knew a lot about the past from a variety of sources, but only partially understood it, and since for the older pupils school history seemed influential and enjoyable but depended largely on books, it may seem appropriate to introduce into the school curriculum from the very beginning the kind of history that makes links between school, home, the locality and museums, and helps children to use these sources in meaningful ways. The Greek researcher said she thought that the development of a well-structured primary history curriculum, which takes into account the role of the family in the education of children and also good practice in museums and other public media, should be encouraged.

Yet, in spite of the justification in terms of constructivist educational theories and recent work that has been done to apply these to the teaching and learning of history, it is not easy to put these theories into practice in countries where the past is still painful, still not understood, dealt with or discussed by adults and is still divisive: countries where safe, received opinions have become a cast of mind. The reality of this was very clear at the Strasbourg meeting of researchers in history education in 1995 (Council of Europe 1995). One participant said that, during that conference, he had talked for the first time about his past to his own family; two compatriots could not bear to sit next to each other because of their different approaches to history teaching during the previous regime; another professor exclaimed 'People simply do not understand what it was like'.

In such circumstances it is easy to understand why family and local history and home–school links are potential dynamite. Books such as *History at Home* (David 1996) offer suggestions that have been successful in England (bed-time stories with historical content, which can lead to discussion about the past or taking a walk around the local area), but to what extent are they transferable? The meeting in Strasbourg concluded that 'For younger pupils history must start with the local environment' and that 'surveys have revealed that pupils are interested in their own family through the ages' (Council of Europe 1995: 30). But a frustrated participant at the Braunschweig Conference (1998) asked with passion, 'How do you construct connections between past and present? What *should* I have told my 8-year-old daughter about the Holocaust?' A trip around the locality for one 6-year-old in Bucharest included seeing bullet traces in the walls, which were not explained, and another said 'I talk to my grandparents about history; that is *happy* events in the past.' The Romanian researcher said that the children's remarks that they do not understand and they want to understand 'show a kind of critical thinking on a very sensitive issue'. She was very surprised at the careless way in which they spoke about history, in an informal context to someone they met for the first time. As for involving parents and out-of-school sources in history education, she pointed out that in Romania parents are important but they have limited time and, as in other former Communist countries, social and economic insecurity has damaged the fabric of society. Although the new curriculum aims to integrate ethnic minorities there is a great deal of difference between urban and rural communities and ethnic minority groups. And she asks whether children should be encouraged to find out about the past from out-of-school sources in countries where there is no critical tradition of the media.

Asking and answering questions about photographs, buildings, sites and museums in order to identify reasons for, and results of, events, which the English Key Stage 2 curriculum requires (DfE 1995: 77), is a luxury that those who have not lived in a totalitarian state can hardly begin to appreciate. We still have no clear idea of how to deal with Nazi and communist atrocities, yet in cemeteries, memorials and museums across Europe they are a dominant part of local history that cannot be ignored. Indeed it has been argued that even memorials set in stone contain an element of dishonesty and that history should be constantly confronted. But is this appropriate for young children, or is local history to be selective? Can it be? Should it be? 'The unctuous brutalisation of public and private life in, say Ceauşescu's Romania abolishes any effective barriers between public and private spaces. ... Remembrance is criminalised for time has begun anew' (George Steiner, the *Observer*, 30 August 1998: 14).

Yet whatever decisions are made about the content of what is taught, it seems essential that pupils begin to learn the methodology of historical enquiry and develop an interest in the past in primary school. Margaret Donaldson has said from the beginning that pupils should learn to develop deductive reasoning: the 'pleasures of the mind' (Donaldson 1978). She argued that this process is piecemeal, gradual and complex, that it should be embedded in a child's immediate concerns, not externally imposed, and that the child should not assume that the questioner knows the answers. This process values individual identity and responsibility, and underpins mutual understanding, tolerance and an open society. In Braunschweig in 1998, as in Strasbourg in 1995, when the English National Curriculum was mentioned, at any Key Stage, everyone sat up. They enquire: 'Do you ask questions?'; 'Discuss interpretations?'; 'Different media?'; 'Range of sources?'; 'How old are these children?' Then they want to know how this can be done. Can they have a photocopy of the pages?

The Polish House (Sikorski 1997) offers some inspiring insights into how personal and national fates might be interwoven for young children through the discussion of artefacts and buildings. The author vividly describes a collection of sabres, traditional furniture, oriental carpets and millstones salvaged from the ruins of Gdańsk in 1945, and kept in his uncle's cellar during his communist childhood. 'Each object came alive in Uncle Klemen's hands; from the markings he could tell from which Polish workshop they came.' And he describes his responses to the multilayered history of Lwów, through which he journeyed on his return to Poland in 1989: its churches, frescoes of the city's heroic defence against Tartars and Swedes, statues of Armenian nobles, of stone lions celebrated in Polish songs, nineteenth-century bourgeois opulence; statues of Lenin, etc. 'It is because communism tried to abolish history that I revel in old things', he writes as he becomes immersed in restoring the dilapidated eighteenth-century manor house that his family has bought.

Two encouraging papers by Francois Audigier of the Institut National de Recherche Pedagogique in Paris strongly advocate that history education should begin with the interests and questions of the child in order to develop critical, independent thinking (Audigier 1997a). He argues that they should learn through active teaching strategies based on constructivist models, that they should begin with their locality and that they should learn to understand different perspectives, in order to develop hierarchies of identity, and develop tolerance and mutual understanding for a future we can't predict. Most interestingly, he believes the initiatives for such an approach to teaching history must be in elementary schools, since secondary history teaching in France is still dominated by chronology and exposition (Audigier 1997b).

Of course we should not be complacent about the contribution that the English history curriculum could make for many reasons. First, we need to be sensitive to tensions and divisions within our own communities. For example, Carmel Gallagher, assistant director of Northern Ireland's curriculum and assessment body, speaking at the Historical Association Conference in 1997 of her experience in implementing the history curriculum in the province, said that most children still have meanings imposed on them; such sensitive topics as the Great Irish Famine need skilful teaching. She has spoken of her strong belief in the influence of personal biography, and how the time and circumstances in which we are born and the things that happen around us provide all sorts of messages that we need to decode and analyse (Gallagher 1998). Second, we still require significant professional development in order to teach civics and the personal, spiritual, cultural and moral dimensions of the revised National Curriculum (Blyth 1998a). Third, in the past English history teaching has been described as 'smug'; its characteristic separation of British and European history has been criticised as inappropriate for an age of international contacts and interdependencies (Berghann and Schissler 1987: 30), and it has been seen in Europe as nationalistic. The German Minister for Culture claimed recently that the British 'are the only nation in the world that has decided to make the second world war a sort of spiritual core of its national self' (Tony Paterson and Dominic Kennedy, *The Times*, 15 February 1999: 3). And finally, research has shown that many English 8-year-olds have an amazingly ignorant concept of Europe (Holden 1997); that they have stereotypical ideas based on images in the media and travel brochures and that they are aware of these misconceptions (Johnson 1998).

Nevertheless Leeuw-Roord (1994) has said that the British spiral curriculum for history is an exemplary model, which progressively provides pupils with skills that are transferable to everyday life, and that although some other countries may have similar objectives they do not have the teaching materials developed in England to put theory into practice or relate learning objectives to the age of the pupils. Maybe it is time to reappraise our perspectives and extend our international contacts, for we have much to offer to history curriculum development in other countries. Perhaps the best practical way forward is for small-scale collaborative case studies set up by individuals.

One excellent example of this is provided by Shifra Sagy, from Ben-Gurion University, and Elia Awwad, a Palestinian psychologist from Bethlehem (Sagy *et al.* 1998). They had found in a survey of Palestinians, Jewish-Israelis and Israeli-Palestinians that each group was most interested in the history of its own nation and country, in contemporary and modern history, and in the 'history of my family' (Borries 1997). Answers to questions about their priorities correlated with their interest in family and national history, and revealed a high level of ethnocentrism. Apart from the Israeli-Palestinians, peace at all costs was low on the agenda. Faced with this 'educational challenge' Sagy and Awwad described a project they have designed for Israel and Palestine, Greece and Turkey, involving forty-eight teachers and 1800 pupils of all ages. The teachers will be active partners in designing materials to investigate 'how we became who we are, how they became who they are and why the boundaries must change'. Activities may involve, for example, comparing, discussing and evaluating two different stories of an event. 'Don't take too much account of your textbooks', Sagy advised.

If such a project can be planned, and if such issues can be grasped honestly and with courage in areas of acute conflict by pupils of all ages, surely a similarly sanguine approach to history education can be attempted elsewhere in Europe, maybe initially through very small collaborative projects between teachers and researchers with creative vision. There have been forty years of rhetoric. There is a need for more empirical case studies involving skilled practitioners and based in real classrooms.

Questions

1   Should history be an essential part of the primary curriculum? Is the structure of the English National Curriculum for history transferable?
2   What kinds of small-scale collaborative projects might provide evidence that enquiry-based history should be an essential component of a primary curriculum?
3   Is it a purpose of history to make us aware of a shared European cultural heritage?
4   Are the aims of history education intrinsic (i.e. to understand past societies on their own terms) or extrinsic (i.e. to prepare pupils for citizenship and liberal democracy).
5   Should families be supported in teaching children about the past? How could this be done? How can bias and prejudice be avoided?
6   Should young children be introduced to twentieth-century history?
7   What should be the balance between local, national, European and global history?

Further reading

Cooper, H. (1995) *History in the Early Years*, London: Routledge.
  Case studies show how teachers can build on pre-school children's understanding of the past, gained through out-of-school sources.
Cooper, H. (1995) *The Teaching of History in Primary Schools: Implementing the Revised History Curriculum*, London: David Fulton.
  An overview of research linking theories of cognitive development to children's thinking in history, showing how theory can be applied to practice. Forthcoming is a third edition of this book.
Phillips, R. (1998) 'Contesting the past, constructing the future: History, identity and politics in schools', *British Journal of Educational Studies* 46: 40–53.
  An examination of the relationship between 'official' history taught in schools and the 'unofficial' histories that influence children in the community.
Slater, J. (1995) *Teaching History in the New Europe*, London: Cassell.
  Discussion, drawing on Council of Europe Seminars: What is Europe? Why Learn History? How? What kind? Who decides?

14 History in Europe

The benefits and challenges of co-operation

Ruth Watts

'We are wastefully and dangerously unaware of the richness and quality of much that is taking place in Europe' (Slater 1995: 51). So said John Slater, a history HMI closely involved in the myriad European initiatives on the teaching and learning of history, but painfully conscious that most history teachers, teacher educators and mentors in England and Wales worked in blissful ignorance of them. This chapter is based on the premise that we need to know of, and be able to benefit from, such projects. We should not be satisfied with partial dissemination, nor dismiss European ideas as either irrelevant or too contentious. The first section of this chapter, therefore, will report on some of the most important initiatives, while the second, including a relevant case study, will relate these to the concerns of history teaching in England and Wales. A third section will discuss how far the Council of Europe's obvious desire for closer European unity might either adversely distort the teaching of European history or benefit history through co-operative ventures. Finally, how English and Welsh history teachers can participate more fully in European activities in history will be explored.

What European initiatives are there in the teaching and learning of history?

Initiatives for the teaching and learning of history abound in Europe. In 1998 alone, three obviously relevant activities in the Intergovernmental Programme of the Council of Europe comprised 'Learning and Teaching about the History of Europe in the 20th Century', a major topic in Key Stage 3, GCSE and 'A' level syllabuses; 'Education for Democratic Citizenship' and 'Higher Education for a Democratic Society', topics currently dear to the DfEE and in which history can play a major role. All of these projects will use a range of methods of co-operative working across Europe and should result by the year 2000 in various reports, materials, awareness-raising campaigns and networks to achieve their objectives (Council of Europe FR-67075). Partly because of a lack of dissemination, however, probably relatively few of the British history community are aware of these ventures and even fewer will participate in them. It is pertinent, therefore, to survey the scene and discover what is of particular significance in European historical initiatives.

Without doubt, the major force for projects on the teaching of history has been the Council of Europe. Almost since its foundation in 1949, this has activated its concern for good history teaching through a series of meetings, conferences and workshops attended by representatives of countries across Europe. In subsequent decades attention was focused on the issue of textbooks free from stereotyping, bias and indoctrination, the place of history in the school curriculum, and the teaching of history in the 'new' Europe, respectively. Of the many important developments, not least was that of the George Eckert Institute for International Textbook Research. This official European centre for exchanging information on history and geography textbooks became a significant player in the advancement of European history teaching. Other initiatives included public exhibitions on European culture, annual awards to museums, and meetings on human rights and on the Jewish, Islamic and Arab contributions to European culture. The latter have illustrated that turn towards examination of what it is to be European, reflected in the Bruges conference of 1991 on 'History Teaching in the New Europe' (Low-Beer 1997: 5, 9–16; Slater 1995: 25–49).

The most significant development from the work of the Council of Europe in history, however, must surely be the birth of Euroclio (The European Standing Conference of History Teachers' Associations). This new organisation was inspired chiefly by Maitland Stobart, long on the Council of Europe. He was so convinced of the good effects of thoughtful history teaching and vice versa, that he urged history teacher educators from all over Europe to meet and debate crucial methods and issues. The international board of Euroclio, run on a shoestring but, luckily, strongly backed by the Netherlands Ministry of Education, has achieved not only excellent annual conferences and a regular publication, but also representation of actual teachers in its meetings. Euroclio's membership is open to associations of history teachers throughout all levels of education in member states of the Council of Europe's Council for Cultural Co-operation (CCC). Other associations involved in history whose aims agree with Euroclio's can become Associate Members. Individual membership is possible only in countries where there is as yet no History Teachers' Association. In 1998 Euroclio was likely to have thirty-nine full members and nine associated members. England and Wales provided three of the former in the Historical Association (HA), the Association of History Teachers in Wales, and the Standing Conference of History Teacher Educators in the UK (SCHTE) (Euroclio *Bulletin* 10, 1998: 3–4, and 9, 1998: 3; Euroclio *Annual Report* 1997: 22–3; http://www. glasnet.ru/~euroclio/; Low-Beer 1997: 37, 74).

Euroclio aims to strengthen in turn history's position in schools throughout Europe, the European dimension in history teaching, greater European awareness and the intellectual freedom of teachers – a particularly significant aim in a subject so closely connected to politics and culture. Other objectives are concerned with finding ways to promote discussion and debate across Europe on all issues relevant to history teaching and to disseminate the findings from these and other information as widely as possible (Slater 1995: 73–4).

These objectives are also echoed by those of the International Society for History Didactics, founded in 1980 to foster scholarship and international co-operation in history education. Its simply produced publications have articles written in the major languages of Europe, although its research is not confined to that continent. *The International Yearbook of History Education*, edited at the University of London's Institute of Education, likewise includes Europe in a wider context. Such ventures as these provide a research-based backcloth for teaching practices (*Information* 1980–98; Dickinson *et al.* 1996).

These are the most directly related European initiatives affecting history but various projects in the European Community, especially those under SOCRATES and ERASMUS, and those promoting school exchanges, may help those involved in history enhance their learning. The Thematic Network for Teacher Education in Europe (TNTEE) and UNESCO are keen to promote, respectively, European networks and education for international understanding. (For further details on some of these see Slater 1995: 51–78; http://tntee.umu.se/).

Are such initiatives relevant to the concerns of history teachers in England and Wales?

It would appear, therefore, that a fairly impressive range of activities related to history is emerging in Europe but, despite the undoubted enthusiasm of their protagonists, these do not always win necessary support even in Brussels (see, for example, Eurclio *Bulletin* 9, 1997–8: 6). Furthermore, however laudable Euroclio's aims, there is real alarm that the reality, particularly with regard to dissemination and participation, is far different from what is intended. Even more problematic is whether potential participants believe these European initiatives relate to their busy, multi-tested world. A brief analysis of some of the most significant projects on which the Council of Europe and Euroclio have expended much time and energy should clarify their relevance. In particular, a project based largely on the opinions of 15-year-old pupils will be examined as a case study.

One instance of the abiding concerns of the Council of Europe from the 1950s has been over history textbooks. There has been anxiety over a range of issues, such as the emphasis on political and national, even nationalistic, history; the neglect of the history of minorities, women, culture and much of Eastern, Central and Southern Europe; and bias both religious and implicit. This was especially felt because history was perceived to be so significant a subject in what continued to be a divided Europe. Despite some extremely important achievements, however, the issues raised were not resolved and, indeed, have become increasingly consequential since the end of the cold war. The perennial issue of governmental control over history textbooks may have eased in Eastern European countries but some now have no textbooks at all. In some other European countries textbooks are written by teams of 'men, living in capital cities' according to the Council of Europe workshop in Braunschweig in 1990 (Low-Beer 1997: 10–12; Slater 1995: 90).

How far are these concerns seen as important in England and Wales? Some, like the neglect of much European history, may appear quite irrelevant to teachers already coping with overloaded syllabuses in a diminishing time-slot. Yet the concept of what is Europe and how we ought to teach about it is one that should be considered at a time of potentially far-reaching continental changes. Textbook writers and teachers have begun to tackle the lack of different perspectives and omissions, particularly on women and minorities, but there is still much to be done (Osler 1994: 219–35). In particular, the matter of implicit bias is growing more significant with the increasing use of the 'new textbook', the CD-ROM, where provenance may be virtually unknown.

It could be exceedingly helpful to teachers, therefore, to be both more aware of these issues and able to tap into a cross-European debate on them. This can be done literally by accessing Euroclio on the Internet. There, for example, the president of Euroclio, Joke van der Leeuw-Roord's updated 1996 paper on the Council of Europe's in-service training programme for teachers skilfully analyses the issues of 'What makes a good history textbook?' using material from Euroclio meetings. Leeuw-Roord's checklist on the characteristics of a good history textbook emphasises that it should be challenging, active and creative. This is relevant to authors and teachers alike, especially as statistics across Europe have shown that students overwhelmingly perceive history lessons as relying heavily on textbooks, yet rate textbooks lowest in what they enjoy in history. Leeuw-Roord's further comments – that in contrast to the dull, dense factual accounts offered elsewhere, Western European history books now offer 'loose fitting incidents with sources as evidence' but no comprehensive account of the past – are equally pertinent. English and Welsh textbooks, after all, whilst vastly improved in colour and presentational terms in the last decade, often fail to give either a full or interesting context (Leeuw-Roord 1996).

Leeuw-Roord's concern that teachers use the textbook like the Bible echoes anxiety arising out of the Braunschweig workshop over the de-professionalisation of teachers if they have to rely too heavily on textbooks. The chilling control of the past, and thus the present and future, some history teachers in Europe have had to face may thankfully be absent in England and Wales. Nevertheless, the latter have increasingly felt heavily circumscribed in what they may do in the classroom (see for example Phillips 1998a: 111–17). Teachers may feel that since the 1995 revisions of the National Curriculum such control is diminishing, but constant thought must be given to the content and methods expected or wanted in history. A comparison with what is happening elsewhere can lead to deeper understanding of our own situation.

This is true also of other issues central to the debates of European conferences on the teaching of history in the 1990s, including how to teach pupils to be active learners, multicultural aspects of history teaching, where history fits in with other disciplines, initial teacher training in history, the use of ICT – all matters discussed elsewhere in this book. The same concerns surface throughout Europe as, for example, Joke van der Leeuw-Roord's paper for the Lviv conference on 'History teacher education in Europe' and Julieta Savova's report on the 1998 Vienna conference on 'Initial training for history teachers' both demonstrate. These authors also stress fresh concerns on the challenge of new interpretations of history, multi-perspectivity, gender, human rights, lifelong learning, environmental concerns and the European dimension (Euroclio *Bulletin* 9, 1997–8: 10–11).

The value of appreciating the varying responses and solutions of different European countries to such issues can lie in teasing out the fundamental lessons to be learnt from them. Graeme Easdown, for example, found this at the Council of Europe and Euroclio conference held in Finland, in March 1998, on 'History teaching and information technology'. He became increasingly anxious that exceedingly high expectations of the value of the Internet for both teaching and learning, and for cross-European communication, were coupled with an uncritical and passive acceptance of the Internet as a source of information rather than 'an interactive resource to be exploited by both teachers and pupils'. This was especially so from Eastern European delegates, but Western Europeans apparently also needed greater understanding of both the problems and pedagogical opportunities of ICT. Otherwise pedagogical change will be based on the provision of advanced and sophisticated technologies, whose use is dictated by outside experts rather than the teachers themselves actively accommodating ICT use to the objectives of historical learning. On the other hand, as Easdown pointed out, use of the Internet could promote both regular discussion and exchange between the members of European teacher and history teacher educator organisations and informal European networks, and this would benefit all European countries (see also Euroclio *Bulletin* 10, 1998).

A case study: 'Youth and History'

Such European networking, conferences and exchanges are certainly the aim of the European Committee on Culture and Education, as shown in their 1996 recommendations on history and the learning of history in Europe. A good example of how this works in practice can be seen in the 'Youth and History' Project, a comparative European project on how adolescents and their teachers view their history teaching. Research experts from Germany, Norway and Hungary united in 1994–5 to direct this 'Youth and History' Project, in which 32,000 15-year-old students from twenty-seven European states were asked to complete a questionnaire concerning their historical consciousness and political attitudes. Their teachers completed a smaller questionnaire. The results were analysed and then detailed in two volumes published jointly by the Korber-Siftung Foundation and Euroclio (Leeuw-Roord 1998: 15–24; Angvik and Borries 1997).

Motivated by a desire to understand through a comparative approach how adolescents actually experience history and learn to make sense out of the past, the research was based on the theory that interpretations of the past and expectations of the future mutually interact. Therefore, students in school should learn how interpretations can vary and how to negotiate and discuss these rationally. Such modern and open learning and teaching was expected more from liberal Western countries than elsewhere. Closed questions in a uniform questionnaire was chosen as the method best suited to multinational research undertaken with limited time and money. The results make fascinating reading and in themselves offer source material for understanding late twentieth-century history. For example, the low credence given to Hitler as a 'mad criminal' in Eastern and parts of central Europe who suffered so much under him would seem to require some historical investigation. Although, as anticipated, contrasting answers came from traditional and religious societies and those who were modernised and secular, some interesting complexities were also discovered (Leeuw-Roord 1998: 17–21, 28, 30–1, 42, 44–9; Angvik and Borries 1997).

Subsequently this research became the basis for a joint Euroclio and Korber-Siftung Foundation conference held with generous hospitality in Pécs, Hungary in September 1997. Representatives from about forty-nine European associations and institutes, including seven from the UK, were present. The conference was divided into four sessions, each based on an overarching question. These were:

1   Is history teaching up-to-date?
2   Do teachers and students attend the same history lessons?
3   Can students fit into the shoes of someone else?
4   Are teachers able and willing to innovate the learning and teaching of history?

Participants discussed these in four groups of mixed nationalities, all speaking English except for one group who spoke French. The geographical mix was potentially uneasy since many past and present enemies sat side by side: Russia, the Ukraine and Georgia, for example. That fruitful debate ensued rather than the scoring of national points demonstrates the value of such co-operative international conferences. Each group reported at the end in a plenary session that then drew up a list of recommendations (see Euroclio *Bulletin* 9, 1997–8: 24–6.

The conference found that, although the survey results showed a fairly consistent correlation between the answers of teachers and their students, teachers had a much higher estimation of their own teaching being 'modern', fascinating, fun and relating to the world around them than their students did. The latter assumed the transference of knowledge to be their teachers' main objective with source-work and those activities students prefer, such as use of media and site visits, seldom used. Even more enlightening was the very high value put on family history by students in contrast with their teachers' low conception of this (Leeuw-Roord 1998: 70–92, 103–18).

The usefulness of such a conference was particularly seen in the debate on students' understanding of historical values and attitudes. Generally students' weak responses led delegates to doubt whether it was possible to strengthen empathetic understanding at this age. Tony McAleavy's brilliant presentation of pupils' work on the American Indians, however, proved that pupils could attain quite sophisticated understanding through imaginative styles of teaching. This also served to counteract the rather negative and somewhat startling view that the results seemed to show of British and other 'liberal' countries' history teaching. It appeared that students in the latter found history to be less interesting and relevant than their European counterparts and claimed little understanding of their own culture or the context of past events and situations. This seemed to contradict the assumptions and aspirations of many at the conference who wished to introduce more innovative methods but were prevented from doing so by political, economic and pedagogical problems. On the other hand, the results may be demonstrating more the achievement of critical attitudes engendered in students than whether their experience of history is better or worse than those used to more traditional methods (Leeuw-Roord 1998: 82–3, 86–90, 93–102, 119–42, 159–60).

Furthermore, the actual data was problematic since there were wide variations in who, and how many, had answered in each country. In England, for example, 868 students were questioned – hardly a representative sample of a country, even though the sample was taken as scientifically as possible. The problems and confusions of the early years of the National Curriculum might also have influenced the replies. It was, also, generally acknowledged that everywhere there could be different interpretations of the questions (Angvik and Borries 1997: 377–87, *passim*; Leeuw-Roord 1998: 146, 149).

This project was valuable in many ways, nevertheless. It has already led to three books, a conference and numerous articles (Angvik and Borries 1997; Leeuw-Roord 1998; and for example Euroclio *Bulletin* 9, 1997–8: 24–6). It brought together academics and 'teaching experts' but also based the whole process on students' perspectives, a vital ingredient all too often left out of discussion on pedagogy. For those present in Pécs the stimulating discussion that took place in the groups and ensuing networking was most valuable (see Leeuw-Roord 1998: 171–90 for these reports). Dissemination of the recommendations and follow-up research and experiment is taking place across the continent (see 'Does IT enhance history teaching?' at http://www.glasnet.ru/~euroclio/quest10.htm). Tony McAleavy represented the HA and is history adviser for Gloucestershire; Sue Bennett, also present, is now at the Qualifications and Curriculum Authority (QCA) and present editor of the Euroclio *Bulletin*.

Some of the data discussed at Pécs should provoke thought amongst politicians in both Europe and Britain. Adolescents across Europe anticipated a big growth in pollution and population but a decreasing influence of science, technology, 'great' people and revolutionary events, and, in countries where democracy has supposedly long existed, appeared to have little interest in its history. Only Ukrainian and Arab youth seemed to have much faith in political reform at all (Leeuw-Roord 1998: 114, 117, 126–33). This is fascinating when politicians are stressing teaching citizenship and technology in schools but are being blamed themselves for lukewarm attitudes on the environment.

Teachers studying the detailed results of this project would find the data about the formation and complexity of attitudes across Europe equally thought-provoking. Those in Pécs from countries no longer under significant Soviet presence, for example, believed that using newer methods of teaching history would help form the identity of their own nation, although hopefully without inculcating nationalistic attitudes (Watts 1998: 171–4). At the same time, understanding that different countries have different needs for which they use history could also lead to questioning the aspirations behind some of these European ventures.

Are European aspirations likely to enhance or distort the teaching of European history?

In the 1996 *Recommendations* the ECC stated firmly that: 'People have a right to their past, just as they have a right to disown it', adding that history 'has a key political role to play in today's Europe. Historical awareness is an important civic skill'. It has been such positive cognisance of the important contribution that history teaching 'can, and should, make' to education generally and, particularly, 'education for democratic citizenship' that has led the Council to stress history's role in its various projects on democratic and civic education. The learning of history has been recommended both for its content and for its development of key critical skills and attitudes necessary for the intelligent workings of a tolerant democracy. There have been long-standing concerns about bias and prejudice (though documents often refer only to 'he'). Since the end of the cold war and in the shifting boundaries and politics of the 1990s, the earlier stress against history as propaganda and for a greater European context seems all the more pertinent. The concepts and issues of nation, nationalism and individual identity that gnaw at the heart of European identity have led in the 1990s to urgent demands for the inclusion of minority history, education for mutual understanding in divided societies, and the teaching of recent and European history. Historical perspectives and skills have been seen as significant for helping pupils develop the rational and critical understanding necessary to sort out the likely mix of myths and prejudices that they cull from their individual experience (Slater 1995: 31–3; Low-Beer 1997: 25–57).

Such concerns can lead to very fruitful projects where students from differing backgrounds exchange views in a truly historical spirit of enquiry. An excellent example is the European Studies Project begun in Ireland, Northern Ireland and England in 1986, and now extending to 300 schools across Europe. Students study agreed topics from their own perspective and then compare information electronically. They thus gain a comparative perspective and learn much about each other at the same time. Topics analysed have included the Russian Revolution, National Socialism and the cold war (Low-Beer 1997: 52; Austen 1995: 22–33; Euroclio 7, 1996–7: 15).

Involvement in such studies is marvellous if it helps replace long-held enmities by mutual understanding, but not if the past is trawled only to produce a historical account that ignores conflict. This could be particularly dangerous at a time of closer, though contested, European unity. The Council of Europe, although ostensibly upholding the diversity of national identities, does wish to 'introduce the European dimension as a state of mind and an attitude based on the awareness of mutual influences'. The example of an attempt to write a European history that could be used interchangeably in every country, however, might mitigate the fear that a history displaying some peaceful pan-European ideal that never existed in reality, or some bland European jargon that prevents real understanding, could actually be written. Frederic Delouche's attempt with twelve historians from the twelve countries of the European Union to put together a uniform 'History of Europe' was published in 1992 and translated from the original French into ten different languages by 1996. When Joke van der Leeuw-Roord subsequently examined the French, Dutch, English and German versions of the Second World War to see whether they lived up to their intent to avoid nationalistic history, however, she found that the different translations could not eschew subtle omissions, additions and variations in language that added a national viewpoint to the text. Achieving a 'European dimension in history education' was possible not through having an identical publication but through comparing these slight subjective alterations as interpretations of history (http://www.glasnet.ru/~euroclio/text1.htm).

Current initiatives on the actual teaching of European history exemplify these issues further. In their 1996 Recommendations the ECC recommended inclusion 'in all European history textbooks' of 'the basic elements of the different histories of Europe' once these were 'accepted by everyone' and, in syllabuses, 'the history of the whole of Europe, that of the main political and economic events, and the philosophical and cultural movements which have formed the European identity'. Subsequently, at the Standing Conference of the European Ministers of Education meeting in Norway in June 1997, it was believed the time opportune to disseminate the project, 'History Teaching in the New Europe', recommending that education authorities 'should review their curricula to ensure that they reflect the richness and diversity of Europe'. Aiming to 'promote shared political, social and cultural values in Europe as a whole' they, nevertheless, categorically rejected the 'idea of trying to impose a uniform or standardised version of European history on schools in member states'.

At Budapest the first major cross-European seminar associated with this project examined both its aim of interesting and engaging secondary school students in those 'forces, movements, events and individuals that have shaped Europe in the 20th Century' and the recommendation that practical advice and examples of innovative approaches and good practice should be provided for curriculum developers, textbook authors and history teachers. The seminar subsequently focused on how to organise and produce teaching packs on four different twentieth-century themes; case studies illustrating innovative approaches to teaching twentieth-century European history; a simulation guide on the Paris Peace Conference of 1919; and a handbook for history teachers including case studies, experimental lesson plans, teaching units and useful information. Drawing on research and case studies already completed, those attending realised that there were many potential challenges in collaborative work of this sort, especially in a continent that has had, and still experiences, bitter divisions. Yet such challenges are an integral part of any history teaching on any period. Besides, the trials of various approaches and materials, case studies and collaboration taking place across Europe are leading to some solutions.

The Budapest seminar also discussed enthusiastically a proposed handbook for history teachers on teaching about European history in the twentieth century. This is intended to include advice on a wide range of topics, pedagogical approaches and resources, and case studies reported in full context. Hopefully, as Robert Stradling wished, the whole handbook will rest on the professional expertise of teachers and will lead to a wider range of perspectives on European history and concerted European collaboration in developing resources, curricula and a clear strategy for teaching sensitive and controversial issues. (See http://culture.coe.fr/hist20/ then follow the links 'more' and 'Teaching of the History of Europe in the 20th Century.)

It might be suspected that all these idealistic recommendations and heady gatherings in Europe might reflect talkshops for a few, more than any substantial gain for hard-pressed teachers. A brief glance at one case study should indicate the potential value of European collaboration and exchange. In February 1997, Sean Lang organised a four-day conference in Cambridge on the Paris Peace Conference of 1919. The participants were sixth-formers from seven schools across Europe including his own, Hills Road Sixth Form College. Students learned how the 1919 Peace Treaties were reached through a role-play simulation where the scene was set as much as possible as it was but the outcomes left open, ignoring hindsight. Participants took the role of another country from their own although they also gave a five-minute presentation on their own country. The imaginative, reflective planning that went into this seems to have resulted in equally thoughtful participation and outcomes, which can best be appreciated by reading Lang's report in full. That such methods can engage students totally in topics crucial to understanding their period was illustrated by the Slovene student who delighted in such 'an amazing way of learning' and the intelligence and skills it inspired. The report also gives detailed advice to teachers on how to set up, organise and follow up such a conference. Such methods could be adapted for other topics and used with varying groups of schools whether international or not. This is available on the web through http://culture.coe.fr/hist20/ then following the links 'more' and 'the simulation of the Paris Peace Conference of 1919'.

It is this kind of collaboration that the ECC is urging. It undoubtedly takes much time and effort but reaps tremendous rewards in the deepening of historical understanding, especially of the intense divisions and yet similarities in experience that make up European culture. Real historical enquiry and intelligent comprehension of European issues is possible provided that sensitivity to the past is maintained and a full picture is sought, not only eschewing partial views of European events but also placing the latter in a global context. If only more teachers knew what was going on, or, even better, participated actively, it would be easier to ensure historical integrity and prevent potentially dynamic opportunities withering or becoming the preserve of a privileged few.

How can history teachers in England and Wales participate more fully in European activities in history?

How understanding of these projects can be spread and teachers actively participate in them, so that practitioners' insights, experience and needs are adequately expressed, will be briefly explored by showing where to find information on European initiatives in history. Access to the major sites and documents in turn should lead the interested history teacher or educator to further materials and possibilities.

The easiest way to gain knowledge of the activities and materials of the Council of Europe is to go to the history website of the ECC (http://culture.coe.fr/). This in itself leads to a plethora of materials and useful information, as for example, the 'Calendar of Events' on the project, 'Learning and Teaching about the History of Europe on [*sic*] the 20th Century' (http://culture.coe.fr/hist20/). Knowing what events are planned in future gives the reader chance to investigate participation, or contact those who will be participating. For instance, the 'Report of the seminar on "Initial training for history teachers in thirteen member states of the Council of Europe"' gives not only a detailed report of the problems and challenges perceived by history teacher educators who attended, but also suggested solutions, and provided the membership and addresses (telephone, fax and e-mail) of those in the different working groups. (If inaccessible through the homepage, try http://culture.coe.fr/hist20/eng/E%20rapport% 20séminaire%20Vienne%20-%20Savova.htm.)

This theme could be followed up by reading Euroclio's *Bulletin* 9 (1997–8), entitled 'History Teacher Education' in Europe, which can also be found on the World Wide Web, this time on Euroclio's homepage (http://www. glasnet.ru/~euroclio/). The homepage itself gives regular, up-to-date details of Euroclio activities and those of the Council of Europe regarding history. 'Teaching materials' includes much valuable material, for example a paper on using sources to develop the critical thinking of students. Past issues of the *Bulletin* can also be downloaded. For example, *Bulletin* 8, entitled 'Preparing for the 21st Century', includes a long report on the Euroclio conference in Budapest in 1997 on the teaching of democratic principles in history. This is accompanied by interesting, detailed case studies giving valuable comparative material to 'A' level teachers on the 1848 revolutions in Austria and Hungary (see Further reading).

The Euroclio 'What's new?' page itself gives full details about the organisation, its board and multifarious activities. In November 1998, for example, amongst other news, the site also offered 'Various skills in the teaching and learning of history' by Leonard Grech and Sandro Scriberras, an interactive game for history students, an Internet discussion on the Northern Ireland Peace Agreement, a list of historical sites on the World Wide Web compiled by Roger Austen, and details on research support offered by the European Union.

Actual participation in seminars and projects depends, in the case of Council of Europe ventures, on applying individually, though usually through the National Liaison Officer. For Euroclio, applications must be made through the appropriate member organisation. SCHTE in the UK, for example, has sent different members of the committee to various conferences. They then report back to the Standing Conference. The committee has taken part in consultation on future progress and intends to become more actively involved in future. If teachers want greater participation they must press the Historical Association and their national teacher associations to act similarly.

The ECC *Recommendations* support such involvement and suggest establishing in member states an on-line library of history, 'national history museums on the lines of the German "House of History" in Bonn', and setting up a code of practice for history teachers together with a 'European charter to protect them from political manipulation'. The Council is also publicising its Documentation Centre (Fax: 03 88 41 27 80) and the George Eckert Centre. Addresses for these and other useful European ventures can be found in Slater alongside a bibliography of Council of Europe documents (Slater 1995: 155–72 ; see also 48–9).

Conclusion

There are, therefore, many initiatives in Europe to improve and utilise the learning and teaching of history, and there are ways for teachers and teacher educators to tap into these. At present, however, dissemination and participation has been partial and limited. Active participation in these ventures is urgent not only so that British history teachers and educators themselves can benefit but also that they may share their own valuable experience and contribute to future developments. They need both to enlighten British politicians and institutions on the value that the Council of Europe puts on history in developing rational, intelligent, critical citizens in a thriving democracy, and ensure that history is never used to propagate ideology.

Questions

This chapter ends, therefore, with the following challenges for history teachers and history teacher educators in England and Wales.

1   How can they use European initiatives to persuade their own government(s) to support the teaching of history more strongly?
2   How can they compel their respective associations to disseminate news of European activities in history more fully and increase participation?

3　How can they obtain and use the reports and research coming from Europe to the best advantage of their students?

4　How can they ensure that the time, money and effort invested by Europe on history teaching and learning recognises the multiplicity of identities and interpretations, and does not serve the ideology of one sector?

Further reading

Leeuw-Roord, J. van der (ed.) (1998) *The State of History Education in Europe*, Hamburg: Korber-Siftung.

This explains the results of the 'Youth and History' survey, not only the largest European cross-cultural history project but also a rare instance of a project based on pupil perceptions. It provides the researchers' interpretations and commentaries of experienced history educators on the project and raises essential issues in the learning and teaching of history.

Slater, J. (1995) *Teaching History in the New Europe*, London: Cassell.

This is very useful for finding out European initiatives in history teaching from 1950 to 1994, especially the work of the Council of Europe. It includes the names of most relevant organisations and many useful addresses.

Much material on history in Europe can be accessed from the following two websites. For further comments on these see the section immediately before this chapter's conclusion (pp. 185–6). The first website is at:
http://culture.coe.fr/

All of the sites used on the Council of Europe's history activities are obtainable once this has been accessed. Click respectively on the links for English/Education/Learning and Teaching about the History of Europe on [*sic*] the 20th Century. They thus become:
http://culture.coe.fr/hist20/
followed by the name of the document.htm. The links include 'calendar of events', 'project group' and 'more'.

The last will lead to 'the simulation of the Paris Peace Conference of 1919' (Sean Lang) and 'Teaching of the History of Europe in the 20th Century' (Robert Stradling). Also of interest is the ECC Newsletter 'On Teaching 20th Century European History' at http://culture.coe.fr/Infocentre/pub/eng/enle6_6.htm (changing the numbers in the URL can give access to other documents).

The second website is
http://www.glasnet.ru/~euroclio/
This gives access to all of the activities set up by Euroclio as well as its issues of *Bulletin*. Again, once the homepage has been opened, access to many further sites is possible. They include the following:

What's new? (Whatnew.htm)
What is Euroclio?
Euroclio bulletins
Teaching materials

A search of some of these sites can prove to be very fruitful. For example, 'Euroclio bulletins' gives the text of Euroclio *Bulletin* 8 (Summer 1997), entitled 'Preparing for the 21st Century'. This in turn allows access to studies on the 1848 Revolutions (see: '5. Presentation by members: 1848 as a case'; or http://www.glasnet.ru/~euroclio/austria.htm and /belgium.htm). *Bulletin* 10 (Summer 1998) *History Teaching and Information and Communications Technology* is at http://www.glasnet.ru/~euroclio/bul10.htm, and contains many useful documents.

The 'Teaching materials' option on the main page includes

Leeuw-Roord, J. van der, 'What makes a good history textbook? Reflections on the use and writing of history textbooks in Europe' (1996).

Leeuw-Roord, J. van der, 'The comparison of different versions of Frederic Delouche "History of Europe"'.

McKellar, I.B. 'The struggle for sources in Scottish schools'.

McKellar, I.B. 'The 1956 Hungarian Rising: using sources to develop the critical thinking of students'.

The site is constantly updated with case studies, materials for all levels of the history classroom, projects and information about other websites.

Part III

Issues in the training of history teachers

15 Current issues in the training of secondary history teachers

An HMI perspective

Carole Baker, Ted Cohn and Mark McLaughlin

Between 1996 and 1998 a team of five subject specialist HM Inspectors (HMI) inspected every secondary course of initial teacher training (ITT) for history teachers in England. Singly or in pairs, they visited every course at least twice, interviewed tutors, mentors and trainees, examined course documents, read trainees' written assignments, pored over teaching files, read external examiners' reports, and observed tutors teaching, mentors working with trainees and trainees teaching pupils in classrooms. The inspection was the most complete and detailed investigation ever undertaken by HMI of how secondary history teachers are trained in England, and produced a mass of information about what is actually happening in history courses, as well as judgements about the quality of the training process, upon which to reflect and try to identify some of the current major issues in the training of history teachers.

In 1996–7 HMI inspected twenty-one courses, including the Open University's distance-learning course and two of the new School-Centred Initial Teacher Training (SCITT) schemes. The following year they undertook nineteen inspections, three of which were re-inspections, and including three more SCITTs. The largest of the courses inspected, the Open University, had over a hundred trainees, whilst the smallest, one of the SCITTs, had only three. The number of trainees on most courses fell within the fifteen to thirty range, with the London Institute of Education the largest of the traditional providers with sixty-nine trainees, whilst SCITTs had numbers in single figures. All the courses led to the award of Qualified Teacher Status (QTS) and all except one to the award of the Post-Graduate Certificate in Education (PGCE). Every inspection was organised on broadly the same lines – Stage 1 focused on the training process in the partnership (in the Higher Education Institution (HEI) and school), and Stage 2 on the standards achieved by the trainees on their final, assessed, block teaching practice. The criteria employed were set out in the joint Teacher Training Agency/Office for Standards in Education (TTA/OFSTED) *Framework for the Assessment of Quality and Standards in Initial Teacher Training* (1996/97 and 1997/98), and the inspection methodology was described and explained in the *Guidance for Secondary ITT Subject Inspections* published by OFSTED. During the course of the inspection the Secretary of State's requirements for the award of Qualified Teacher Status (QTS) were revised, and Circular 10/97 was replaced by Circular 4/98, and competences by standards.

The inspectors investigated and reported on six cells in the *Framework*: the quality of the admissions policy and the selection procedures (S1); the quality of the training process in developing the knowledge, understanding and skills set out in the competences (1996/97) or standards (1997/98) for the award of QTS (T2); the accuracy and consistency of the assessment of trainees (T4); and the three competence or standards cells (C1–3 or ST1–3) (these are: subject knowledge and understanding; planning teaching and classroom management; and assessment, recording and reporting on pupils' progress). Each cell was awarded a grade on a four-point scale from: very good with several outstanding features (1); good with no significant weaknesses (2); adequate but requiring significant improvement (3); to poor quality, not complying with the Secretary of State's current criteria (4). Finally, the inspectors provided summary oral feedback to the providers at the end of the inspection and issued a published report on each course.

Broadly speaking, history teacher training is mostly of good or very good quality in England, as are the standards achieved by trainees. Some courses achieved Grade 1s in some cells but not in others, only two courses gained a profile of six Grade 1s, although several more had between three and five Grade 1s. Four courses needed to be re-inspected because they either had a profile of Grade 3s in the standards cells, or were judged to be non-compliant in a particular cell. The strongest cell, with most Grade 1s and 2s, was S1 and the weakest was C3 (or ST3), which was the trainees' competence or standard cell relating to the assessment and recording of pupils' progress. History compared well with other secondary subjects and particularly favourably in respect of the quality of the trainees it attracts. Nearly all the history trainees were academically well qualified, with at least second-class honours degrees, and on many courses over three-quarters had first-class or upper second-class honours degrees in history, whether studied as a single subject or in combination with other subjects.

It is as well to acknowledge at the outset that the issues thrown up by the inspections were to some extent, but not entirely, determined by the kinds of questions posed by the inspectors. The inspectors did not approach the courses with a completely open agenda; rather they sought information and evidence that would help them arrive at judgements in relation to the criteria set out for each cell in the *Framework*. They had, in other words, a strong notion of what they were looking for, and the criteria contained implicit assumptions about what constitutes good practice in secondary history teacher training. Nonetheless, there are always unintended consequences of inspection and findings that do not fit neatly into frameworks, whether published or implicit.

One of the first of these issues arose out of the inspection of cell S1, with implications for judgements about quality elsewhere, and especially in relation to cell C1/ST1. It turned on the kind of history degree that would provide the most appropriate and secure foundation for those intending to be secondary-school history teachers. Many of the applicants for ITT did not, or do not, hold what might be described as traditional single-subject history degrees. There is currently a far wider range of undergraduate degrees offered in British universities, in which the study of history features more or less strongly, than used to be the case even twenty years ago. History, or sometimes 'historical studies', is studied in combination with a host of other subjects from biology to business studies. Where modularisation prevails, it permits a wealth of associations. Furthermore, many first degrees featuring history can focus on particular periods (the Victorian for example) or aspects of the study of the past such as war studies or Byzantine studies. Very modern or contemporary history and international relations courses are common. Degrees based on geographical area studies – North American, Latin American, African, Russian – are also popular. Those making decisions about suitability for training, who have to chose between applicants, are faced with an almost bewildering array of first degrees, and obliged to make decisions about which constitute the best fit with the requirements of the National Curriculum and the more popular GCSE and 'A' Level syllabuses taught in schools. The criteria by which such decisions are made are rarely stated, although they can be articulated by tutors, and are applied in practice, other things being equal. The 'other things' refer usually to the applicants' attributes, qualities and previous experiences, especially contact with young people.

Once on the course, the trainees' familiarity with the periods and topics they are called upon to teach can be extremely variable. Some trainees are decidedly apprehensive as they approach some topics, and tackling unfamiliar material at advanced level can generate acute anxieties. Courses have devised a range of strategies to deal with this aspect of subject knowledge in the sense of familiarity with content, but there is a limit to what can be achieved in a crowded one-year programme. Audits are frequently employed at the outset of courses to identify gaps in trainees' subject content knowledge of particular historical periods and topics, and reading or intensive study are often prescribed to fill the gaps identified. But reading takes time, and trainees complain that time, opportunity and even energy are valuable commodities in short supply on courses where they are taught intensively when not in school and are heavily committed when they are.

Striking the right balance between the amounts of time devoted to the school-based elements of the training and those spent in lectures, seminars and workshops, and using that time most effectively, also concern course planners. The Secretary of State's requirements set out in the relevant circulars allow little room for manoeuvre in respect of the overall amount of time that trainees must spend in schools, but the pattern of such attachments can vary, and there is much more scope for flexibility in the provision of Education and Professional Studies (EPS) and subject applications programmes. The number, length and distribution throughout the year of subject applications-taught sessions vary considerably between PGCE courses. Some courses adopt what might be described as a minimalist approach, with the trainees committed to no more than one three-hour subject applications session a week at the HEI or lead school when they are not involved in classroom-related school experience; others devote a whole day a week, or even longer, to subject applications work, when the trainees are not engaged full-time with school experience. The mark of very good courses is not so much the amount of time they devote to subject applications work, but the extent to which the time available is used effectively, the relationship between the centrally provided sessions and what the trainees are expected to do in schools and the coherence of the whole programme, including EPS, in helping the trainees achieve the standards and to teach more effectively. Nonetheless, the demands made on trainees' time could be more consistent, and the contribution that mentors can and should make to the trainees' knowledge and understanding of issues raised in subject application sessions enhanced, as in the most effective programmes, to avoid repetition and reduce pressure on all involved in the training process.

It has become a cliché to observe that subject mentors are key figures in the training of history and other teachers, and that the better the mentors the better the course. But it is worth repeating because the inspections bore out this truism time and again. The most effective training partnerships were those that were able to recruit able subject mentors from strong departments, provide them with good-quality initial and continuing training, bind them closely to the course and secure their loyalty, furnish them with professional development opportunities and treat them with respect. But the achievement of these highly desirable outcomes is far from easy. It requires effort, time, tact, skill, credibility, support and sensitivity. That it can be done at all is a credit to many of those involved in training history teachers. The mentors have to be recruited in the first place and there is often competition for their services – from within the school and the area where the school is located, for example – for these people are often much in demand. Once engaged, they need to be inducted and, thereafter, their knowledge, skills and understandings developed, extended, refined and eventually disseminated. At the same time they have to be retained and motivated. Some partnerships are very skilled at, and imaginative in, the ways they retain, develop and motivate their mentors. Joint observations and debriefing of trainees involving tutors or area mentors/moderators, regular meetings with a professional value-added element, newsletters, participation in the selection process and centre-based teaching, and the accreditation of prior learning leading to formal qualifications are just some of the strategies employed. The new 'Move me on' feature in *Teaching History*, the periodical published by the Historical Association, is a valuable recognition of the importance of mentors, and is revealing about the depth and subtlety of mentors' understandings. It is also an excellent vehicle for celebrating and disseminating good practice.

Recognising good mentoring practice and distinguishing between good, adequate and indifferent practice is difficult and highly skilled. It is also potentially contentious and always sensitive, so it is an aspect of the training process that partners often choose to avoid. Some mentors are so obviously skilful, proficient, efficient and effective that they are easy to identify. Others are not nearly so good, and inspectors found the quality of feedback to trainees varied to an unacceptable extent. It was often insufficiently subject-specific and not related to the trainees' achievement of the standards. Defining, precisely, what it is that the most effective subject mentors do that is distinctive, and setting up arrangements for them to share their expertise systematically on a regular basis with others is more difficult to achieve and undertaken less frequently. Many partnerships are committed to improving the practice of the less effective mentors and have strategies, usually oblique, non-confrontational and co-operative, for developing their skills and enhancing their knowledge and understanding. The least effective mentors are usually 'dropped' more or less diplomatically, but sometimes with great difficulty and not before they have had lengthy contact with trainees. Assuring quality in mentoring is an issue for all partnerships, but difficult to achieve when mentors are either not paid at all, or are low-paid or under-paid volunteers in the ITT process, nominated by the school, the headteacher or head of department rather than selected by the partnership, and frequently heavily committed in respect of teaching and other associated activities.

If the subject mentors' wider role in the training of intending teachers is now generally recognised, the responsibilities they have in relation to their colleagues within their departments are not always fully appreciated. Trainees usually work with several teachers in a history department, not all of whom are trained mentors as defined by the partnership, but who, nevertheless, contribute to their training and assessment. The only training that these class teachers, not all of whom may be front-line history specialists, usually receive is that provided by the mentor. But mentors are invariably extremely hard-pressed and do not have the time, even when they have the skills, knowledge and inclination, to induct and continue to provide the kind of support their colleagues need. Partnerships have concentrated on the needs of mentors, understandably, but need to find ways of providing for the 'significant others' in trainees' school experiences if they are to raise standards of training overall. There is talk about so-called 'training departments', where a culture of training prevails, where all are committed to the achievement of high training standards, where familiarity with current ITT requirements is the norm and where trainees and teachers are conscious of and keen to be engaged in a mutually beneficial enterprise. But such departments are rare. There were outstanding examples, however, where trainees benefited throughout their attachment from quality teaching coupled with critical analysis of a high standard that contributed significantly to their progress. Few departments exhibit all, or even most, of these characteristics.

History departments do not regard initial teacher training as their core activity and, under pressure, mentors and other teachers alike accord it a lower priority. That lower priority is often a reflection of the school's perception of what is more and what is less important. The overwhelming majority of schools have the best of intentions in respect of their responsibilities for teacher training, and the drawing up of contracts has heightened partners' awareness of their duties to the trainees and their responsibilities to each other. Schools are subject to a range of pressures, however, and some pressures are more intense and irresistible than others. The pressure from parents to ensure that their children are taught by the 'best teachers', which often means the most experienced teachers and not 'students', for example, or the department's desire to achieve high standards in public examinations or to attract the most able pupils when they make decisions about which subjects to study for General Certificate of Secondary Education (GCSE) or Advanced Level ('A' Level). League tables and OFSTED inspections simply add to the list. Such pressures can impact on training and the opportunities available to trainees. Trainees may, for example, have restricted access to certain sets in Year 9, to examination groups in Year 10 and Year 11, and to sixth-form classes particularly in Year 13. Furthermore, the funding that each trainee brings into the school is required for a host of purposes and may not find its way to the departments in which the trainees are based, may not be used to compensate the subject mentors for their extra duties, or deployed to provide them with the non-contact time they so sorely need. The deployment of ITT funds within schools is a major issue for the partnership model in general.

The better training schools and departments regard ITT trainees as a valuable resource. They see them as bringing in new ideas, new resources, contact with the most recent developments in history teaching, energy, enthusiasm, commitment, stimulation and opportunities for staff development. They also keep their eyes and ears open for potential new members of staff. At the same time they are very aware of the responsibilities they bear and the cost, human as well as material, of undertaking a training role. However, some schools and departments overlook or insufficiently exploit the benefits of being involved in ITT. The potential of drawing members of staff from departments other than history into the trainees' programmes, for example, of linking ITT with provision for Newly Qualified Teachers (NQTs) and the wider Continuing Professional Development (CPD) programme, the spin-off for the development of classroom observational skills linked to appraisal, and the use of trainees as pupil mentors on a one-to-one basis. There is strong evidence that being involved in ITT, participating in a training partnership, can stimulate change and promote good practice not only at the departmental level , but also at the school level. Some SCITTs recognise this very clearly and a major reason, in more than one case, for becoming involved in school-centred training schemes was to extend opportunities for staff development and to raise pupils' standards of achievement by improving the quality of teaching and learning.

In assessing trainees, the majority of history courses are good, and fewer have significant shortcomings than in the average secondary subject. Nonetheless, nearly one course in five displayed some weaknesses. Some trainers, and especially school-based mentors, were insufficiently familiar with the standards; and mentors' colleagues in schools, who have a significant training role, were nearly always much less knowledgeable about and familiar with the standards than the mentors. Some mentors were also uncertain about their role in the assessment process, and apprehensive about making judgements that might have conflicted with HEI tutors' judgements. Trainers' grasp of what constituted good practice, beyond the pass/fail boundary, needed strengthening, as did moderation within schools and across partnerships. Moderation was not always provided by a history subject specialist within the schools or across partnerships.

Every PGCE secondary course inspected had one or more external examiner. These external examiners were nearly always generic – concerned with the course as a whole rather than the subjects within it, although individual external examiners nearly always had a subject specialisation that, sometimes, was history. The generalist or generic external examiners were not able to comment with confidence on subject-specific knowledge, pedagogical issues and, especially, on the issue of comparability of standards between the partnerships of which they had experience. Their comments on the course were usually of a generic nature and, if they referred to history at all, were bland and at a high level of generality. Lack of funding prevents courses from having a subject specialist external examiner for every subject every year, but some courses were able to circumvent that difficulty by ensuring that external examiners' subject specialisations were rotated regularly, or by employing external subject consultants on a less formal basis to provide an outside perspective.

A very high proportion of the history trainees inspected by HMI were of such good quality that it was quickly apparent that they were, or could be, a valuable addition to the school and department providing training. But trainees' strengths, as well as their shortcomings, need to be identified early and thoroughly, the former exploited and the latter redressed. Some of the disadvantages of relatively narrow courses of study in history can, paradoxically, be strengths. Individual trainees encountered had, for example, a detailed knowledge and understanding of periods or aspects of history, or of the history of relatively unfamiliar geographical areas, which could have been shared with the rest of the group or used to good effect within a school history department. Inspectors met graduates who were very strong in aspects of Byzantine, Islamic, African and Medieval Studies, for example, all highly relevant to the teaching of particular units of the National Curriculum; and with trainees who were graduates in information technology, computer applications, graphics and desktop publishing as well as accountancy, tourism and criminology. On the other hand, many graduates lack that broad grasp of the chronology and sweep of British and European history that was a feature of traditional medieval and modern history degrees. They were frequently very aware of contemporary developments in the wider world, the impact of the two world wars, communism, nazism, colonialism, post-colonialism and the cold war, but less secure on earlier medieval and modern developments in the world, and largely ignorant, with exceptions of course, of ancient history. These shortcomings revealed themselves in the teaching of the ancient, medieval and early modern periods especially. There was a tendency to fall back on stereotypes – in teaching about medieval people and society, for example, or explanations about the nature of the religious conflicts in England in the sixteenth and seventeenth centuries. The issue for trainers is how to harness and exploit trainees' strengths while addressing their shortcomings, all in the course of a training year that lasts nine months.

In order to meet the standards set out in Circular 4/98 trainees are required to:

> use teaching methods which sustain the momentum of pupils' work and keep all pupils engaged through [*inter alia*] ... selecting and making good use of ... Information and Communications Technology (ICT) and other learning resources ... [and] ... exploiting opportunities to improve pupils' basic skills in literacy, numeracy and ICT.

The inspection of courses revealed that many trainees are personally very skilled in the use of ICT. They can word-process, use spreadsheets and a range of software, including CD-ROMs, and are comfortable with e-mail and the World Wide Web. There is, of course, a range in the levels of knowledge, proficiency and confidence, from individuals who are impressively accomplished to those who, if not terrified – for terror is much rarer than it used to be – are rather less secure in either knowledge or skills. Many trainees use their skills to good effect in producing written assignments – nearly all word-processed now – and in the preparation of teaching materials for use in the classroom. Work-sheets and overhead transparencies, for example, are often, usually even, word-processed and of high quality in presentational terms, easy to read, often supported by illustrations, and attractive to the pupils. Trainees also use CD-ROMs and the Internet to acquire information about particular topics or historical characters, which is not so easily accessible through printed materials. Trainees' opportunities to use ICT directly in the teaching of history, however, and to develop the pupils' skills in the use of ICT through their teaching of history are significantly more limited. The problem often resides at school and, more specifically, departmental levels. Trainees frequently have very restricted, often totally insufficient, access to the school hardware and, although the use of ICT in the teaching of history has increased, sometimes dramatically, in recent years, its regular and systematic use is still at an embryonic stage in most history departments. Some trainees' ambitious plans to use ICT in their teaching are frustrated by logistical and administrative difficulties involving access to computers that the full-time members of staff find just as difficult to overcome. Opportunities to become familiar with a range of history teaching packages *in situ*, and to gain confidence in the use of ICT for teaching purposes are, therefore, very variable – too variable at present.

History trainees' teaching and classroom management capabilities are broadly good. They usually, for example, deliver clear presentations, explain carefully and deliver instructions effectively. Mentors and class teachers are comfortable and confident in dealing with these aspects of teaching and frequently provide very sound advice. However, the trainers could undertake more direct coaching; they could be less oblique and more direct and explicit with the assistance and advice they offer. Many are too kind, and too anxious not to give offence. In their understandable concern not to undermine the confidence of trainees, they often concentrate on strengths and gloss over short-comings. Their comments lack that critical edge that extends trainees and leads to improvement. This may be one reason why trainees have a tendency to 'plateau' – to achieve a certain, acceptable level of proficiency at which they remain for the rest of their time on the practice. Questioning technique furnishes a pertinent example. Many trainees – assisted, advised and supported by their mentors, tutors and class teachers – acquire a reasonable level of proficiency. They grasp the difference between closed and open-ended questions, between directed and non-directed, and are more or less skilled in the ways they use these kinds of questions in class. However, few go much beyond this relatively straightforward repertoire onto a higher plain, using responses as springboards for further questions, deploying questions that stretch the pupils' thinking in specifically historical ways. Articles in more recent issues of *Teaching History* seek to address the question of how to promote higher-level thinking in history, and the improvement of trainees' and teachers' questioning skills would greatly assist.

Trainees' planning was usually diligent, more or less thorough, and displayed an awareness of the need to address issues of progression. However, although aware, trainees found it very difficult to plan for and achieve progress through their teaching, in practice. School history departments, increasingly, have developed, piloted, implemented, evaluated and revised detailed schemes of work of their own, which are often of a high quality but that leave trainees with a limited amount of medium- and longer-term planning to do. They are obliged to operate within boundaries laid down, and have insufficient practice in preparing and planning the work of a group of pupils over a period of time so as to advance their knowledge of, and thinking in, the subject. The progression that is built into the schemes with which they are presented is not always fully explained to the trainees and made explicit, and, because they have not had to wrestle with planning for progression directly, they are not developing the skills and insights to enable them to recognise it in the classrooms. They need to be shown more examples of what progress is, and what constitutes good practice in bringing it about. They also need to consider why the approach embedded in the particular practice they are observing and involved in has been adopted, and provided with opportunities to weigh its strengths and shortcomings.

The aspect of their practice in which trainees were least confident, practised and proficient was in the assessment recording and reporting (ARR) of pupils' progress (ST3). History trainees were, on the whole, stronger in this cell than the trainees in other subjects, but inspection indicated, nonetheless, that there is room for improvement. The trainees were nearly always very diligent in their marking of pupils' work and conscientious about keeping records of what pupils had done. However the marking varied in quality – from that which was careful, thorough and helped pupils to understand how they might improve, to marking that did little more than signify that a piece of work had been handed in. Records also varied in their usefulness. Some trainees kept records to meet their professional obligations – entirely understandable and justifiable – but failed to reflect on why they kept the records, or whether keeping them in this or that particular form was either the most efficient means or helped them and their pupils achieve their ultimate teaching and learning objectives respectively. Those trainees who adapted and modified departmental practice in the keeping of records found the whole process of record-keeping much more useful, informative, interesting and beneficial in shaping and informing their planning and teaching than did those who simply adopted, and conformed to, the practice that prevailed.

Gauging the levels – both National Curriculum and GCSE or 'A' level related – at which students were working was another aspect of ARR practice in which trainees' proficiency and confidence varied to quite a significant degree. It is, of course, a higher-level skill and one that experienced teachers find demanding. Nonetheless, trainees have to make a start and to be able to demonstrate, by the end of their training year, that they can operate at a reasonable level of proficiency. They would not be expected to become GCSE or 'A' level markers in their first year of teaching, for example, but they are expected to be familiar with GCSE and 'A' level assessment requirements. Some trainees' skills were developed very systematically by their tutors and subject mentors, working closely together and pushing forward the trainees' understanding through regular practice, close monitoring and discussion. Other trainees were much less fortunate and did not have their knowledge, skills and understanding established securely or consolidated and developed as systematically. In some cases the trainees were largely self-taught in this aspect of their practice, proceeding by trial and error, and looking to more experienced colleagues to confirm that they were 'more or less on the right lines'.

The demands upon, and expectations of, ITT are onerous and ambitious; however, it can and will be argued that it is the initial training 'year' that lasts nine months, not the training. The renewed emphasis on induction in the recently issued (1998) Green Paper, *Teachers: Meeting the Challenge of Change*, the introduction of the Career Entry Profile, which has been launched more or less successfully, the importance now attached to appraisal, all linked to school-based CPD policies, should mean that the initial preparation of history teachers can be viewed in the context of the 'three i's' of training – initial, induction and in-service. There are indications of overload in initial training and some trainers, faced with the mountain of knowledge that trainees are expected to acquire and the daunting range of competences or standards they are required to master, fall either into a state of weary resignation or pick and mix as best they can. The most effective partnerships share the burden, have a strong, clear, shared vision of what is required, what is desirable and what would signify high achievement, and are able to communicate that to their trainees and to all the partners. They do this through their documentation, in written communications between the partners and through constant discussion and networking. There is no magic formula: success stems from infinitely painstaking listening, talking and negotiation. Establishing and maintaining successful partnerships is an extremely time-consuming and frustratingly slow process at times, but there would appear to be no alternative within the present partnership model of training.

The quality of training in history is well above the all-subject secondary average. The proportion of very good training is much higher and the proportion of adequate training is much lower than in most other subjects. History trainees are predominantly good in subject knowledge; in planning, teaching and class management; and in marking pupils' work, providing feedback, and monitoring pupils' progress. This is all excellent news. There is, nonetheless, room for improvement. Some of the issues identified in this chapter indicate where there is scope for improvement – broadening mentors' perspectives on good teaching, for example, or providing better access to the full age and ability range for all trainees. The less good news is that history graduates find it more difficult to secure posts than anyone else. Competition is fierce and career progression in history is often slow. Many history graduates move on in their chosen profession by moving out of history teaching into pastoral and administrative posts. It has, alas, been ever thus, but the proposals in the Green Paper aimed at enabling good teachers to remain in the classroom may stem, if not reverse, this trend.

16 Good practice in the school-based training of history teachers

*Carole Baker, Ted Cohn and
Mark McLaughlin*

This chapter is concerned with the elements of subject-related training that take place in schools rather than HEIs and the lead school in SCITTs. It seeks to describe aspects of good practice identified in the recent HMI inspections of initial teacher training history courses, and it focuses particularly upon the role of the lead person, responsible directly for the training of history trainees, in teaching practice schools. Several terms are used to describe this person in different HEI and SCITT partnerships, but the most common one is subject mentor, and this is the term that will be adopted here. In considering the roles and responsibilities of the subject mentor, we will begin by placing these within the wider context of the subject mentor's school and the HEI or SCITT partnership. Other roles of the subject mentor to be considered include the development of: trainees' subject knowledge; their skills in planning, classroom management and teaching; and their skills in the assessment, recording and reporting of the progress of pupils. Lastly, the role of subject mentors in monitoring and assessing the progress that trainees make towards achieving the required competences or standards will be discussed.

Recent changes in the organisation of teacher training in England, and, in particular, the requirement that trainees spend at least two-thirds of their training course in schools, have given schools enhanced responsibilities for the training of teachers. The term partnership reflects the essential qualities of good training, however it is organised, which are close collaboration between all those involved in the training, and shared understandings and purposes. Partnerships and consortia have adopted a number of strategies to achieve these outcomes. Documentation that clearly delineates the roles and responsibilities of all of those involved in the training is a universal feature of the best training. Increasingly, this documentation is being revised to identify how the subject mentor's role should alter as the trainee becomes more confident and competent in the basic teaching skills of classroom management and organisation, in order to help them develop higher-order skills. Good documentation is an essential, but not sufficient, condition to ensure that subject mentors fully understand and internalise the nature and scope of their responsibility for training.

Regular meetings of subject mentors with those responsible for the overall subject training in the lead school or HEI are as necessary as high-quality documentation. A very important part of these meetings is imparting information to subject mentors about changes, such as the move from competences to standards with the introduction of Circular 4/98, and alterations to documentation in the light of these changes. Where these meetings are successful, however, they often involve much more than the imparting of information. There are discussions and opportunities for negotiation about how particular requirements will be implemented, so that subject mentors feel involved in decision making. Examples of good practice across the partnership or consortium are identified and shared. For instance, at one meeting, examples of effective ways of collecting evidence of the attainment of particular standards by the trainees were scrutinised and discussed, while at another meeting effective ways of logging mentor review sessions were demonstrated. Sometimes a part of meetings are devoted directly to the professional development of subject mentors, such as one where ways of improving pupils' writing in history were considered. Occasionally trainees are involved as well, and in one instance trainees and subject mentors worked collaboratively on exploring the uses of ICT in teaching history. Another valuable feature of regular meetings is the opportunities they provide for informal discussion and sharing of good practice between subject mentors, which help to counteract any sense of professional isolation. Sometimes a meeting for subject mentors has been arranged between the trainees' two main teaching practices, and this has been used productively by subject mentors from trainees' first and second teaching practice schools to discuss the progress and training needs of the trainees for whom they are responsible.

A strategy that has greatly helped create a sense of common purpose in HEI partnerships, which are all considerably bigger than SCITT partnerships, is the creation of a subject co-ordinating and planning committee, comprising the subject tutor or tutors from the HEI and selected subject mentors from partnership schools. Such committees provide subject mentors with a direct input into initial planning and can be a valuable source of rapid monitoring and review about developing issues and concerns. Sometimes committees have a formal management and review function, and subject mentors on the committee take a leading role in explaining changes in subject mentor roles and in answering queries raised by other subject mentors.

Good collaboration across partner institutions is an essential feature of good training, but so is good collaboration within individual schools. Where there is good practice, the particular roles of subject mentors, and others with more general professional training responsibilities in schools, are clearly delineated and the training is closely co-ordinated, so that, for instance, discussion of how the school approaches special educational needs is combined with discussion of how special educational needs is addressed in history. Inspection evidence indicates that this collaboration is usually at least sound, and is often good. In one school subject mentors observed non-history trainees teaching their subjects, as well as observing history trainees, and met regularly with the senior mentor with overall responsibility for all trainees as a group to discuss trainees' progress and identify common issues and particular concerns. These discussions provided a valuable forum for subject mentors to test developing judgements and to put forward the evidence to support these judgements, which helped to establish and sustain consistency in practice across different subjects and to support and advise inexperienced subject mentors.

The best training occurs where what is done centrally, in the HEI or lead school, and what is done in other schools complement and reinforce each other effectively. This was a good feature of a number of partnerships, particularly during the period where trainees spent part of their time in schools and part of their time in HEIs or the lead school, between or before major teaching practices. Evidence about different GCSE syllabuses, differing approaches to special educational needs, the teaching of particular history topics, and the marketing of history at Key Stage 4, for instance, were used well to help identify commonalities and differences, and to develop an understanding of good practice. Assignments that trainees undertake for assessment purposes often expect them to reflect upon and use school experiences, in conjunction with relevant research work done in the HEI or lead school. Where subject mentors have been involved in providing guidance and support, it has usually been productive, significantly improving trainees' understanding. It was much less common for subject mentors to ask trainees to reflect upon work done in other aspects of their training, in considering how they might improve a particular aspect of their teaching or solve a particular problem.

Subject mentors can also make an important contribution to the centrally based training in a HEI or lead school, and inspection evidence showed that this provided a valuable extra dimension to this aspect of the training. For instance, in one session a subject mentor provided insights into the different demands of three different 'A' level history courses he had taught, and another subject mentor discussed what trainees needed to consider when applying for their first job, drawing on his own experience of helping to appoint staff.

The development of trainees' subject expertise is an area of great importance. It is referred to in Chapter 1 and is the focus of Chapter 3. Subject mentors often provide valuable guidance to trainees about how to improve their subject knowledge of a particular series of events or period of history with which they are not familiar and that they will be teaching. They frequently help trainees to identify the sort of subject knowledge that is particularly useful for teaching purposes, such as a concise and clear overview, brief extracts from key documents, or descriptions of key events and figures, or interesting historical anecdotes. Subject mentors are less likely to address systematically the wider areas of weakness in subject knowledge, but in the best practice this has become a strong feature of the subject mentor's role, with a twin focus on developing trainees' knowledge of historical periods and events with which they are not familiar, and consolidating their understanding of the historical concepts and skills that underpin the history curriculum in schools.

The development of trainees' expertise also includes the key skills of literacy, numeracy and ICT. Trainees are usually introduced to these as part of their centrally based training programme, but these then have to be practised and developed in the school context. Literacy, and in particular the development of writing skills, is generally the best developed area. In some instances trainees have brought ideas from their central training that have been adopted successfully in the school more generally. Less attention has been paid to the development of reading, but good mentors make this a strong focus as well. It is very uncommon for significant attention to be paid to the development of numeracy skills, reflecting in part the continuing reluctance to pay sufficient attention to quantitative data as a resource for teaching history. The development of ICT skills is also a weak area, but this often reflects the lack of sufficient hardware and the lack of appropriate software in schools, and that many subject mentors lack the necessary skills and opportunities to use ICT effectively in the classroom themselves.

There is overwhelming inspection evidence that detailed planning is an essential part of good teaching. Trainees are usually introduced to planning in their HEI or lead school and provided with good exemplars of planning at the level of individual lessons, series of lessons, units of work and, sometimes, schemes of work for a particular course. Where this work is combined with the scrutiny of curriculum planning in the schools in which trainees are working during, for instance, a period when the trainees spend part of the week in their teaching practice schools and part in the HEI or lead school, it greatly enhances the trainees' understanding of the role of planning in effective teaching. The role of subject mentors in this is two-fold. First, they must ensure that trainees' lesson planning is well thought out and appropriate in terms of the subject matter to be taught, the tasks set for pupils, the structure and organisation of lessons, and the resources needed to support the teaching. This is familiar ground for subject mentors and the great majority carry out this role well, providing a judicious mixture of guidance and support that allows the trainee to retain a sense of ownership of the material they are to teach, while ensuring that it is relevant and well matched to the learning needs of the pupils. Second, they often provide good advice and guidance about how to organise the series of lessons for which the trainees are responsible, to ensure that the relevant part of the history curriculum is covered.

Opportunities for trainees to produce their own medium-term plans to support their teaching are often limited by the detailed nature of curriculum planning in history in schools. Nevertheless, it is important for mentors to discuss with trainees how their teaching of a particular part of the history curriculum contributes to the pupils' developing understanding of historical concepts, such as chronology, conflict, continuity, change and power, and the historical skills of interpretation, analysis and communication. An example of one aspect of this was where a subject mentor explained very clearly how the school's scheme of work was used to provide a structured framework, which allowed an element of choice for individual teachers, but achieved common learning outcomes in a large school. The trainees' observation of lessons was then planned so that they could observe this in operation in the department.

The interplay between knowledge, concepts and skills in history is a difficult and complex area, which trainees are often not ready to tackle until they feel comfortable with the knowledge they are imparting and with their classroom management. It is an aspect of the training that mentors can develop particularly during the middle and latter part of later teaching practices, and is often done best in conjunction with discussions about constructing the scheme of work for history and assessment. It is an essential part of the training, because it leads the trainee to an understanding of the infrastructure which provides the underlying continuity, coherence and progression in the learning experiences in history of pupils, which are clearly exemplified in the key elements of the National Curriculum at Key Stage 3.

It is in school that trainees have their major opportunities to observe good teachers in the classroom. During their first teaching practice trainees normally spend a considerable amount of time observing teaching. Trainees need to observe a range of teaching strategies being used effectively to teach history, but they also need opportunities to discuss with the teachers they observe reasons for the particular teaching strategies adopted, the aims of lessons, and the intended and actual learning outcomes. This helps trainees to analyse, reflect upon and adapt what they have observed in their own teaching. Early on, it is important for trainees to focus upon strategies for effective classroom management. Often these have become a natural part of a good teacher's teaching repertoire, which they no longer think about. However, for a trainee teacher these strategies need to be made explicit, so that they understand what is being done and why it is being done. Managing the beginnings and endings of lessons and changes of activity are well recognised critical areas of classroom management in a good lesson. Nevertheless so are other aspects, such as the organisation of furniture, the composition of small groups and how the learning needs of particular pupils are addressed. Increasingly, observation should be closely structured to focus the attention of trainees on these critical areas of classroom management. Often observation is not restricted to the teaching of history, but also includes observing good teachers teaching a variety of subjects. Trainees find that this can give them valuable extra insights, as in the case of one trainee who said that observing English teaching had heightened his awareness of the importance of language in the teaching of history and given him some useful ideas about how to improve the quality of pupils' writing. Sometimes trainees also spend a day accompanying a pupil to all of his or her lessons, which gives them an understanding of the range and variety of activities that pupils encounter during a day's lessons, which they find helpful, and, more than occasionally, salutary.

Usually, as a teaching practice proceeds the amount of observation that a trainee does reduces to a trickle when they take on a full teaching commitment. There is evidence, however, that when trainees have gained some teaching experience and have begun to develop basic levels of competence, they are much more perceptive in their analysis of other teachers' lessons and are able to adapt and use what they have learned more quickly and effectively in their teaching. Partly this is because the more advanced teaching skills, such as the effective use of questioning to clarify meaning, test understanding or illustrate a point, are often only fully appreciated and able to be incorporated into their teaching by trainees once they have mastered the basic principles of classroom management.

One technological aid that is very seldom used in schools to analyse and improve teaching is the video camera. Video provides powerful direct evidence of teaching, which can be used very effectively to rectify weaknesses and consolidate strengths. It is also very helpful in analysing good teaching, particularly when combined with observation of the lesson by the trainee. Many of the subtle nuances of good teaching, such as position in the classroom, effective use of the voice and eyes, and the range and quality of talk with pupils and between pupils, are not noticed during a single observation. Good teachers are often no longer fully aware of the good habits, which have become ingrained in their teaching behaviour, and only through discussion of the longitudinal evidence provided by video evidence do these become explicit and need explanation.

Trainees are required to demonstrate how to use a range of teaching strategies competently, and the advice and guidance that the subject mentor provides is critical to their success in achieving this. Trainees normally begin by teaching lessons that have a simple structure and organisation, and then proceed to lessons that are more complex. Sometimes they become comfortable with one teaching strategy, having found it successful, and are loath to try out others. Sometimes they want to try out strategies for which they are not yet fully ready, for instance because their classroom management is not sufficiently secure. Collaborative teaching with a subject mentor or another teacher is often helpful in encouraging the trainee to be more adventurous early in their teaching experience. For instance, in one lesson a trainee introduced a lesson about the causes of the English Civil War. The teacher role-played the views of a London Puritan merchant and a Royalist aristocrat to illustrate views of two important opposing groups. This role-play, together with written sources, was used as a resource for small-group work, with the teacher supporting two groups where there were potentially troublesome pupils. The trainee then organised feedback from groups about their perception of the causes of the war and the teacher discussed with pupils at the end of the lesson what they had learnt. One of the hidden benefits of collaborative teaching for trainees is that it often gives them enhanced credibility in the eyes of pupils, because they are seen to be taking an equal part in the lesson with the teacher, and sometimes a leading part.

One of the most difficult aspects of training for subject mentors and other teachers is to determine how much to tell a trainee about their teaching and what to have them focus upon at any one time. Advice that concentrates upon copying the actions of good teachers, without explaining fully the purpose of these actions, makes it difficult for trainees to respond thoughtfully to pupils' actions or develop teaching strategies that best suit their own personality. Advice that provides detailed and complex instructions can confuse trainees, so that they are not clear about what they should focus upon, particularly in their early lessons. The first major concern of the great majority of trainees is whether a class will listen to them and do what they are asked to do. It is reasonable for subject mentors to begin with the fundamentals of classroom management, ensuring that lessons have a tight agenda, with well-planned beginnings and endings, a simple structure, clearly thought through strategies for managing changes of activity and appropriate tasks well resourced. Subject mentors usually provide very helpful guidance and advice about classroom management and the organisation and resourcing of lessons, so that trainees often make rapid progress in achieving these basic teaching skills. It is less common for subject mentors to move on to focus systematically on developing trainees' higher-order teaching skills, such as the effective use of questioning, to test understanding, explore issues and consolidate knowledge. They often pay insufficient attention to the progress that pupils are making as a result of the teaching of the trainees, particularly across several lessons, and make that a focus of discussion. As a result, trainees do not always make as much progress later in their teaching practices as they do early on. This has been a long-term concern in initial teacher training and some partnerships are developing strategies that require subject mentors to focus more strongly on higher-order teaching skills, and on teaching and progress in learning across several lessons.

School-based training plays a vital part in developing trainees' assessment, reporting and recording (ARR) skills. Trainees are usually introduced to the generic legal requirements in the HEI or lead school. Sometimes they practise the marking of some aspect of pupils' work as a part of their centrally based training, but it is in the schools in which they practise teaching that trainees develop their understanding of, and skills in, assessment, recording and reporting most effectively. A very important part of this work is the regular marking of pupils' work. Trainees have to learn how to use marking effectively to aid progression in pupils' learning, a difficult task that many experienced teachers still struggle with. Subject mentors nearly always ensure that trainees comply with the assessment procedures of the department, but do not always provide as much support and guidance with this aspect of ARR as they might. It is often an area that is more appropriate to the later stages of a trainee's teaching experience, because it requires trainees to have become secure in their classroom management and teaching. Collaborative marking can be very helpful in demonstrating to trainees how they can develop their strategies so that they are more effective in their marking.

As well as the regular marking of pupils' work, there is also the summit of assessment, represented by the end of Key Stage 3 assessment, course-work at GCSE, and sometimes GCE 'A' level, departmental and school tests, and reporting to parents, which trainees need to experience and become competent in doing. The changing requirements for school experience, which now include two substantial teaching practices in different schools, make it more likely that trainees will be in a school when end of Key Stage assessments are being determined, and some subject mentors are providing good opportunities for them to take on a supervised assessment role. It is often possible to manufacture similar opportunities for trainees to mark course-work at GCSE and GCE 'A' level, as a double marker, and to take part in the marking of departmental and school tests. Sufficient time needs to be devoted to discussing the purposes and outcomes of these types of assessment, as well as trainees experiencing them as participants. In the best training, opportunities for all of this are now planned systematically.

An aspect of assessment that sometimes causes particular difficulties is reporting. Occasionally, teaching practices do not coincide in either school placement with any reporting to parents, or this takes place so early in the teaching practice that trainees have little they can contribute. Where trainees have taught a class for some time, they have found it a very valuable experience when they have been allowed to report back to parents about the work pupils have done for them, under the guidance and supervision of the regular teacher. Similarly, trainees are not always in school when written reports are prepared for parents. If they are, they can make a helpful contribution by being asked to write a first draft of a report, to relevant criteria, on what pupils have achieved in the lessons they have taught, for at least some classes. There is considerable merit in asking them to do this in any case, to aid the regular teacher's knowledge of what pupils have achieved and to practise report writing. As with oral reporting and assessment generally, it is not enough that trainees have the experience. Subject mentors must also discuss with them how the various aspects of formative and summative assessment, recording and reporting to parents fit together, as well as how they are linked to teaching and learning. It is very important in this regard that subject mentors help trainees to develop an understanding of the symbiotic relationship between teaching, learning and assessment.

Subject mentors have a major responsibility for the assessment of trainees, to evaluate the progress they are making towards achieving the standards. This is normally fulfilled through evaluations of individual lessons, regular discussions about progress with trainees and more formal assessment reviews, which provide summative judgements about how far trainees have progressed towards achieving the standards.

Trainees are observed teaching regularly by subject mentors and other teachers whose classes they teach. Oral feedback about the teaching is nearly always provided, and often written evaluations as well for the great majority of lessons observed. Trainees nearly always find these helpful, particularly with regard to classroom management and organisation. Feedback proves most helpful, however, when they are directly related to aspects of the standards. This helps to sharpen and focus the evaluations and provides evidence that can be consolidated relatively easily for summary reviews and the effective setting of targets for future progress. Similarly, the regular weekly discussions, which mentors very commonly hold about the progress a trainee is making, benefit from being focused around the standards.

The more formal reviews at significant points in training courses, such as the end of a teaching practice, must be directly related to the standards. In the best practice, these reviews draw on a wide range of evidence for their judgements. The most important evidence comes from the direct observation of the work of the trainee, but there are other helpful sources of evidence on which the subject mentor can draw. One subject mentor, in an incisive but positive review of a trainee's progress at the end of her first teaching practice, drew also on her own evaluations of lessons she had taught and on her more general reflections on the progress she was making, as well as previous reviews. This evidence was used very effectively to evaluate the trainee's teaching in terms of her progress towards achieving the standards, and led to a stimulating discussion about various aspects of teaching and learning. This was followed by the setting of agreed targets that identified very clearly where the trainee should build upon her strengths and could address areas of relative weakness or limited experience, in order to continue her progress in achieving the standards at the start of her second teaching practice.

During the two years of the inspection, target setting has become an increasingly common feature of the training courses inspected, but targets are still often written in a language that is too vague and general for them to be particularly helpful to trainees. Where targets are highly focused on aspects of the standards and expressed in terms of outcomes, which could be easily monitored and evaluated, they prove much more effective in helping trainees to make progress in the development of their teaching skills.

The quality of evaluations of classroom management and organisation made by subject mentors and others is usually good and sometimes very good. An area of evaluation that is much weaker is that concerned with the progress that pupils make in the lessons which trainees teach. Early in trainees' teaching experience it is often necessary to focus upon classroom management and organisation of their teaching because, until trainees are secure with these aspects of teaching, it is difficult for them to focus their attention productively upon other issues. As trainees become secure in these areas, it is important that evaluation moves on to focus more upon what progress in learning pupils make as a result of the trainee's teaching, as this is the essential purpose of teaching. Where this happens, trainees are more likely to move from being merely competent to becoming good or very good classroom practitioners.

In the best training courses subject mentors are part of a staff development community, which centres on the trainees, and includes subject mentors, other history teachers and those responsible for more general professional issues in school, other subject mentors and lead subject mentors in SCITTs or subject tutors in HEIs. The major focus is the training and assessment of trainees, but subject mentors can gain much from the opportunities this provides for them to analyse and reflect upon their own teaching, and to work collaboratively with others involved in the training. Subject mentors carry onerous responsibilities for the training of their trainees, but they can also have exciting opportunities for professional development and fulfilment in carrying out their role.

17 Inspecting subject knowledge

Carole Baker, Ted Cohn and Mark McLaughlin

Chapter 15 indicated the range of concerns inspectors have about trainees' prior qualifications and experience in history, and their interest in how one-year training courses help trainees deal with significant inadequacies in subject knowledge. Inspectors have to judge whether, by their final assessed teaching practice, trainees have fulfilled the requirement to demonstrate that they have a:

> secure knowledge and understanding of the concepts and skills in their specialist subject(s) at a standard equivalent to degree level to enable them to teach it (them) confidently and accurately at … Key Stage 3 and Key Stage 4 and, where relevant, post-16 for trainees on 11–16 or 18 courses.
> (Circular 4/98, Annex A, A1(i))

Inspection, as well as research, indicates that without such knowledge the quality of teaching and learning in the classroom suffers. Thus, in inspecting each of the cells described in Chapter 15, inspectors take full account of subject knowledge.

In dealing with the selection of trainees, inspectors first come to a judgement about the adequacy of history trainees' prior qualifications and experience, as well as their intellectual capacity. They ask, in particular, whether previous qualifications and experience suggest that trainees will be able to demonstrate the required level of subject knowledge and understanding by the end of training. Inspectors do not merely assure themselves that trainees possess a degree – the basic entry requirement of Circular 4/98 – but they also examine the class and subject focus of the degree as well as the possession and relevance of any higher degree. In fact, as the recent series of inspections reveal, the great majority of history trainees hold good honours degrees, with 50 per cent or more having first or upper second degrees. Moreover, in most cohorts a small number also possess postgraduate degrees, including doctorates. Additionally, almost all trainees' degrees include a significant and discrete history component and, where history has been studied in conjunction with another subject, that subject is usually highly relevant to the school history curriculum, for example politics or archaeology. Such subject combinations can give an extra dimension to teaching. A detailed knowledge of politics can enable trainees to enhance pupils' understanding of key events such as the Labour victory of 1945 for example; a thorough grounding in archaeology can help trainees tackle topics, such as the Anglo-Saxon settlement, where archaeological evidence is crucial in understanding events.

Overall, in looking at trainees' prior subject knowledge, inspectors adopt a flexible approach, taking careful account of experience, such as working in a local record office or successfully completing an 'A' level history course immediately before admission to training. While, ideally, candidates would enter training with an overview of British, European and world history as well as a detailed knowledge of the content areas included in the school curriculum, inspectors are well aware that most lack both. In particular, few know much about the medieval and early modern periods. Inspectors, therefore, look carefully to see whether entrants have a clear understanding of the nature of the subject and its guiding principles; and whether they have sufficient experience of learning history to enable them make good gaps in specific aspects of subject knowledge and, at the same time, acquire a 'mind map' of the past. As a result, they register concern where trainees' previous experience of history is very limited, for example to a brief introduction to the history of Southeast Asia as part of a degree in Southeast Asian studies and language.

Given the generally high number of candidates for each place on most history PGCE courses, providers can be highly selective. Even so some make a better job of selection than others. Inspectors scrutinise selection procedures to ascertain whether history subject knowledge is taken sufficiently seriously. They examine how well applications and references are screened – for subject knowledge and understanding as well as suitable experience with young people. Discussion with trainees and trainers, together with examination of relevant documentation, indicates that most providers are tightening up on selection arrangements. Most interviewers now probe candidates' knowledge of subject content and, increasingly, providers include, as part of the selection process, written tests or tasks, for example on National Curriculum content areas, or structured discussion based on the reading of specialist articles or the handling of an artefact or picture. Such exercises offer additional insights into candidates' understanding of the principles governing historical study. In examining the effectiveness of selection arrangements, inspectors also look at the ways in which providers seek to ensure consistency of judgement. In terms of subject knowledge, this can be achieved most effectively where history specialists are used, where all interviewers are guided by the same set of subject knowledge questions and subject-specific published selection criteria, where interviewing involves two interviewers who consult each other before and after the interview process, and where interviewers complete a common report pro forma that requires comment on subject knowledge.

Inspectors also have to make a judgement about the adequacy of the training process in helping trainees acquire the history subject knowledge they need. The current *Framework for Inspection*, acknowledging this, requires inspectors to judge the extent to which trainees' subject knowledge is audited at the outset of training, and then assessed and monitored and, if necessary, brought up to the required levels. How do inspectors do this? As noted, it is highly unlikely that trainees embarking on a PGCE history course will possess already the full range of subject knowledge necessary to teach school history effectively. Thus, inspectors look to see how well providers identify trainees' subject knowledge needs. All providers now audit trainees' subject knowledge early in the course, usually against the demands of the National Curriculum at Key Stage 3 and the most common topics found in GCSE and 'A' level syllabuses. The best audits are designed to judge trainees' depth of subject knowledge rather than superficial coverage, and also their levels of confidence in teaching particular topics to particular age groups. To be effective an audit needs to be undertaken in some detail, and trainees need careful guidance on its completion, particularly where history specific skills are included.

Whatever the level of detail provided in an audit form, or the quality of guidance given to trainees, inspectors will raise questions about the effectiveness of the audit if it depends entirely on self-assessment. Inexperienced trainees are in no position to gauge accurately the depth and range of the subject knowledge they possess, nor its relevance for teaching the school curriculum. A few providers overcome this difficulty – at least in part – by undertaking some form of audit at interview. Such a strategy has another advantage. Candidates accepted on to the course can be required to undertake targeted reading and research beforehand, and thus reduce the time needed during training to make good major subject knowledge gaps.

Since the purpose of the initial audit, wherever located, is not merely to identify those aspects of school history where trainees lack sufficient knowledge, but also to provide a basis for monitoring their progress in remedying deficiencies, inspectors look carefully at arrangements for monitoring. In the best practice any initial audit is merely the start of a course-long process of profiling, which includes fixed points where targets and action plans are set and reviewed by trainees in collaboration with trainers, and profiles are taken with trainees to each placement school to ensure progression. Whatever the procedures, the real effectiveness of any profile is determined by the perceptiveness and quality of the comments provided by trainee and trainer; the specificity of targets set; the devising of suitable action plans; and the regular review and revision of previous targets. Even where procedures are generally effective, the process can be undermined if, as is too often the case, insufficient attention is paid to the effects of subject knowledge on teaching and where neither targets nor action plans address subject knowledge needs sufficiently closely.

Inspectors examine not merely the auditing and profiling procedures, but also the effectiveness of arrangements put in place to help trainees make good subject knowledge deficiencies. If such arrangements are to work well, much depends on the subject expertise of trainers both in school and in higher education. This is one of the reasons why inspectors scrutinise curricula vitae, examine arrangements for the selection of subject mentors, raise questions about the scope and quality of subject-specific mentor training and look to see whether subject mentors' subject expertise is extended – through subject newsletters or bulletins, electronic communication or short and specific guidance notes from tutors, for example. Inspectors also consider carefully the quality of contributors from outside a training partnership, whether, for example, they are chosen for subject expertise as well as general teaching skill.

When observing training sessions, including those undertaken by subject mentors, inspectors have further opportunities to examine trainers' subject expertise. The most effective trainers (tutors or subject mentors) demonstrate and utilise substantial subject knowledge, including knowledge of relevant research – sometimes their own – to enhance trainees' knowledge, for example of the range of available primary resource material. They also pose questions and make comments that focus trainees' attention on subject teaching as well as on classroom management, and their questions and comments derive from high levels of subject knowledge. Where this is the case, trainees and trainers invariably engage in highly effective professional discussion about the teaching of the subject.

In examining the training process, inspectors also identify the methods employed by a training partnership to help trainees enhance subject knowledge, and then judge how effective these methods are. In so doing, they use discussion and the scrutiny of documentation, as well as the observation of training.

First, they consider any contribution made by higher education, in particular whether the training is designed to enhance subject knowledge, and whether higher-education training sessions themselves combine practical advice on teaching with the extension of trainees' historical knowledge and understanding of the nature of the discipline. Some trainers are particularly skilful in developing trainees' subject pedagogy in this way. Thus one training session, a semantic study of the concept of empire, drawing on the Roman and Victorian periods, not only showed trainees how to use museums and artefacts effectively, but also enhanced their understanding of such significant concepts as cultural diversity and similarity and difference. Another session gave trainees experience of setting and testing hypotheses when teaching 'A' level. In small groups, they used a variety of secondary sources including the Internet to form different interpretations of aspects of the First World War, de-construct opposing hypotheses and consider the relevance of this approach to the classroom. A third session on GCSE history not only gave trainees a clear view of the nature and requirements of GCSE history syllabuses, but also effective opportunities to enhance their own subject knowledge of the First and Second World Wars, as well as the cold war.

Inspectors also judge whether higher education trainers draw on a suitably wide range of material, including textbooks and articles. They consider whether such material is structured appropriately and whether bibliographies are classified helpfully. In particular, they ascertain whether trainees are encouraged to read beyond the school textbook or information sheet and whether the extent, level and quality of their reading is checked regularly. Where training includes field-work, inspectors ask whether sufficient use is made of field visits to improve subject knowledge and understanding, as happened in one university during visits to the local record office, the Imperial War Museum, a nineteenth-century pit re-construction and a 'hands-on' Second World War blitz centre; or in another, where training included not only visits to local museums and important historical sites, but also required trainees to undertake a local study, thus widening their expertise in the use of local resources and helping them see how local history can illustrate national events and confirm or challenge general interpretations.

Inspectors also look to see whether the subject expertise of individual trainees is used to benefit the wider group. This occurs where tutors require trainees to lead seminars and thus develop their own and others' subject knowledge; where they expect trainees, either singly or in small groups, to compile teaching packages on curriculum topics such as the Norman Conquest, and then undertake micro-teaching; or where they identify trainees' particular strengths, share this information and encourage trainees to draw on each others' subject expertise, thus developing a consultancy model.

Second, as Chapter 16 indicates, inspectors assess the contribution made by school experience to trainees' subject knowledge. Subject mentors are in day-to-day contact with trainees, and thus in a position to identify clearly where gaps in subject knowledge undermine teaching. The most effective recognise that they have a responsibility to enhance limited conceptual understanding, or extend expertise in unfamiliar content areas. They draw trainees' attention to suitable reading or to the specialisations of other teachers in the history department and introduce them to departmental resources as well as the school library. Additionally, they show trainees how visits to museums or historical sites can extend their understanding. Such subject mentors use their detailed schemes of work to support trainees in identifying what to look for in their wider reading and require trainees to devise learning resources, including audio and video materials, which demand high levels of subject knowledge, and enhance it at the same time. In the very best cases, subject mentors give other subject teachers careful guidance on the part they should play in identifying gaps in subject knowledge and helping trainees make these good. Subject mentors are helped to take sufficient account of the subject knowledge of trainees and its impact on teaching and learning, where pro forma such as lesson observation forms and school report forms include a requirement to focus on trainees' development of subject knowledge as well as teaching skills. Whether this is the case or not, completed written lesson observations, school reports or reports of meetings between school-based trainer and trainee show clearly whether the effects of subject knowledge strengths and weaknesses on teaching are taken sufficiently seriously.

Occasionally, discussion with trainers and trainees, as well as scrutiny of documentation, reveals another approach to the enhancement of trainees' subject knowledge in schools. Placements are arranged with this in mind. For example, trainees are paired on the basis of complementary subject knowledge, or weaknesses in subject knowledge are a factor in the placement of a particular trainee in a particular department.

The third focus of inspection – the assessment of trainees' progress both in and out of the classroom – also throws light on the significance attached by providers to subject knowledge. Inspectors spend a considerable time reading trainees' assignments and files. In so doing, and in subsequent discussion with trainees, they are able to identify levels of subject knowledge and understanding, and detect the extent to which weaknesses have been identified and made good. The best teaching files show clearly where and how trainees have remedied deficient subject knowledge. Some providers even require trainees to include reading notes in their files to show the extent and level of the research they have undertaken for topics taught. Where files show that trainees have been over-reliant on school textbooks, their teaching often lacks depth and range. They are unable to select interesting anecdotes or set what they are teaching in a broader context. Trainees' files also show whether they have considered key concepts, key questions or key words with sufficient care. This is apparent most frequently in the setting of learning objectives. Inspectors look carefully to see whether such objectives are historically accurate and appropriate. Subsequent discussion often reveals that inadequate planning is the result of limited knowledge and understanding. Whether trainees themselves recognise the impact of their level of subject knowledge on the quality of their teaching is sometimes evident in the evaluation of lessons or sequences of lessons. In the best training, the most proficient comment regularly on the relationship between subject expertise, the quality of teaching and the extent of pupils' learning.

In scrutinising written assignments, inspectors are interested in the demands of the task as well as the quality of trainees' responses, in terms of subject knowledge as well as professional skills. Some of the best assignments are designed to enhance both. One provider, for example, includes an assignment that requires trainees to develop an area of subject knowledge weakness, analyse the learning process involved, and then consider the implications for teaching in the classroom; another sets a series of school-based exercises designed to extend both subject knowledge and professional expertise. These tasks are linked closely to the HEI-based programme and help both university tutors and subject mentors monitor trainees' progress in meeting a range of required standrds, including subject knowledge. Inspectors also note carefully where providers fail to exploit the potential of assignments to develop subject know-ledge, not recognising fully the contribution it makes to high-quality teaching. Frequently, trainees are set, as an assignment, the task of producing a scheme of work and a sequence of lessons, yet they are rarely expected to demonstrate the research they have undertaken to extend their subject knowledge and understanding to the level necessary for effective planning. However, even where a written history assignment is not designed to target subject knowledge, close scrutiny reveals the level of trainees' subject expertise, not least in the range of texts, articles and other materials consulted. Inspectors are always suspicious where bibliographies are sparse or non-existent.

The marking of written assignments and files also throws light on the importance placed on adequate subject knowledge. In the best practice, marking relates to clearly stated criteria that encapsulate subject knowledge standards; trainers comment on the way a trainee's subject knowledge contributes – or not – to his/her planning and teaching; and subject knowledge strengths and weaknesses, together with their implications, are noted and discussed. Such marking also includes constructive suggestions on how a trainee might extend subject expertise or reading, as in one case where a trainer suggested the use of parliamentary debates as another source of evidence for teaching about the coming of the railways.

Recent inspection has shown that assessment of trainees' classroom practice does not always take sufficient account of subject knowledge. Some providers, recognising this, are now developing subject specific exemplifications of the standards outlined in Circular 4/98 and concomitant guidance on completing lesson observation forms, records of mentor meetings and school reports. One intention is to help trainers judge how far levels of subject knowledge contribute to the quality of trainees' teaching, and thus improve the assessment of subject knowledge, as well as subject teaching, in the classroom.

In observing the standards displayed by trainees in the classroom, inspectors identify clearly the contributions made by subject knowledge to teaching performance. They follow up their conclusions – as appropriate – in subsequent discussion.

First, and perhaps most importantly, where trainees have high levels of subject knowledge they plan and teach confidently, knowing themselves to have mastery of a particular topic. This confidence underpins their planning and teaching. The impact is particularly evident when observing trainees teaching 'A' level pupils, but is not by any means confined to this age group. The contribution of substantial subject knowledge to effective teaching is very apparent when an inspector is able to observe a trainee teach two lessons, one where he or she has mastery of subject content, and the other where he or she has read up the topic only recently and briefly. The contrast, in terms of confidence as well as skill, is usually marked.

Second, where trainees have high levels of subject knowledge, they are more likely to structure individual lessons and sequences of lessons effectively and select teaching methods that develop pupils' understanding and skills appropriately. This was the case where one trainee designed a lesson for very able Year 10 pupils that involved small groups working in turn on collections of different types of source material, each collection illustrating different causes of the Second World War. Not only did the lesson run smoothly, but the quality of learning was evident in a lively class discussion that explored motivation and causation at a sophisticated level. Such a lesson was only possible because of the trainee's breadth of subject knowledge and depth of understanding of complex historical concepts.

Third, inspectors gain insight into trainees' subject knowledge through the quality of the materials they produce. One example of this was a sophisticated simulation game on the Black Death devised by a trainee to give very able Year

7 pupils detailed subject knowledge about, and understanding of, medieval life and society. Another was where a trainee, teaching about the relationship of Henry II and St Thomas à Becket, developed highly effective learning materials at different levels of difficulty, and thus motivated pupils of all abilities to make good progress.

Fourth, inspectors look to see how far the content of trainees' teaching reflects depth of subject knowledge. Trainees with suitable subject knowledge rarely slip into error. They select suitably detailed and relevant anecdotes and make effective use of analogies. They are sensitive to nuances of interpretation and flit easily between periods, comparing and contrasting particular aspects of different periods. Recent inspection examples include a comparison of German and British perceptions of Dunkirk with British and Iraqi perceptions of the Gulf War; and of the role of Henry VIII with that of Hitler.

Fifth, inspectors also ask how well trainees cope with unexpected questions. Those with high levels of subject knowledge either respond accurately to complex queries, for example to a Year 12 student's question on the composition of Henry VIII's income, or are confident enough to acknowledge ignorance in dealing with unexpected and eccentric questions, such as one on the age of Edward VI on his death. Subject knowledge weakness and a lack of subject confidence are exposed where trainees flounder in response to such queries, providing incorrect or generalised answers.

Sixth, inspectors consider whether trainees are adept in helping pupils master the language and organising concepts of history. Where trainees have developed an effective conceptual framework, they recognise potential difficulties of understanding, for example related to chronology or anachronism, or to skill – such as in moving from narrative to analytical writing – and teach accordingly. They respond to pupils' difficulties by amending future teaching, in one case seen recently, using timelines to counter uncertainties over chronology. They also take account, in their planning and teaching, of the need to help pupils acquire essential terminology, for example through displays of key words or by pertinent questioning.

Seventh, inspectors also recognise that trainees need depth of understanding if they are to seize on the potential of a topic to promote pupils' spiritual, moral, social and cultural development. The best trainees are able to plan for, as well as grasp, opportunities to deal with such issues. In teaching the Crusades, for example, they select a balanced range of source materials; in examining modern China or medieval crime and punishment, they help pupils consider human rights. They also devise tasks to encourage pupils make moral judgements – should Cromwell be seen as cruel and ruthless or a national hero, for example. Such trainees are confident enough to examine stereotyping, through the selection of appropriate extracts from cowboy films in examining images and perceptions of Native Americans, for example.

Eighth, inspectors ask whether their teaching shows that trainees have a clear understanding of the nature of history. Where this is the case, trainees pay close attention to key elements, in particular the more difficult such as interpretation. They also demonstrate an ability to relate the present to the past, for instance recognising the long-term effects of historical events such as the Reformation.

When coming to a judgement about the standards attained by trainees in assessing and recording pupils' progress in history, inspectors use as evidence written assignments and observation of classroom performance, as well as discussion with trainees. Does this evidence demonstrate subject expertise and a recognition of its significance in teaching and learning history? Suprisingly few trainees take sufficient account of historical accuracy in their assessment and recording of pupils' attainment in history, however, and even fewer use their assessment to plan and teach in such a way that pupils deepen their historical understanding and extend their historical skills systematically.

Finally, moderation arrangements are examined by inspectors to see whether they throw any light on the significance attached by a training partnership to the importance of trainees' standards in terms of subject knowledge. This can be seen in the extent to which subject specialists are used to verify judgements, written assignments are second marked by subject specialists, or judgements on the standards trainees attain in school are confirmed by subject specialists. Inspectors are concerned where general, rather than subject-specific, external examiners are used year on year. Without subject expertise, it is extremely difficult, if not impossible, to evaluate history trainees' progress and attainment, not merely in subject knowledge but also in subject pedagogy. Subject-specific external examiners, where used effectively, review assignments, comment on course structure and content, meet trainees and interrogate them, and moderate the assessment of practical teaching, taking account throughout of subject knowledge. In addition they report and offer guidance on the attention paid to subject knowledge in selecting, training and assessing trainees, as well as how to improve teaching in the classroom through improving trainees' subject expertise.

This chapter has emphasised the significance attached to subject knowledge in the inspection of all aspects of the training of secondary history teachers and seeks to show how inspectors go about their task. It describes what inspectors do, not researchers. Some of the questions that the researcher might ask cannot be addressed during the short process of inspection and have not been considered here. That is not to say that inspectors are unaware of such questions. What sort of degree background provides the best basis for future history teaching? Does a degree that provides an overview of world, European and British history provide a more suitable basis for history teacher training than one that concentrates on one period? What constitutes appropriate history subject knowledge? What is the precise relationship between history subject knowledge and effective subject teaching? These questions are for others to explore.

Bibliography

ACCAC, CCEA, QCA (1999) *Subject Criteria for History*.

Ainscow, M. (1998) 'Would it work in theory?: Arguments for practitioner research and theorising in the special needs field', in C. Clark, A. Dyson and A. Millward (eds) *Theorising Special Education*, London: Routledge.

Aldrich, R. and Dean, D. (1991) 'The historical dimension', in R. Aldrich (ed.) *History in the National Curriculum*, London: Kogan Page.

Ambrose, S.E. (1984) *Pegasus Bridge, 6 June 1944*, London: George Allen & Unwin.

Anderson, R.C. (1977) 'The notion of schemata and the educational enterprise', in R.C. Anderson, R.J. Spiro and W.E. Montaque (eds) *Schooling and the Acquisition of Knowledge*, Hillsdale, NJ: Lawrence Erlbaum.

Andretti, K. (1993) *Teaching History through Primary Evidence*, London: David Fulton.

Angvik, M. and Borries, B. von (eds) (1997) *Youth and History*, 2 vols, Hamburg: Korber-Siftung.

Ashby, R., Dickinson, A.K. and Lee, P. (1996) 'There were no facts in those days: Children's ideas about historical explanation', in M. Hughes (ed.) *Teaching and Learning in Changing Times*, Oxford: Blackwell.

Ashby, R. and Lee, P. (1987) 'Children's concepts of empathy and understanding in history', in C. Portal (ed.) *The History Curriculum for Teachers*, Lewes: Falmer Press.

Askar, P., Yavuz, H. and Koksal, M. (1992) 'Students' perceptions of computer assisted instruction environment and their attitudes to computer assisted learning', *Educational Research* 34(2): 133–9.

Atkinson, D. (1988) *Votes for Women*, Cambridge: Cambridge Educational.

Audigier, F. (1997a) 'L'Enseignement de l'histoire entre plusieurs logiques', *Le Bulletin d'Euroclio* 8: 12–18.

—— (1997b) 'L'Union de l'histoire, de la géographie et de l'education civique à l'école Élémentaire: Revée? Pensée? Practiquée? Delaissée?', Symposium of the Consortium of Institutions for Development and Research in Education of Europe, Strasbourg, 28–30 May.

Austen, R. (1995) 'Building bridges in cyberspace and on the ground: Working with student teachers in Northern Ireland', in D. Kerr and C. O'Neill (eds) *Professional Preparation and Professional Development in a Climate of Change*, Lancaster: SCHTE in UK.

Bage, G. (1993) 'History at KS1 and KS2: Questions of teaching, planning, assessment and progression', *Curriculum Journal* 4(2): 269–82.

Baker, K. (1993) *The Turbulent Years: My Life in Politics*, London: Faber & Faber.

Banham, D. (1998) 'Getting ready for the Grand Prix: Learning how to build a substantiated argument in Year 7', *Teaching History* 92: 6–15.

Barker, B. (1978), 'Understanding in the classroom', in A. Dickinson and P. Lee (eds) *History Teaching and Historical Understanding*, London: Heinemann.

Bayliss, P. (1998) 'Models of complexity: Theory-driven intervention practices', in C. Clark, A. Dyson and A. Millward (eds) *Theorising Special Education*, London: Routledge.

Beaber, L. (1998) 'Building community with the Internet', *Information, International Society of History Didactics* 19(1): 64.

BECTA/Historical Association (1998) *Defining Effectiveness in History using IT: Approaches to Successful Practice*, Coventry: BECTA.

Bereiter, C. and Scardamalia, M. (1987) *The Psychology of Written Composition*, Hillsdale, NJ: Lawrence Erlbaum.

Berghann, V.R. and Schissler, H. (1987) *Perceptions of History, an Analysis of School Textbooks*, Oxford: Berg.

Bernot, L. and Blancard, R. (1995), in H. Cooper (ed.) *History in the Early Years*, London: Routledge.

Biot, C. (1987) 'Co-operative group work: Pupils' and teachers' membership and participation', *Curriculum* 8: 2.

Blair, T. (1995) 'A week in politics', Channel 4, 18 February.

Bloom, A. (1987) *The Closing Of The American Mind*, New York: Simon & Schuster.

Blunkett, D. (1998) 'Letter to all headteachers of Key Stage 1 and Key Stage 2 schools in England', 13 January.

Blyth, A. (1998a) 'Growing towards citizenship; Humanities in the revised curriculum, *Education 3–13* 26(3): 3–8.

—— (1998b) 'Editorial', *Primary History* 18: 2.

Blyth, A., *et al.* (1976) *Place, Time and Society 8–13: Curriculum Planning in History, Geography and Social Science*, Bristol: Collins/ESL Bristol for the Schools Council.

Blyth, J. (1994) *History 5–11*, London: Hodder & Stoughton.

—— (1988) *History 5–9*, London: Hodder & Stoughton.

Blyth, J., Cigman, J., Harnett, P. and Sampson, J. (eds) (1991) *Ginn History*, Aylesbury: Ginn.

Board of Education (1937) *Handbook of Suggestions*, London: HMSO.

—— (1931) *Report of the Consultative Committee on the Primary School*, London: HMSO.

—— (1927) *Handbook of Suggestions for Teachers*, London: HMSO.

—— (1923) *Report on the Teaching of History*, Pamphlet 37, London: HMSO.

—— (1905) *Suggestions for the Consideration of Teachers and Others Concerned in the Work of Public Elementary Schools*, London: HMSO.

Booth, M.B. (1993) 'History', in A.S. King and M.J. Reiss (eds) *The Multicultural Dimension of the National Curriculum*, London: Falmer Press.

—— (1987) 'Ages and stages: A critique of the Piagetian approach to history teaching', in C. Portal (ed.) *The History Curriculum for Teachers*, Lewes: Falmer Press.

—— (1983) 'Skills, concepts and attitudes: The development of adolescent children's historical thinking', *History and Theory* 22(4): 101–17.

—— (1978) 'Children's inductive historical thought', *Teaching History* 21: 3–8.

Booth, M. and Husbands, C. (1993) 'The history national curriculum in England and Wales: Assessment at Key Stage 3', *The Curriculum Journal*, 4, 1: 21.

Borries, B. von (1997) 'Political Attitudes and Decision', in M. Angvik and B. von Borries (eds) *Youth and History. A Comparative European Survey on Historical Consciousness and Political Attitudes among Adolescents*, Hamburg: Korber Stiftung.

—— (1994) 'Reconstructing history and moral judgement: On relationships between interpretations of the past and perceptions of the present', in M. Carratero and J. Vose (eds) *Cognitive and Instructional Processes in History and the Social Sciences*, Hillsdale, NJ and Home UK: Lawrence Erlbaum Associates.

Bourdillon, H. (ed.) (1994) *Teaching History*, London: Open University Press.

Bousted, M. and Davies, I. (1996) 'Teachers' perceptions of models of political learning', *Curriculum* 17(1): 12–23.

Bradley, N. (1947) 'The growth of the knowledge of time in children of school age', *British Journal of Psychology* 38: 67–78.

Brandt, G. (1986) *The Realization of Anti-Racist Teaching*, Lewes: Falmer Press.

Braunschweig Conference (1998) 'Education for international understanding. What do we know about pupils' historical consciousness and geographical awareness and the role of textbooks in the teaching of history, geography and civics?', Conference at Georg Eckert Institute, 8–10 June.

Breese, S. (1998) 'In search of Englishness; In search of votes', in J. Arnold, K. Davies and S. Ditchfield (eds) *History and Heritage: Consuming the Past in Contemporary Culture*, Shaftesbury: Donhead.

Bright, M. (1997) 'IT revolution in the classroom', the *Observer*, 13 July.

British Library (1998) *Making of the United Kingdom*, CD-ROM, London: British Library.

Brosnan, M. (1998) *Technophobia, the Psychological Impact of Information Technology*, London: Routledge.

Bruner, J.S. (1986) *Actual Minds, Possible Worlds*, Cambridge, MA: Harvard University Press.

—— (1974) *Toward a Theory of Instruction*, Cambridge, MA: Harvard University Press.

—— (1960) *The Process of Education*, New York: Vintage Books.

Byrom, J. (1998a) 'Working with sources: Scepticism or cynicism? Putting the story back together again', *Teaching History* 91: 32–5.

—— (1998b) *Changing Minds Teacher's Book, Britain 1500–1750*, London: Addison Wesley Longman.

—— (1997) *Medieval Minds*, Think Through History Series, London: Longman.

Byrom, J., Counsell, C. and Riley, M. (1997) *Medieval Minds: Britain 1066–1500*, London: Addison Wesley Longman.

Calderhead, J. (1984) *Teachers' Classroom Decision Making*, London: Holt, Rienhart & Winston.

Carpenter, B. Ashdown, R. and Bovair, K. (eds) (1996) *Enabling Access: Effective Teaching and Learning for Pupils with Learning Difficulties*, London: David Fulton.

Carpenter, M. (1866) *The Last Days of the Rajah Rammohun Roy*, London.

Carrington, B. and Short, G. (1989) *Race in the Primary School*, Windsor: NFER Nelson.

Carvel, J. (1998) the *Guardian*, 7 November.

Central Advisory Council for Education (England) (1967) *Children and their Primary Schools: A Report (Plowden Report)*, London: HMSO.

Chitty, C. (1989) *Towards a New Education System: The Victory of the New Right?*, London: Falmer Press.

Clare, J.D. (1997) 'History is Important', *Teaching History*, July.

Clark, C., Dyson, A. and Millward, A. (eds) (1998) *Theorising Special Education*, London: Routledge.

Clark, R. (1994) 'Media will never influence learning', *Educational Technology Research and Development* 42(2): 21–9.

—— (1983) 'Reconsidering research on learning from media', *Review of Educational Research* 53(4): 445–59.

Cloonan, M. and Davies, I. (1998) 'Improving the possibility of better teaching by investigating the nature of student learning: With reference to procedural understanding in politics in higher education', *Teaching in Higher Education* 3(2): 173–83.

Cochrane, P. (1995) *The Times Educational Supplement*, 23 June.

Cohen, M. (1999) the *Guardian*, 12 January.

Collins (1995) *English Dictionary*, London: Collins.

Coltham, J. and Fines, J. (1971) *Educational Objectives for the Study of History*, London: Historical Association.

Cooper, H. (1998) 'Concepts, Modèles, Raisonnements', in F. Audigier (ed.) *Concepts, Modèles, Raisonnements*, Paris: Institut National de Recherche Pédagogique.

—— (1995a) 'The National Curriculum and action research', in *The Teaching of History in Primary Schools: Implementing the Revised National Curriculum*, London: David Fulton.

—— (1995b) *History in the Early Years*, London: Routledge.

—— (1995c) *The Teaching of History in Primary Schools: Implementing the Revised National Curriculum*, second edn, London: David Fulton.

—— (1993) 'Removing the scaffolding, a case study investigating how whole-class teaching can lead to effective peer group discussion without the teacher', *The Curriculum Journal* 4(3): 385–401.

—— (1991) 'Young children's thinking in history', unpublished Ph.D. thesis, University of London.

Cooper, H., David, R., Huggins, M. and Thorley, J. (1997) 'An investigation of what young children in a range of European countries know about the past and how they acquired that knowledge', paper presented at the European Conference for Educational Research, Frankfurt.

Cooper, P. and McIntyre, D. (1996) *Effective Teaching and Learning: Teachers and Students' Perspectives*, Milton Keynes: Open University Press.

Copeland, W. (1997) in A. Martin, *et al.* (eds) *Information Technology and the Teaching of History: International Perspectives*, Amsterdam: Harwood.

Council of Europe Council for Cultural Co-operation (1995) 'Report of meeting of experts on educational research on the learning and teaching of history', Strasbourg, 19–20 June.

Council of Europe FR-67075 (1988) *Intergovernmental Programme of Activities for 1998 EDUCATION*, Strasbourg: Council of Europe (document without reference, not archived).

Counsell, C. (1998a) *Teaching History* 93, November.

—— (1998b) 'Big stories, little stories', *The Times Educational Supplement*, 8 September 1998.

—— (1997) *Analytical and Discursive Writing at Key Stage 3*, London: Historical Association.

—— (1996) 'Progression in secondary school history education: A qualitative study of history teachers' theories of action', unpublished M.Ed. dissertation, University of Bristol, Graduate School of Education.

Counsell, C. and the Historical Association Secondary Education Committee (1997) *Planning the Twentieth Century World*, London: Historical Association.

Cox, K. and Hughes, P. (1998) 'History and children's fiction', in P. Hoodless (ed.)*History and English in the Primary School. Exploiting the Links*, London: Routledge.

Crawford, K. (1995) 'A history of the Right: The battle for control of National Curriculum History 1989–1994', *British Journal of Educational Studies* 43(4): 433–56.

Crick, B. (1978) 'Basic concepts for political education', in B. Crick and A. Porter, *Political Education and Political Literacy*, London: Longman.

Crick, B. and Porter, A. (1978) *Political Education and Political Literacy*, London: Longman.

Culpin, C. (1994) 'Making progress in history', in H. Bourdillon (ed.) *Teaching History*, London: Open University Press.

Curriculum Council for Wales (1993) *Progression and Differentiation in History at Key Stage Three*, Cardiff: CCW.

—— (1991) *Non-Statutory Guidance to History in the NC*, Cardiff: CCW.

Curtis, S. and Bardwell, S. (1994) 'Access to history', in H. Bourdillon (ed.) *Teaching History*, London: Open University Press.

Davey, A. (1983) *Learning to be Prejudiced: Growing up in Multi-Ethnic Britain*, London: Edward Arnold.

David, R. (1996) *History at Home*, Northampton: English Heritage.

Davies, I. (1997) 'Education for European citizenship: Issues in history education', *Evaluation and Research in Education* 11(3): 119–28.

—— (1996) 'Values and the teaching and learning of European history', *Children's Social and Economics Education* 1(1): 51–60.

Davies, I., Gregory, I. and Riley, S. (1997) 'Concepts of citizenship: Results of research on teacher perceptions in England', paper for British Education Research Association 1997 conference at the University of York.

Davies, I. and John, P. (1995) 'History and citizenship', *Teaching History* 78: 5–7.

Davies, I. and Sobisch, A. (eds) (1997) *Developing European Citizens*, Sheffield: Sheffield Hallam University Press.

Davies, R. (1998) 'Why is history essential?', *Welsh Historian* 28: 4–5.

Davitt, J. (1999) 'A digital education', the *Guardian*, 12 January.

DES (1991) *History in the National Curriculum (England)*, London: HMSO.

—— (1990a) *The Final Report of the History Working Group. History for Ages 5 to 16* , London: HMSO.

—— (1990b) *National Curriculum History Working Group, Final Report*, London: HMSO.

—— (1989) *Aspects of Primary Education. The Teaching and Learning of History and Geography*, London: HMSO.

—— (1988) *Curriculum Matters 5–16: History*, London: HMSO.

—— (1985a) *History in the Primary and Secondary Years. An HMI View*, London: HMSO.

—— (1985b) *GCSE: The National Criteria: History*, London: HMSO.

—— (1982) *Education 5 to 9: An Illustrative Survey of 80 First Schools in England*, London: HMSO.

—— (1978a) *Primary Education in England. A Survey by HM Inspectors of Schools*, London: HMSO.

—— (1978b) *Special Educational Needs: Report of the Committee of Enquiry into the Education of Handicapped Children and Young People (The Warnock Report)*, London: HMSO.

—— (1967) *Children and their Primary Schools. A Report of the Central Advisory Council for Education (England)*, London: HMSO.

Deuchar, S. (1987) *History and GCSE History: A Critique*, York: Campaign for Real Education.

Dewey, J. (1966) *Democracy and Education*, London: Free Press/Macmillan.

DfE (1995) *Key Stages 1 and 2 of the National Curriculum*, London: HMSO.

—— (1994) *The Code of Practice on the Identification and Assessment of Special Educational Needs*, London: HMSO.

—— (1991) *History in the National Curriculum (England)*, London: HMSO.

DfEE (1999) Press Release, 19 March 1999.

—— (1998a) *The National Literacy Strategy. Framework for Teaching*, London: HMSO.

—— (1998b) *Teachers: Meeting the Challenge of Change*, London: HMSO.

—— (1997 and 1998) *Teaching: High Status, High Standards: Requirements for Courses of Initial Teaching Training*, Circulars 10/97 and 4/98, London: HMSO.

—— (1995) *History in the National Curriculum, England*, London: HMSO.

Dickinson, A.K. (1998) 'History using information technology: Past, present and future', *Teaching History* 93, November: 16–20.

Dickinson, A.K., Gordon, P., Lee, P. and Slater, J. (eds) (1996) *International Year Book of Education*, London: Woburn Press.

Dickinson, A.K. and Lee, P.J. (1984a) 'Identifying progression in children's understanding: The use of visual materials to assess primary school children's learning in history', *Cambridge Journal of Education* 23(2): 137–54.

—— (1984b) 'Making sense of history', in A.K. Dickinson, P.J. Lee and P.J. Rogers (eds) *Learning History*, London: Heinemann.

Dickinson, A., Lee, P. and Ashby, R. (1997) 'Research methods and some findings on rational understanding', in Pendry, A. and O'Neill, C. (eds) *Principles and Practice: Analytical Perspectives on Curriculum Reform and Changing Pedagogy from History Teacher Educators*, Standing Conference of History Teacher Educators in the UK.

Die Zeit (1996) 'So that you know where East Germany was, five year olds explain why we needed the wall', 4 October.

Donaldson, M. (1978) *Children's Minds*, London: Fontana.

Downes, T. (1993) 'Student teachers' experiences in using computers during teaching practice, *Journal of Computer Assisted Learning* 9(1): 17–33.

Easdown, G. (1994) 'Student teachers, mentors and information technology', *Journal of Information Technology for Teacher Education* 3(1): 63–78.

Ericksen, G. (1994) 'Pupils' understanding of magnetism in a practical assessment context: The relationship between content, process and progression', in P. Fensham, R. Gunstone and R. White (eds) *The Content of Science*, Lewes: Falmer Press.

Etzioni, A. (1995) *The Spirit of Community: Rights, Responsibilities and the Communitarian Agenda*, London: Fontana Press.

Euroclio (1997) *Annual Report*.

Euroclio *Bulletin* 7 (1996–7) *From Moscow to Belfast … from Budapest to Neuchatel*.

Euroclio *Bulletin* 9 (1997–8) *History Teacher Education in Europe*.

Euroclio *Bulletin* 10 (1998) *History Teaching and Information and Communication Technology*.

European Standing Conference of History Teacher Associations (obtainable from Paul Vandepitte, Driesstraat 9, B-8700 TIELT).

Evans, H. (1997) *The Times Educational Supplement*, 4 July.

Evans, R.J. (1997) *In Defence of History*, London: Granta Books.

Farmer, A. and Knight, P. (1995) *Active History in Key Stages 3 and 4*, London: David Fulton.

Figueroa, P. (1993) 'History: Policy issues,' in P.D. Pumfrey and G.K. Verma (eds) *Cultural Diversity and the Curriculum. The Foundation Subjects and RE in Secondary Schools*, London: Falmer Press.

Fraisse, P. (1982) 'The adaptation of the child to time', in W.J. Friedman (ed.) *The Developmental Psychology of Time*, London: Academic Press.

Friedman, W.J. (1982) 'Conventional time concepts and children's structuring of time', in W.J. Friedman (ed.) *The Developmental Psychology of Time*, London: Academic Press.

Fryer P. (1984) *Staying Power. The History of Black People in Britain*, London: Pluto Press.

Fukuyama, F. (1992) *The End of History and the Last Man*, London: Hamish Hamilton.

Furedi, F. (1992) *Mythical Past, Elusive Future: History and Society in an Anxious Age*, London: Pluto.

Gallagher, C. (1998) 'The future of history? A plea for relevance', paper given at the SHP Conference, Leeds, 3–5 April.

Gates, B. (1995) the *Guardian*, 2 March.

Gibson, I. and McLelland, S. (1998) 'Minimalist cause boxes for maximal learning: One approach to the Civil War in Year 8', *Teaching History* 92.

Goodson, I. (1994) *Studying Curriculum*, Buckingham: Open University Press.

Greater London Council (1986) *A History of the Black Presence in London*, London: GLC.

Gorman, M. (1998) 'The structured enquiry is not a contradiction in terms', *Teaching History* 92.

Gross, R.E. and Dynneson, T.L. (1991) (eds) *Social Science Perspectives on Citizenship Education*, New York: Teachers' College, Columbia University.

Grosvenor, I. (1999) '"Race" and Education', in D. Matheson and I. Grosvenor (eds) *Introduction to Educational Studies*, London: David Fulton.

—— (1997) *Assimilating Identities: Racism and Education Policy in Post 1945 Britain*, London, Lawrence & Wishart.

Grosvenor, I. and Chapman, R.L. (1987) *Asians in Britain*, Olbury: Sandwell Education Department.

Grosvenor, I. and Watts, R. (1995) *Crossing the Key Stages of History*, London: David Fulton.

Hamer, J. (1997) 'History in the primary years: The state of the nation', *Primary History* 17: 13–14.

Happold, F. (1928) *The Approach to History*, London: Christophers.

Hargreaves, A. and Evans, R. (eds) (1997) *Beyond Educational Reform: Bringing Teachers Back In*, Buckingham: Open University Press.

Harner, L. (1982) 'Talking about the past and future', in W.J. Friedman (ed.) *The Developmental Psychology of Time*, London: Academic Press.

Harnett, P. (1998) 'Heroes and heroines: Exploring a nation's past. The History Curriculum in State primary schools in the twentieth century', *History of Education Society Bulletin* 62, November: 83–95.

—— (1993) 'Identifying progression in children's understanding: The use of visual materials to assess primary school children's learning in history', *Cambridge Journal of Education* 23(2): 137–54.

Harrison, C. (1997) 'Differentiation in theory and practice', in J. Dillon and M. McGuire (eds) *Becoming a Teacher: Issues in Secondary Teaching*, London: Open University Press.

—— (1980) *Readability in the Classroom*, Cambridge: Cambridge University Press.

Hassell, D. (1999) the *Guardian*, 12 January (supplement).

Haydn, T. (1999) 'CD-rom in the history classroom: Problems and possibilities', in J. Everett and P. Hillis (ed.) *The Dissemination of Knowledge: History and Computing at the End of the 1990s*, forthcoming.

Haydn, T. (1999) Got to get title of forthcoming book for this ref.

Haydn, T., Arthur, J. and Hunt, M. (1997) *Learning to teach History in the Secondary School*, London: Routledge.

Haydn, T. and Macaskill, C. (1995) *Information Technology and Initial Teacher Education: Bridging the Gap between What is and What Might be*, London: Institute of Education, University of London.

Healy, J. (1998) *Failure to Connect*, New York: Simon & Schuster.

Heater, D. (1990) *Citizenship: the civic ideal in world history, politics and education*, London: Longman.

—— (1974) 'History teaching and political education', *Politics Association*, occasional pamphlet, 1.

Heater, D. and Oliver, D. (1994) *The Foundations of Citizenship*, London: Harvester Wheatsheaf.

Heimlich, R. (1988) *Soziales und emotionales lernen in der Schule*, Weinheim: Beltz verlag.

Hennessy, P., Collinson, P., Bentley, M. and Samuel, R. (1991) 'The history of nations', a discussion chaired by Peter Hennessy originally broadcast on the BBC Analysis Radio Programme', *PUSH Newsletter*.

HMI (1985) *History in the Primary and Secondary Years: An HMI View*, London: HMSO.

Holden, C. (1997) 'Making links: The Romans and a European dimension', *Education 3–13* 25(3): 42–6.

Hoodless, P. (1998) *History and English in the Primary School: Exploiting the Links*, London: Routledge.

—— (1996) *Time and Timelines*, London: Historical Association.

Howells, G. (1998) 'Being ambitious with the causes of the First World War: Interrogating inevitability', *Teaching History*, August.

http//tntee.umu.se/ [Thematic Network for Teacher Education in Europe].

http://www.glasnet.ru/~euroclio/ [Homepage].

Husbands, C. (1996) *What Is History Teaching? Language, Ideas and Meaning in Learning about the Past*, Buckingham: Open University Press.

Information Mitteilungen Communications (1980–98), vols 1–19, International Society for History Didactics.

International Bureau of Education (IBE) (1997) *What Education for What Citizenship? Educational Innovation and Information*, Geneva: International Bureau of Education.

Jahoda, J. (1963) 'Children's concepts of time and history', *Educational Review* 15(2): 87–104.

Jenkins, K. (1991) *Re-Thinking History*, London: Routledge.

Johnson, P. (1998) 'Understanding the roles of emotion in anti-racist education', in N. Clough and C. Holden (eds) *Children as Citizens: Education for Participation*, London: Jessica Kingsley Publishers.

Jonathan, R. (1993) 'Education, philosophy of education and the fragmentation of value', *Journal of Philosophy of Education* 27(2): 171–8.

Kay, A. (1995) 'Computers, networks and education', in 'The computer in the 21st century', *Scientific American*, special issue: 148–55.

Kaye, H. (1996) *Why do Ruling Classes Fear History? And Other Questions*, London: Macmillan.

Keatinge, M. (1910) *Studies in the Teaching of History*, London: Black.

Kerridge, R. (1998) *The Story of Black History*, London: Claridge Press.

Kimber, D., Clough, N., Forrest, M., Harnett, P., Menter, I. and Newman, E. (1995) *Humanities in the Primary School*, London: David Fulton.

Knight, P. (1996) 'The National Curriculum is excellent: Secondary history teachers, teacher educators and the National Curriculum', in D. Kerr, (ed.) *Current Change and Future Practice: Fresh Perspectives on History Teacher Education, History and History Teaching*, University of Leicester School of Education/Standing Conference of History Teacher Educators.

—— (1991) 'Teaching as exposure: the case of good practice in junior school history' *British Educational Research Journal* 17(2).

—— (1989a) 'Empathy: Concepts, confusion and consequences in a National Curriculum', *Oxford Review of Education* 15(1): 41–53.

—— (1989b) 'A study of children's understanding of people in the past', *Educational Review* 41(3): 207–19.

Kozma, R. (1994) 'Will media influence learning? Reframing the debate', *Educational Technology Research and Development* 42(2): 7–19.

—— (1991) 'Learning with the media', *Review of Educational Research* 61(2): 179–212.

Lang, P.L.F. (1995) 'Pastoral care and personal and social education: International perspectives', in R. Best, P. Lang, C. Lodge and C. Watkins (eds) *Pastoral Care and Personal and Social Education: Entitlement and Provision*, London: Cassell.

Lawton, D. (1980) *The Politics of the School Curriculum*, London: Routledge & Kegan Paul.

LeCocq, H. (1999) 'Note-making, knowledge-building and critical thinking are the same thing', *Teaching History* 95.

Lee, P., Ashby, R. and Dickinson, A.K. (1997) 'Research methods and some findings on rational understanding', in C. O'Neill and A. Pendry (eds) *Principles and Practice: Analytical Perspectives on Curriculum Reform and Changing Pedagogy from History Teacher Educators*, SCHTE.

—— (1996a) 'Progression in children's ideas about history', in M. Hughes (ed.) *Progression in Learning*, Clevedon, BERA Dialogues, 11: 50–81.

—— (1996b) 'Children making sense of history', *Education 3–13* 24(1): 13–19.

—— (1996c) 'Children's understanding of "because" and the status of explanation in history', *Teaching History* 82(1): 6–11.

Leeuw-Roord, J. van der (ed.) (1998) *The State of History Education in Europe*, Hamburg: Korber-Siftung.

—— (1994) 'A letter from the continent', *The Times Education Supplement: History Extra*.

Levstik, L. and Pappas, C. (1987) 'Exploring the development of historical understanding', *Journal of Research and Development in Education* 21(1): 1–15.

Lewis, E. and Theoharis, J. (1996) 'Race in a world of overlapping diasporas: The history curriculum', in A. Booth and P. Hyland (eds) *History in Higher Education*, Oxford: Blackwell.

Lewis, M. and Wray, D. (1994) *Working with Writing Frames: Developing Children's Non-Fiction Writing*, Leamington Spa: Scholastic.

Lindsay, G. and Thompson, T. (1997) *Values into Practice in Special Education*, London: David Fulton.

Little, V. (1990) 'A National Curriculum in history: A very contentious issue', *British Journal of Educational Studies* 38(4): 319–34.

Little, V. and John, T. (1986) *Historical Fiction in the Classroom*, Teaching of History Series, Number 59, London: Historical Association.

Lomas, T. (1999) 'Primary update', *Primary History* 21(6).

—— (1998) 'The challenges facing History Teachers', *Welsh Historian* 28: 6–10.

—— (1993) *Teaching and Assessing Historical Understanding*, London: Historical Association.

Low-Beer, A. (1997) *The Council of Europe and School History*, Strasbourg: Council of Europe.

Lowenthal, D. (1998) *The Heritage Crusade and the Spoils of History*, Cambridge: Cambridge University Press.

—— (1985) *The Past is a Foreign Country*, Cambridge: Cambridge University Press.

—— (1981) *The Past is Another Country*, Cambridge: Cambridge University Press.

Lynn, S. (1993) 'Children reading pictures: History visuals at Key Stages 1 and 2', *Education 3–13* 21(3): 23–9.

Lunzer, E.A., Gardner, W.K., Davies, F. and Greene, T. (1984) *Learning from the Written Word*, Edinburgh: Oliver & Boyd, for the Schools Council.

Lyotard, J. (1984) *The Postmodern Condition*, Manchester: Manchester University Press.

McAleavy, T. (1998) 'The use of sources in school history 1910–1998: A critical perspective', *Teaching History* 91: 10–16.

—— (1994) 'Meeting pupils' learning needs: Differentiation and progression in the teaching of history', in H. Bourdillon (ed.) *Teaching History*, London: Open University Press.

—— (1993) 'Using the attainments targets in Key Stage 3: AT2 interpretations of history', *Teaching History* 72.

McKiernan, D. (1993) 'History in a National Curriculum: Imagining a nation at the end of the twentieth century', *Journal of Curriculum Studies* 25(1): 33–51.

McLaughlin, T.H. (1992) 'Citizenship, diversity and education: A philosophical perspective', *Journal of Moral Education* 21(3): 235–50.

Madian, J. (1995) 'Multimedia – why and why not?', *The Computing Teacher*, April: 16–18.

Marcus, G.J. (1975) *Heart of Oak*, Oxford: Oxford University Press.

Martin, D. (1999) 'Why should we use historical fiction to teach English and history?', *Primary History* 22.

Mason, J. and Purkis, S. (eds) (1991) *A Sense of History*, London: Longman.

Mellar, H. and Jackson, A. (1994) 'The changing picture of information technology experience in post-graduate teacher training', *Journal of Computer Assisted Learning* 10(1): 14–22.

Millar, R. (1991) 'A means to an end: The role of processes in science education', in B. Woolnough (ed.) *Practical Science*, Milton Keynes: Open University Press.

Millar, R. and Driver, R. (1987) 'Beyond processes', *Studies in Science Education* 14: 43–52.

Ministry of Education (1959) *Primary Education. Suggestions for the Consideration of Teachers and Others Concerned with the Work of Primary Schools*, London: HMSO.

Morris, S. (1992) *A Teacher's Guide to Using Portraits*, London: English Heritage.

Mulholland, M. (1998) 'Frameworks for linking pupils' evidential understanding with growing skill in structured, written argument: The evidence sandwich', *Teaching History* 91: 17–19.

Myers, K. (1996) *School Improvement in Practice: Schools Make a Difference*, Lewes: Falmer Press.

Naughton, J. (1999) the *Observer*, 10 January.

NCC (1993a) *Teaching History at Key Stage 1. NCC Inset Resources*, York: NCC.

—— (1993b) *Teaching History at Key Stage 2. NCC Inset Resources*, York: NCC.

—— (1993c) *Teaching History at Key Stage 3*, York: NCC.

—— (1991) *History Non-Statutory Guidance*, York: NCC.

—— (1990) *Education for Citizenship*, York: NCC.

NCET/Historical Association (1998) *History Using IT: Searching for Patterns in the Past; Using Data Handling in History*, Coventry: NCET/Historical Association.

—— (1997) *History Using IT: Improving Students' Writing in History Using Word Processing*, Coventry: NCET/Historical Association.

Nichol, J. (1998) 'Nuffield Primary History: The Literacy through History Project and the Literacy Hour', *Primary History* 20: 14–17.

Norman, K. (1992) *Thinking Voices: The Work of the National Oracy Project*, London: Routledge.

Norwich, B. (1994) 'Differentiation: From the perspective of resolving tensions between basic social values and assumptions about individual differences', *Curriculum Studies* 2: 289–308.

—— (1990) *Reappraising Special Needs Education*, London: Cassell.

Oakden, E. and Sturt, M. (1922) 'The development of the knowledge of time in children', *Journal of Psychology* 12(4): 309–36.

Oakeshott, M. (1956), in P. Laslett, (ed.) *Philosophy, Politics and Society*, Oxford: Basil Blackwell.

O'Brien, T. (1998) 'The millennium curriculum: Confronting the issues and proposing solutions', *Support for Learning* 13(4): 147–52.

OFSTED (1997) *Annual Report 1995–96*, London: HMSO.

—— (1996a) *Subjects and Standards Report, Primary Schools*, London: HMSO.

—— (1996b) *Subjects and Standards Report, Secondary Schools*, London: HMSO.

—— (1995a) *Annual Report 1993–94*, London: HMSO.

—— (1995b) *History: A Review of Inspection Findings 1993/1994*, London: HMSO.

—— (1993) *History Key Stages 1, 2 and 3*, London: HMSO.

Oppenheimer, T. (1997) 'The computer delusion', *Atlantic Monthly*, July.

Osler, A. (1994) 'Still hidden from history?', *Oxford Review of Education* 20(2): 219–35.

Osler, A., Rathenow, H-F. and Starkey, H. (1996) *Teaching for Citizenship in the New Europe*, Stoke-on-Trent: Trentham.

Owston, R. (1997) 'The World Wide Web: A technology to enhance teaching and learning?', *Educational Researcher*, March: 27–33.

Oxford (1993) *Concise Oxford Dictionary*, Oxford: Oxford University Press.

Papert, S. (1993) *The Children's Machine: Rethinking School in the Age of the Computer*, New York: Basic Books.

Parsons J. (1998) 'High take-up of GCSE History at Redwood School', *Teaching History*, November.

Partington, G. (1986) 'History: Re-written to ideological fashion', in D. O'Keefe (ed.) *The Wayward Curriculum: A Cause for Parents' Concern?*, London: Social Affairs Unit.

—— (1980) *The Idea of an Historical Education*, Slough: NFER.

Patrick, H. (1988) 'The history curriculum: The teaching of history 1985–7, *History Resources*, 2(1): 9–14.

—— (1987) *The Aims of Teaching History in Secondary Schools*, Leicester: University of Leicester, School of Education.

Phillips, R. (1998a) *History Teaching, Nationhood and the State: A Study in Educational Politics*, London: Cassell.

—— (1998b) 'Contesting the past, constructing the future: Politics, policy and identity in schools', *British Journal of Educational Studies* 46: 40–53. Also published in, J. Arnold, K. Davies and S. Ditchfield (eds) *History and Heritage: Consuming the Past in Contemporary Culture*, Shaftesbury: Donhead.

—— (1998c) 'The politics of history: Some methodological and ethical dilemmas in elite based research', *British Educational Research Journal* 24: 5–19.

—— (1996) 'History teaching, cultural restorationism and national identity in England and Wales', *Curriculum Studies* 4: 385–99.

—— (1993) 'Teachers' perceptions of the first year's implementation of Key Stage three history in the National Curriculum in England', *Research Papers in Education* 8(3): 329–53.

—— (1992) ' "The battle for the big prize": The creation of synthesis and the role of a curriculum pressure group: The case of history and the National Curriculum, *The Curriculum Journal* 3: 245–60.

Phillips, R., McCully, A., Goalen, P. and Wood, S. (1999) 'Four histories, one nation? History teaching, nationhood and a British identity', *Compare: A Journal of Comparative Education* 29(2): 153–69.

Piaget, J. (1962) *Judgement and Reasoning in the Child*, London: Routledge & Kegan Paul.

—— (1927), *Le Développement de la notion de temps chez l'enfant*, trans. A.J. Pomerans, London: Routledge & Kegan Paul.

Portal, C. (1987) 'Empathy as an objective for history teaching', in C. Portal (ed.) *The History Curriculum for Teachers*, Lewes: Falmer Press.

Price, M. (1968) 'History in danger', *History* 53: 342–7.

Pring, R. (1984) *Personal and Social Education in the Curriculum*, London, Hodder & Stoughton.

QCA (1999) *Five Yearly Review of Standards – History*, London: QCA.

—— (1998a) *Developing the School Curriculum. Advice to the Secretary of State on the Broad Nature and Scope of the Review of the National Curriculum*, London: QCA.

—— (1998b) *A Scheme of Work for Key Stages 1 and 2 History*, London: QCA.

—— (1998c) *Education for Citizenship and the Teaching of Democracy in Schools. Final Report of the Advisory Group on Citizenship*, London: QCA.

—— (1998d) *Maintaining Breadth and Balance at Key Stages 1 and 2*, London: QCA.

—— (1998e) Research into structured papers.

—— (1997) *History Update*, quarterly bulletin to LEA Advisers/Inspectors.

Rauner, M. (1997) 'Citizenship in the curriculum: The globalization of civics education in anglophone Africa: 1955–1995, in C. McNeely (ed.) *Public Rights, Public Rules: Constituting Citizens in the World Polity and National Policy*, New York: Garland Publishing.

Raymond, E. (1998) 'The cathedral and the bazaar', http://sagan.earthspace.net.esr/writings/cathedral-bazaar/.

Richards, C. (1986) 'Anti-racist initiatives', *Screen* 77: 5.

Riley, M. (1997) 'Big stories and big pictures: Making outlines and overviews interesting', *Teaching History* 88, July: 20–2.

Rogers, P. (1987) 'The past as a frame of reference', in C. Portal (ed.) *The History Curriculum for Teachers*, Lewes: Falmer Press.

Rollison, D. (1998) the *Daily Telegraph*, 29 October.

Rothenburg, P. (1991) 'Critics of attempts to democratize the curriculum are waging a campaign to misrepresent the work of responsible professors', *Chronicle of Higher Education* 37, April: 10.

Runnymede Trust (1998) *Commission on the Future of Multi-Ethnic Britain*, London: Runnymede Trust.

Sagy, S., Emda, O., Dan, B. and Awwad, E. (1998) 'Individualism and collectivism in two conflicted societies: Comparing Israeli-Jews and Palestinian Arabs high school students', paper presented to the International Conference on Education for International Understanding, Braunschweig.

Said, E. (1993) *Culture and Imperialism*, London: Chatto & Windus.

Samuel, R. (1998) *Island Stories: Unravelling Britain, Theatres of Memory Volume II*, London: Verso.

Saville, J. (1982) 'William Cuffay', in J. Bellamy and J. Saville (eds) *Dictionary of Labour Biography* VI, London: Macmillan.

SCAA (1997a) *Expectations in History at Key Stages 1 and 2*, London: SCAA.

—— (1997b) *History and the Use of Language*, London: SCAA.

—— (1996) *Review of Qualifications 16–19*, Full Report, p. 85 and pp. 105–6.

Schick, J. (1995) 'On being interactive: Rethinking the learning equation', *History Microcomputer Review* 11(1): 9–25.

Scott, J. (ed.) (1990) *Understanding Cause and Effect: Learning and Teaching about Causation and Consequence in History*, London: Longman.

Schools' Council (1983) *Primary Practice a Sequel to the Practical Curriculum*, Schools' Council Working Paper 75.

Schools' Council History 13–16 Project (1976) *A New Look at History*, Edinburgh: Holmes McDougall.

Scruton, R. (1985) 'World Studies: Education as indoctrination' (London, Institute for European Defence and Strategic Studies).

SEAC (1993a) *Standard Assessment Tests*, Slough: NFER.

—— (1993b) *Children's Work Assessed, Geography and History*, London: SEAC.

—— (1993c) *History from Photographs*, London: SEAC.

Sears, A. (1996) 'Something different to everyone: Conceptions of citizenship and citizenship education', *Canadian and International Education* 25(2): 1–16.

Sharp, C. (1995) *Viewing, Listening, Learning: The Use and Impact of Schools Broadcasts*, Slough: NFER.

Shawyer, G., Booth, M. and Brown, R. (1988) 'The development of children's historical thinking', *Cambridge Journal of Education* 18(2): 209–19.

Shemilt, D. (1987) 'Adolescent ideas about evidence and methodology in history', in C. Portal (ed.) *The History Curriculum for Teachers*, London: Falmer Press.

—— (1984) 'Beauty and the philosopher: Empathy in history and classrooms', in A.K. Dickinson, P.J. Lee, and P.J. Rogers (eds) *Learning History*, London: Heinemann.

—— (1980) *History 13–16 Evaluation Study: Schools Council History Project*, Edinburgh: Holmes McDougall.

—— (1976) *Schools Council 13–16 Project Evaluation Study*, Edinburgh: Holmes McDougall.

Sherwood, M.(1998) 'Sins of omission and commission: History in English schools and struggles for change', *Multicultural Teaching* 16(2): 14–20.

Short, G. and Carrington B. (1996) 'Anti-racist education, multiculturalism and the new racism', *Educational Review* 48(1): 65–77.

Shuter, P. and Child, J. (1987) *Skills in History I*, Oxford: Heinemann.

Sikorski, R. (1997) *The Polish House*, London: Weidenfeld & Nicolson.

Skidelsky, R. (1987) 'History as social engineering,', *The Independent*, 17 March.

Slater, J. (1995) *Teaching History in the New Europe*, London: Cassell.

—— (1989) *The Politics of History Teaching: A Humanity Dehumanised?*, London: ULIE.

Slater, J. and Hennessey, R. (1978) 'Political competence', in B. Crick and A. Porter (eds) *Political Education and Political Literacy*, Longman: London.

Social Exclusion Unit (1998) *Truancy and School Exclusion. Report by the School Exclusion Unit*, London: HMSO.

Sparrowhawk, A. (1995) 'Information technology in the primary school', conference address, Manchester, BBC, 28 March.

Speaker's Commission (1990) *Encouraging Citizenship*, London: HMSO.

SREB [Southern Regional Examination Board] (1986) *Empathy: From Definition to Assessment*, Southampton: SREB.

Stobart, M. (1996) 'Tensions between political ideology and history teaching. To what extent may history serve a cause, however well-meant?', *The Standing Conference of European History Teachers Association Bulletin* 6.

Stow, W. (1998) 'An investigation into aspects of children's understanding of historical time', unpublished MA thesis, Canterbury Christ Church University College.

Stradling, R. (1995) 'The European content of the school history curriculum', report to the Council for Cultural Co-operation of the Council of Europe, Strasbourg.

—— (1987) 'Political education and politicization in Britain: A ten year retrospective', paper presented at the International Round Table Conference of the Research Committee on Political Education of the International Political Science Association. Ostkolleg der Bundeszentrale für Politische Bildung, Cologne, 9–13 March.

Swafford, J. (1998) 'Teachers supporting teachers through peer coaching', *Support for Learning* 13(2): 54–8.

Sylvester, D. (1994) 'Change and continuity in history teaching 1900–1993', in H. Bourdillon (ed.) *Teaching History*, London: Open University Press.

Tate, N. (1998) 'The curriculum and values in society', in *Education Reform in the UK*, London: British Council.

Tawney, R. (1978) *History and Society*, London: Routledge & Kegan Paul.

Taylor, J. (1996) 'Technonerds', Channel 4, 19 March.

Thatcher, M. (1993) *The Downing Street Years*, London: Harper Collins.

Thomas, G., Walker, D. and Webb, J. (1998) *The Making of the Inclusive School*, London: Routledge.

Thornton, S. and Vukelich, R. (1988) 'Effects of children's understanding of time concepts on historical understanding', *Theory and Research in Social Education* 16(1): 69–82.

Tomlinson, S. (1990) *Multicultural Education in White Schools*, London: Batsford.

Torney-Purta, J. (1996) 'The connections of values education and civic education: The IEA civic education study in twenty countries', paper presented at the conference 'Morals for the millennium: educational challenges in a changing world'. Lancaster, July.

Tosh, J. (1984) *The Pursuit of History: Aims, Methods and New Directions in the Study of Modern History*, London: Longman.

Townsend, J. (1998) 'Caught or taught: Infection or subjection? Struggling readers in secondary schools still need that little bit extra', *Support for Learning* 13(3): 129–33.

Troyna, B. and Selman, L. (1989) 'Surviving in the "Survivalist Culture", anti-racist strategies in the new ERA', *Journal of Further and Higher Education* 13(2).

TTA/OFSTED (1996 and 1997) *Framework for the Assessment of Quality and Standards in Initial Teacher Training*, London: TTA.

Vygotsky, L.S. (1978) *Mind in Society*, Cambridge, MA: Harvard University Press.

Walker, B. (1996) *Dancing to History's Tune: History, Myth and Politics in Ireland*, Belfast: Institute of Irish Studies, Queen's University.

Walsh, B. (1998) 'Why Gerry likes history now: The power of the word processor', *Teaching History* 93, November: 6–15.

—— (1997) *British Social and Economic History*, London: John Murray.

Walsh, B. and Brookfield, K. (1998) *Making of the United Kingdom: Teacher's Handbook*, London: British Library.

Warren, J. (1998) *The Past and its Presenters: An Introduction to Historiography*, London: Hodder & Stoughton.

Watson, G. (1998) '"The children love history and we enjoy teaching it." Feedback to QCA from primary teachers about the National Curriculum history', *Primary History* 19: 7–8.

Watts, R. (1998) 'Report of the working group I' in J. van der Leeuw-Roord (ed.) *The State of History Education in Europe*, Hamburg: Korber-Siftung.

Watts, R. and Grosvenor, I. (eds) (1995) *Crossing the Key Stages of History*, London: David Fulton.

Welsh Office (1995) *History in the National Curriculum: Wales*, Cardiff: Welsh Office.

—— (1990) *National Curriculum History Working Committee for Wales: Final Report*, Cardiff: Welsh Office.

West, J. (1981a) 'Children's awareness of the past', unpublished Ph.D. thesis, University of Keele.

—— (1981b) *History 7–13*, Dudley Metropolitan Borough.

Whitty, G., Rowe, G. and Appleton, P. (1994) 'Subjects and themes in the secondary school curriculum', *Research Papers in Education* 9(2): 159–81.

Wicks, B. (1988) *No Time To Wave Goodbye*, London: Allen & Unwin.

Wiegand, P. (1993) *Children and Primary Geography*, London: Cassell.

—— (1992) *Places in the Primary School: Knowledge and Understanding of Places at Key Stage 1 and 2*, London: Falmer Press.

Wilson, M.D. (1985) *History for Pupils with Learning Difficulties*, London: Hodder & Stoughton.

Wood, D. (1988) *How Children Think and Learn*, Oxford: Blackwell.

Wood, S. (1998) 'History and identity in Scottish schools', in J. Arnold, K. Davies and S. Ditchfield (eds) *History and Heritage: Consuming the Past in Contemporary Culture*, Shaftesbury: Donhead.

Wood, S. (1995) 'Developing an understanding of time-sequencing issues', *Teaching History* 79, April: 11–14.

Woodhead, C. (1998) 'Letter to David Blunkett', *The National Curriculum and Inspection*, 5 January.

Wray, D. (ed.) (1990) *Emerging Partnerships*, Avon: Multilingual Matters.

Wray, D. and Lewis, M. (1998) 'Bringing literacy and history closer together', *Primary History* 20: 11–13.

—— (1996) *Developing Children's Non-Fiction Writing: The Use of Writing Frames*, Leamington Spa: Scholastic Press.

Wrenn, A. (1998) 'Shared stories and a sense of place', *Teaching History* 91: 25–30.

www.cthree.freeserve.co.uk/schte/ [SCHTE in UK].

Zinn, H. (1993) 'Why students should study history', *Rethinking Schools* 7.

Index